# Praise for
# *The Valuation Book*

"Looking for a book on company and stock valuation that gets to the point? Here it is. Global practice on a broad theoretical foundation. You will get a high return on your investment in reading time by growing your knowledge and reducing the risk of misjudgments. The value (increase) is definitely higher than the price. Well done!"

—**Wolfgang Kniest, Dipl.-Kfm., CVA, Co-Founder and Managing Director of the European Association of Certified Valuators and Analysts (EACVA)**

"How do you know how much a stock is really worth? My suggestion? Read this book! Four experts break down the secrets to valuation in easily digestible pieces so that everybody understands what really matters."

—**Joachim Klement, Managing Director, Panmure Liberum Investment Bank**

"Valuation is an ART not a SCIENCE… but it does need you to get your tools right to get the best out of that art. The only book you need on the shelf taking you from a novice to valuing businesses like a seasoned banker."

—**Sameer Merchant, CEO, City Investment Training**

"Beautifully written to take me from 0mph to 88mph in one book. Nothing is assumed, everything is explained and the reality of examples used makes every topic pop into focus."

—**Stuart O'Brien, Freelance Accounting and Finance Lecturer**

"An engaging journey through valuation principles that challenges readers to think critically while providing a solid foundation of knowledge."

—Matthew Ashley, former Group CFO, Micro Focus International plc, National Express Group plc, William Hill plc

"*The Valuation Book* strikes the perfect balance between accessibility and rigour, making it a must-read for anyone looking to understand this critical field."

—Geoff Robinson, Founder of TheInvestmentAnalyst.com, 9x #1 ranked Institutional Investor Analyst

"This book is a gem for anyone eager to master valuations. It takes you from novice to expert with crystal-clear language and a user-friendly structure. Packed with comprehensive insights and down-to-earth wisdom from top practitioners and academics, it will skyrocket your knowledge and fuel your passion for diving deeper into this field. Highly recommended!"

—Dr Rodrigo Souza, Senior Lecturer, Roehampton University, London

"What a pleasure to read this concise, clear, and practical guide. This book is an excellent companion for anyone approaching a valuation exercise. While it is aimed at beginners, it offers new and useful insights to readers of all levels and backgrounds. A must-have for any finance and accounting student, educator, or professional."

—Dr Matt Bamber, Associate Professor of Accounting, The Schulich School of Business, York University, Canada

"An insightful book that bridges the gap between theoretical concepts and real-world application in valuation."

—Charles Richardson, former CFO and Strategy & M&A Director, Bupa Global and UK

"An easy-to-read and understand book on how to value firms. Packed with practical examples for issues related to valuation, such as how to value private and young firms and how to approach ethical and environmental concerns in valuation. Highly recommended for both students and professionals."

—Professor Antonios Siganos, Professor of Finance, Edinburgh Napier University

"This book covers all aspects of valuation in a non-rocket science way. Regardless of the reader's starting level, everyone benefits from being served each chapter at the right bite-size to understand the essence of the valuation practice well enough and to explain it simply."

—**Ben Husemann, Head of M&A at Giesecke+Devrient GmbH**

"*The Valuation Book* provides a strong conceptual framework for business valuation in a clear and direct writing style, with insights based on real-life experience and on a solid accounting and financial analysis foundation: a useful guide for valuation specialists as well as investors, students, attorneys, and anyone with an interest in business valuation."

—**Antonella Puca, CPA/ABV, CFA, Managing Partner, BlueVal and Author of *Early Stage Valuation***

"At last – a clear, jargon-free and practical guide to valuation! The book is engagingly written, easy to follow and filled with real-world examples, making it the most accessible and practical book on valuation that I have seen."

—**Deborah Taylor, Finance Instructor, Financial Edge**

"A must-read for anyone seeking to understand the fundamentals of equity valuation. This textbook distils complex concepts into clear, manageable insights for readers of all backgrounds."

—**Professor Frank Hong Liu, Professor of Accounting and Finance, Loughborough University**

"An outstanding resource offering clear guidance and practical insights. It effectively bridges the gap between theory and real-world application, making it ideal for professionals and students eager to deepen their understanding of equity valuation."

—**Professor Andreas Charitou, Professor of Accounting and Finance, School of Economics and Management, University of Cyprus**

"This textbook is an excellent and accessible resource for students, making learning both enjoyable and straightforward. Its clear explanations and engaging content ensure that complex topics are easily understood. Ideal for non-specialists and those enrolled in valuation courses, I highly recommend it for anyone looking to enhance their understanding of valuation."

—**Dr Trang Nguyen, University of Bristol**

"This book is an excellent first step into the world of equity valuation for the uninitiated and, to the specialist, a great reminder of the ever-important (and often forgotten) foundations of financial analysis."

—**Dr Joao Toniato, Head of Global Equity Strategy, Aviva Investors**

# The VALUATION Book

# The VALUATION Book

## HOW TO VALUE BUSINESSES AND SHARES – AN INTRODUCTORY GUIDE FOR INVESTORS, MANAGERS AND MORE

Mark Aleksanyan,
Kenneth Lee,
Matthias Meitner &
Neil Pande

HARRIMAN HOUSE LTD
3 Viceroy Court
Bedford Road
Petersfield
Hampshire
GU32 3LJ
GREAT BRITAIN
Tel: +44 (0)1730 233870

Email: enquiries@harriman-house.com
Website: harriman.house

First published in 2024.
Copyright © Kenneth Lee, Mark Aleksanyan, Matthias Meitner, Neil Pande

The the rights of Kenneth Lee, Mark Aleksanyan, Matthias Meitner, Neil Pande to be identified as the Authors has been asserted in accordance with the Copyright, Design and Patents Act 1988.

Paperback ISBN: 978-0-85719-949-2
eBook ISBN: 978-0-85719-950-8

British Library Cataloguing in Publication Data
A CIP catalogue record for this book can be obtained from the British Library.

All rights reserved; no part of this publication may be reproduced, stored in a retrieval system, or transmitted in any form or by any means, electronic, mechanical, photocopying, recording, or otherwise without the prior written permission of the Publisher. This book may not be lent, resold, hired out or otherwise disposed of by way of trade in any form of binding or cover other than that in which it is published without the prior written consent of the Publisher.

Whilst every effort has been made to ensure that information in this book is accurate, no liability can be accepted for any loss incurred in any way whatsoever by any person relying solely on the information contained herein.

No responsibility for loss occasioned to any person or corporate body acting or refraining to act as a result of reading material in this book can be accepted by the Publisher, by the Authors, or by the employers of the Authors.

The Publisher does not have any control over or any responsibility for any Authors' or third-party websites referred to in or on this book.

# Contents

**Preface to the First Edition** — 1

**Section A: Broad Principles and Building Blocks** — 5
    Chapter 1: The building blocks of valuation — 7
    Chapter 2: Introduction to accounting and why accounting is important for valuation — 15
    Chapter 3: Earnings versus cash flows — 27
    Chapter 4: Assets and capital structure — 35

**Section B: Forecasting** — 45
    Chapter 5: Forecasting earnings — 47
    Chapter 6: Forecasting balance sheets — 57
    Chapter 7: Forecasting – completing cash flows — 69

**Section C: Discount Rates** — 79
    Chapter 8: The impact of risk — 81
    Chapter 9: Standard approaches to determine risk-adjusted discount rates — 89
    Chapter 10: Practical perspectives on risk-adjusted discount rates — 96

**Section D: What Are You Valuing?** — 103
    Chapter 11: What is enterprise value? — 105
    Chapter 12: What is equity value? — 113
    Chapter 13: The enterprise value bridge — 120
    Chapter 14: When to use enterprise value and when to use equity value — 124
    Chapter 15: The different types of valuation models — 130

## Section E: Multiples-Based Valuation — 135

    Chapter 16: The logic of multiple-based valuations — 137

    Chapter 17: Equity multiples — 146

    Chapter 18: Enterprise value multiples — 152

    Chapter 19: Sector-specific multiples — 157

## Section F: Present Value Models: the Dividend Discount and Free Cash Flow Models — 161

    Chapter 20: Stages in present value-based models — 163

    Chapter 21: The logic of the Dividend Discount Model — 168

    Chapter 22: How (and when) does the Dividend Discount Model work? — 177

    Chapter 23: Free cash flow to the firm (FCFF) – talk-through — 182

    Chapter 24: Free cash flow to the firm (FCFF) – walk-through — 190

    Chapter 25: Free cash flow to the firm (FCFF) – food for thought — 202

    Chapter 26: Free cash flow to equity (FCFE) – talk-through — 213

    Chapter 27: Free cash flow to equity (FCFE) – walk-through and food for thought — 219

## Section G: Accounting-Based Models — 235

    Chapter 28: The logic of residual income — 237

    Chapter 29: Turning residual income into a valuation — 243

## Section H: Specialist Topics — 253

    Chapter 30: Valuation in an international context – currency issues — 255

    Chapter 31: Valuation of distressed companies — 263

    Chapter 32: Integrating ESG factors into valuation — 270

    Chapter 33: Valuation of young companies — 277

    Chapter 34: Valuing private versus public companies — 282

## Index — 287

# Preface to the First Edition

Have a look at the plentiful supply of valuation textbooks on the market and you will quickly notice the dominance of weighty tomes, stuffed full of sophisticated formulae. As Steve Penman suggested, valuation methodologies invite the application of formulas out of higher mathematics[1] – it may not *be* rocket science, but it looks like it is! How is such a world to be opened to the non-specialist? What about the early career investor, the non-finance student, the general manager, the lawyer or accountant, to name a few. The objective of our book is very much targeted at this non-specialist audience. Although all of the authors teach detailed valuation classes on a range of topics to both students and practitioners, we know that the most important lessons are the fundamental ones covered in this textbook. These core principles will enable readers to not only build basic models but also to better understand valuation issues and interpret the work of others.

Our experience of existing texts on valuation is that readers are confronted with lengthy chapters that cover vast amounts of technical material, some important, some much less important. This can be very off-putting for the non-specialist. To tackle this, our book is constructed around 34 short chapters, all with an identical structure:

**Bite size** – In a nutshell, the key learning points from the chapter.

**Practitioner focus** – The relevance of this chapter for those undertaking valuations in the real world.

**Core content** – This is the main technical content of the chapter.

**Stretch yourself** – If the reader feels confident then this section pushes the technical boundaries to introduce some more advanced aspects of the topic.

Although we focus on making the text as clear and easy to follow as possible, some coverage of theory and mathematical formulae is unavoidable. However, we have

---

[1] Paraphrased from Penman, S. (2006). Handling valuation models. *Journal of Applied Corporate Finance*, 18(2), 40–55.

kept this to an absolute minimum and focused instead on concepts, challenges and practical application. We also have a number of chapters that present a 'walk-through' of a forecast and model to aid readers who may need to explore valuations conducted by others.

The book can also usefully be divided up into various broad sections, as follows:

## Section A: Broad Principles and Building Blocks (Chapters 1–4)

These chapters cover key valuation and accounting concepts needed to understand how valuations are carried out.

## Section B: Forecasting (Chapters 5–7)

Forecasting is essential for valuation and is based around accounting numbers. These chapters follow logically from the introduction to accounting and show how forecasting is carried out in practice.

## Section C: Discount Rates (Chapters 8–10)

The time value of money and determining discount rates are a central part of valuation. Here we cover the most important aspect of discount rate determination used in practice, including the typical sources used to access data on key inputs.

## Section D: What Are You Valuing? (Chapters 11–15)

The differences between equity valuation and enterprise value are critical yet are often covered at a very high level in textbooks. Here we look at a variety of aspects of these two values and how to reconcile one with the other. Here we also introduce the different types of valuation models you will see in the rest of the text.

## Section E: Multiples-Based Valuation (Chapters 16–19)

Multiples-based and intrinsic valuation-based methods are the commonplace valuations seen in industry. Additionally, practitioners often use multiples as a language of valuation even where other methods are used. We conclude this section with looking at which multiples are used in different sectors.

## Section F: Present Value Models – the Dividend Discount and Free Cash Flow Models (Chapters 20–27)

Most intrinsic valuation models are based on discounting a flow of future economic benefits. Here we explain the general logic of these and then apply it to valuations based around dividend flows and free cash flows. We address the process of building the Dividend Discount Model (DDM) and Discounted Cash Flow (DCF) model and 'walk through' completed models in both enterprise value and equity form.

## Section G: Accounting-Based Models (Chapters 28–29)

The final model type is based on accounting-based numbers, termed residual income. We cover the core conceptual foundation and the application to valuation.

## Section H: Specialist Topics (Chapters 30–34)

This section covers a range of specific topics that would not be relevant in every circumstance. These include foreign currency issues, impact of environmental, social and governance (ESG) issues on valuation as well as valuing immature companies or those in distress.

*We do hope you enjoy the book. Please visit the companion website for the book at www.thevaluationbook.com where we address further issues, provide video content, excel models for your use and delve deeper into the issues covered in the book.*

*Ken, Mark, Matthias and Neil*

# SECTION A
# Broad Principles and Building Blocks

# CHAPTER 1

# The building blocks of valuation

*"A cynic knows the price of everything, and the value of nothing"*
**(Oscar Wilde's definition of a cynic, many years ago)**[2]

## Bite size

This book is about the fundamentals of valuation and right from the start it is vital to be as precise as possible about what we mean by valuation and the terminology surrounding it. In this chapter we go through the fundamental aspects of valuation (what we call 'building blocks'), which provide a strong foundation for the content that follows. A number of these building blocks have specific chapters devoted to them later in the text and so, in this chapter, we are simply introducing the ideas. We shall ensure you do not meet the definition of a cynic by differentiating between price and value!

## Practitioner focus

In our experience, one of the challenges of valuation in the commercial world is the technical language used by practitioners. To the uninitiated it can appear abstract, complex and intimidating. One of the objectives of this book is to enable more people to speak confidently about valuation. To do this you need to understand, and be comfortable with, the use of several key terms, ideas and concepts. In this chapter we

---

2 To be more precise this is taken from Lord Darlington in *Lady Windermere's Fan* (Oscar Wilde, 1891).

have put together what we hold to be ten critical building blocks to understanding valuation models and theory.

FIGURE 1.1 TEN BUILDING BLOCKS OF VALUATION

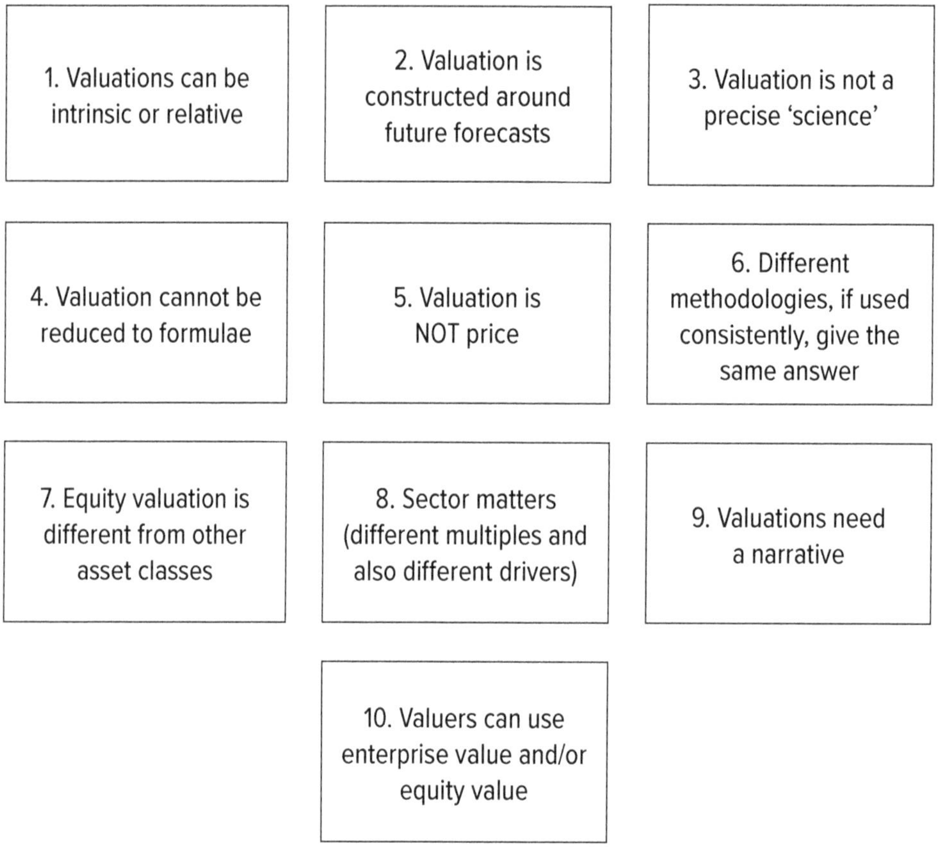

| 1. Valuations can be intrinsic or relative | 2. Valuation is constructed around future forecasts | 3. Valuation is not a precise 'science' |
|---|---|---|
| 4. Valuation cannot be reduced to formulae | 5. Valuation is NOT price | 6. Different methodologies, if used consistently, give the same answer |
| 7. Equity valuation is different from other asset classes | 8. Sector matters (different multiples and also different drivers) | 9. Valuations need a narrative |
| | 10. Valuers can use enterprise value and/or equity value | |

# Core content

## 1. Valuations can be intrinsic or relative

There are two main approaches to valuation – intrinsic and relative – and you need to be clear about which approach you are following. The first, which we will term relative valuation, seeks to value an asset based on how the market values similar assets. For example, if a house on a residential street has sold for $1m, then this might be a good starting point for the valuation of other similar houses on that street or nearby. In the same way, if a UK retailer is valued at 10 times earnings then we might value another

UK retailer at 10 times its earnings. We would need to ensure that the various assets (houses, retail stocks, etc.) were indeed similar for this approach to work, although we can always make some adjustments. Perhaps we might consider one retailer as riskier than another. In that case we could value it on (say) 9 times earnings to reflect this higher risk. As mentioned above, an approach to valuation that is based on the value of other (similar) assets in the market is termed relative valuation. This approach often uses multiples to derive values and we address this in detail later in the text.

The other approach to valuation is to move away from market-based measures of valuation. Instead, this second approach seeks to determine what we think the 'true value' of an asset is, irrespective of its current pricing in the market. For example, we might think that, due to the development of a new online shopping service, one retailer is worth more than another, which is still adopting a model based on physical shops. Consequently, we would undertake our own analysis to determine value using a methodology such as discounted cash flow. This approach is termed intrinsic valuation. As we shall see, many valuations reflect elements of both approaches and we have a number of chapters in the book that are devoted to exploring intrinsic and relative valuation.

## 2. Valuation is constructed around forecasts

The most fundamental rule in equity valuation is that the value of an equity is derived from the future cash flows it is expected to generate. It is only in the process of cash flow generation that an asset has any value. These cash flows could be flows in the form of dividends or free cash flows,[3] for example. Even if we are using a relative valuation approach, the market's valuation of similar assets will itself be based on future flows.

All approaches to intrinsic valuation require an estimate of future flows. Sometimes these estimates can be very simple. For example, a valuation could be based on the assumption that the current level of cash flow will continue forever ('in perpetuity'). Clearly, this would not represent an adequate, nor realistic, valuation of a share for most companies. Therefore, we normally need to construct quite sophisticated forecasts of the future to underpin valuations.

## 3. Valuation is not a precise 'science'

A logical consequence of embedding valuations around future cash flows is that valuations are based upon forecasts of the future. Given the inherent uncertainty of producing such forecasts, valuations do not produce a 'correct' answer. Instead

---

3  Free cash flow is a particular type of cash flow that we explore in detail in Chapters 23–27.

the output of a valuation should be thought of as an estimate of value. There are myriad assumptions that feed into any sophisticated valuation, many of which require significant judgement. This is why valuation processes often use scenario analysis, in other words varying assumptions, and observing the different value estimates they produce. The different scenarios and value estimates are then the basis for discussion and debate.

## 4. Valuation cannot be reduced to formulae

Many valuation textbooks are highly technical and make extensive use of mathematical formulae as well as technical jargon. To some extent this cannot be completely avoided, but the emphasis in this text will be on understanding valuation processes rather than merely using formulae to generate value estimates. The most important elements of a valuation are normally the forecasts of earnings and cash flows that we require. We need to understand how to convert cash flow forecasts into a valuation and this is normally where valuation formulae become important.

## 5. Valuation is NOT price

The price of an asset in the market, for example a share listed on the stock market, is driven by a range of factors including fundamentals, momentum and sentiment. Momentum refers to the observation that if a stock is going up or down then investors' panic, fear, herding behaviour and greed can drive this trend further. Sentiment refers to the idea that markets often favour companies with certain characteristics at particular points in time. This is very different from a valuation that is driven by an analysis of the operations of a company and expected future cash flows. Whereas we can simply observe price from a data source such as Bloomberg or LSEG, a comprehensive valuation comes from detailed analysis of financial statements, combined with economic data and other insights.

## 6. Different methodologies, if used consistently, give the same answer

There are a range of well-established valuation methodologies, a number of which we will address in this textbook. Each individual methodology appears to have its own advantages and weaknesses. However, if used consistently with equivalent assumptions, then they should produce the same value estimates. So, for example, a discounted cash flow valuation and a discounted dividend valuation, if constructed consistently, should produce the same answer. This can be difficult to see, given the complexity of some of the issues involved. It can also be a challenge to ensure that assumptions are always consistent. Nonetheless, it is important to realise that this underlying uniformity does exist.

## 7. Equity valuation is different from other asset classes

Equity investors are the residual claimants of the firm's returns. What do we mean by this? The return that equity investors are entitled to represents what remains after the claims of all other providers of capital (i.e. providers of bank loans, holders of corporate bonds and other creditors) have been settled. In other words, equity investors bear a greater risk in comparison with providers of debt capital. The eventual outcome for equity investors therefore depends on the debt-equity mix of how the company's assets are financed, and the company's ability to generate returns on the total capital invested in the company. The latter depends on a wide range of factors such as management quality, competitive landscape, business model, new products, growth rates, international expansion and the broader economic outlook, to name a few. Therefore, it is very difficult to predict with precision the ultimate outcome as it depends on so many unknowns. Contrast equity with another important asset class, fixed income securities. Essentially, these represent debt (loans). The return for a fixed income investor is the interest on the debt security. Therefore, the concerns of a fixed income investor (and valuer) will focus on the ability of the company to service the debt and repay the principal. Although issues such as company expansion plans and management quality will still be of interest, the focus is much narrower in terms of how these possible future developments impact debt servicing. This means that the valuation of fixed income securities deals with far fewer important uncertainties and it requires fewer assumptions compared with the valuation of equity.

## 8. Sector matters (different multiples and also different drivers)

Although in the text we tend to use more straightforward industries to explain valuation methodologies, it is important not to ignore the potential complications and adaptations required to value stocks in certain sectors. The valuation of banks, insurance companies, highly cyclical companies, immature companies, real estate and extractive industries all present unique challenges for the valuer (see Chapter 19). Although there remain commonalities between the valuation approaches, the unique characteristics of these sectors alter important aspects of forecasting and valuation.

However, to begin with, it is very useful to avoid the distraction of more complex sectors in order to understand core valuation processes and procedures. We shall consider some of these more specialist sector valuations in later chapters of the book.

## 9. Valuations need a narrative

Although the focus of this text is exploration of and understanding the mechanics of valuation, it is important to note that this is only half the story. Valuation also needs a narrative, a story to provide the numbers with context or, as one of the most renowned valuation experts, Aswath Damodaran, termed it: "valuation that is not backed up by a story is both soulless and untrustworthy".[4] In the absence of a narrative a valuation just becomes a set of calculations. Given the complexity of valuations for listed companies, communicating these calculations without a story becomes very cumbersome. Instead, with the aid of a well-crafted narrative, we can communicate the most important aspects of a valuation. For example, we might like to communicate where our valuation differs from the consensus in the market, where we are different from other valuers. Therefore, we should see valuation as consisting of two important elements – the forecasts and valuation computations and value estimates on the one hand and the underpinning narrative on the other.

## 10. Valuers can use enterprise value and/or equity value

If we want to value the shares of a company we have a choice about what to value – enterprise value or equity value. What is the difference? Enterprise value represents the value of the operations of the business irrespective of their financing. Equity value represents the valuation of the residual ownership in the business. It is the value most relevant to shareholders as it represents their investment in the business.

Importantly, irrespective of which choice we make – enterprise value or equity value – we can still ascertain the value of the equity. This is achieved through what is called the enterprise value bridge, which takes us from enterprise value to equity or vice versa. As we shall see, there are important advantages to calculating enterprise value first and then converting this value to equity in comparison to valuing equity directly. We address all these concepts in detail in the text, but it is important to note that the decision to focus on estimating enterprise value or equity value is a very important building block of many valuations.

---

4   Quote from: Damodaran, A. (2017, p.vii). *Narrative and Numbers: The value of stories in business.* Columbia University Press.

# Stretch yourself

Throughout the text we shall include a stretch-yourself section to push readers to consider a particular concept in more detail. This is more difficult in the opening chapter as much of the detail on valuation concepts is yet to come!

Nonetheless, let us consider building block 9 – the suggestion that valuations are more than just their numerical content, they also require a narrative. Much of the thinking around this comes from the work by Aswath Damodaran already referenced above. In his articulation of the importance of the narrative component of valuation, Damodaran (2017) sees five steps in this process that are worth reviewing:

## Step 1: Develop a narrative for the business you are valuing

This will capture how the business is expected to develop over time. We have already mentioned the importance of forecasts for any valuation, and we can imagine that this narrative will form an early-stage basis for the forecasts that we need to conduct for our valuation.

## Step 2: Test the narrative to see if it is possible, plausible and probable

Some narratives will simply fail on further analysis. Therefore, they should be tested by, for example, discussion with well-informed professionals in the field. Narratives should be rejected, altered and developed based on these discussions.

## Step 3: Convert the narrative into drivers of value

We now move on to the stage at which we introduce numbers into our work. In this step we are seeking metrics that can be used to capture, understand and assess the performance and future prospects of the company in relation to the narrative. We can then go from narrative to numbers and numbers to narrative.

## Step 4: Connect the drivers of value to a valuation

Now we are into main valuation phase where we convert forecasts into an intrinsic valuation, which is a major part of the content of this book.

## Step 5: Keep the feedback loop open

This involves fine-tuning the narrative based on information from experts and data relating to actual performance, competitive landscape and the broader economic outlook. The output of this step will feed back into Step 1 and the process will begin again.

# CHAPTER 2

# Introduction to accounting and why accounting is important for valuation

## Bite size

This chapter provides an initial insight into the importance of financial statements, and the basic concepts that underpin them, for the purposes of valuation. It raises the issue of different accounting treatments across different countries and provides an introduction to the income statement and balance sheet.

## Practitioner focus

As will quickly become apparent to any professional dealing with valuations, accounting terminology and measures are critical to valuation calculations. Stephen Penman, a world-renowned professor from Columbia University, put it eloquently when he said: *"Valuation is a set of methods for determining the appropriate price to pay for a firm. Accounting is a set of methods for producing the information for that determination"*.[5] The truth is that real-world valuations cannot be undertaken without a good knowledge of accounting basics and a detailed knowledge of certain accounting metrics, such as return measures, which are covered in detail in later chapters.

---

5  Penman, S., (2011) Accounting for Value. New York, NY: Columbia Business Publishing.

# Core content

## 1. The nature of financial reporting and accounting standards

Accounts are prepared in order to provide useful information about a business to various groups of stakeholders, including management, shareholders, employees, suppliers, banks and financial analysts. Essentially, the accounts contain a historical record of the financial transactions of a company. The idea is that gaining an understanding of past performance assists with the prediction of future performance. From Chapter 1 we know that for those undertaking valuations, forecasting the future is a critical component. Accounting becomes essential to this process as the past performance and financial position of a business provides the foundation for that forecasting process.

Although the basic concept is straightforward, preparing accounts for large companies can be a very complex process. Therefore, there are regulations and principles governing how to prepare financial statements and these can, and do, vary from country to country.

All of the rules governing financial statement preparation in a particular country are called GAAP or Generally Accepted Accounting Principles. Given that there are different rules in each country we end up with terms such as US GAAP, UK GAAP or Japanese GAAP. Arguably the most important 'GAAP' is actually a broad-based, cross-border set of accounting standards called 'International Financial Reporting Standards' (IFRS).[6]

Since 2005, the European Union (EU) has required all EU-listed companies to prepare their financial statements under IFRS. This means that, given the moves towards IFRS in many parts of the world (e.g. Asia Pacific region) two major GAAPs now exist: US GAAP and IFRS. In general, US GAAP standards tend to be more rule-based and specific than IFRS, with detailed standards on individual sectors and substantial application guidance. IFRS tend to be less detailed, and more principle-based, leaving some scope for company managers to determine an appropriate way to implement the rules. Having said that, IFRS are still very detailed and technical documents.

---

6 In addition to IFRS, some older standards remain, called International Accounting Standards (IAS).

# 2. The components of financial statements

The accounting standard IAS 1, *Presentation of Financial Statements*, addresses the component parts of financial statements.

FIGURE 2.1 THE STRUCTURE OF FINANCIAL STATEMENTS

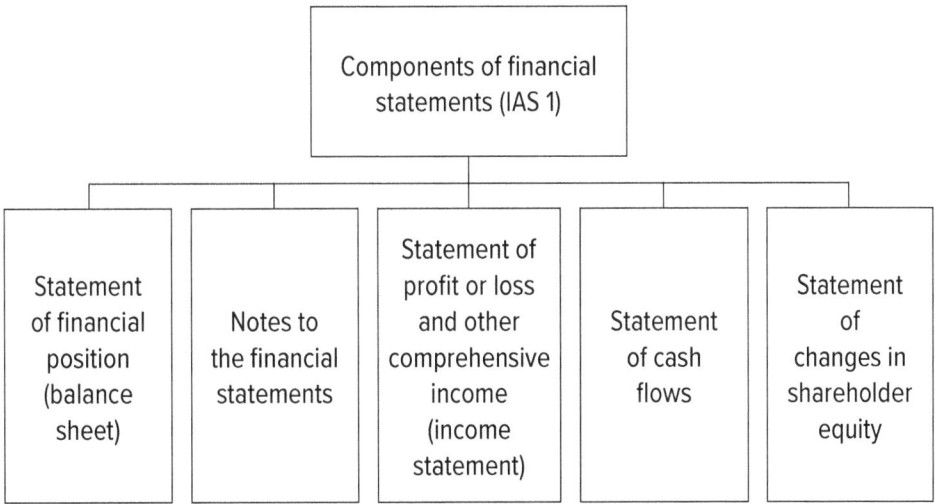

We shall address each of these in the context of how they might help a professional undertaking a valuation.

## 2.1. The statement of financial position

This statement is often termed the balance sheet; it shows the assets of a business together with the liabilities and equity. We can see this in the balance sheet example for Coca-Cola in Table 2.1. Assets are subdivided into current assets (expected to be used over a normal operating cycle or 12 months) and non-current assets, which are longer term in nature. For those undertaking valuations, assets represent the resources of a business that are available to management. If we are going to forecast a company to grow, then we would need to consider what extra resources (assets) would be needed to support this growth. In the Coca-Cola example (Table 2.1) we can see the listing of current and non-current assets which, when combined, represent total assets, that is all of the resources the company controls.

The classification of balance sheet assets can be seen in Figure 2.2.

FIGURE 2.2 ASSET CLASSIFICATION

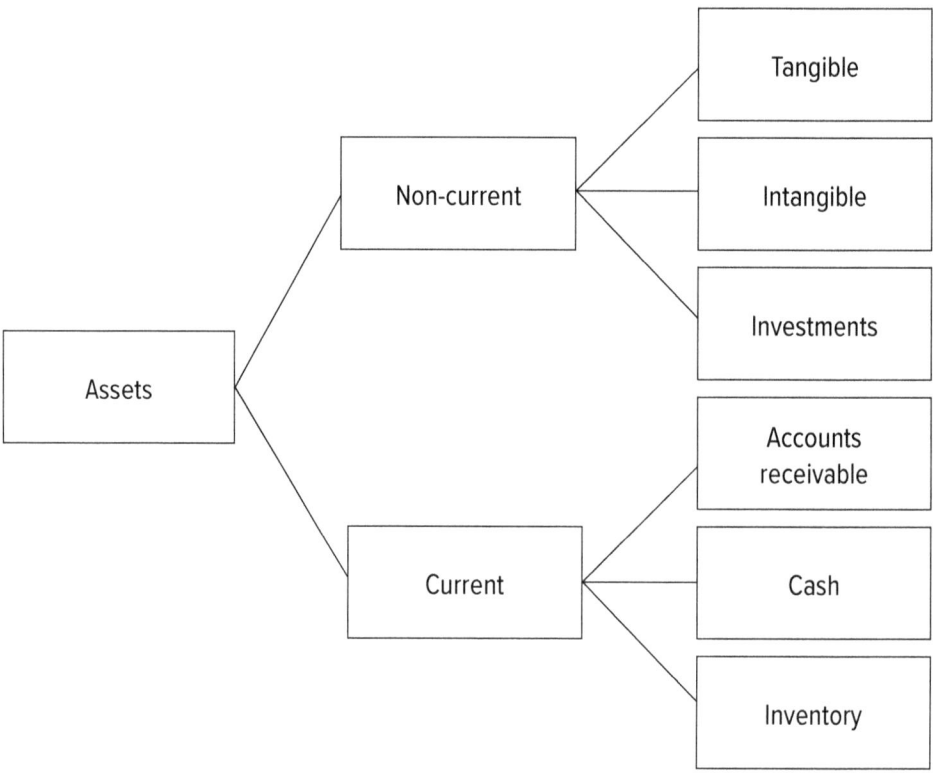

The other side of the balance sheet shows how the assets of a company have been financed. It discloses the amounts owed to third parties ('Liabilities') and amounts attributable to the owners (shareholders) of the business ('Equity'). The liabilities are classified and presented based on their timing – into current and non-current. Some of these liabilities will be financing in nature (for example, long-term debt) and others will be more operational (for example, accounts payable). We shall see later on that the distinction between operating items and financing items is important for valuation, especially if using enterprise value. Lastly, we have the equity section, which represents the ownership interest of the shareholders. As valuers we are trying to estimate an appropriate *market* value for the equity whereas the Equity section of the balance sheet represents the *book* value of equity. The relationship between the two is captured in a ratio called price to book (P/B) multiple, something we shall cover when we get to the section on valuation multiples.

## TABLE 2.1 STATEMENT OF FINANCIAL POSITION (BALANCE SHEET) – COCA-COLA

| **CONSOLIDATED BALANCE SHEETS** – (in millions except par value) | Dec. 31, 2021 | Dec. 31, 2020 |
|---|---|---|
| **ASSETS** | | |
| **CURRENT ASSETS** | | |
| Cash and cash equivalents | $ 9,684 | $ 6,795 |
| Short-term investments | 1,242 | 1,771 |
| **Total cash, cash equivalents and short-term investments** | **10,926** | **8,566** |
| Marketable securities | 1,699 | 2,348 |
| Trade accounts receivable, less allowances of $516 and $526, respectively | 3,512 | 3,144 |
| Inventories | 3,414 | 3,266 |
| Prepaid expenses and other current assets | 2,994 | 1,916 |
| **Total current assets** | **22,545** | **19,240** |
| Equity method investments | 17,598 | 19,273 |
| Other investments | 818 | 812 |
| Other non-current assets | 6,731 | 6,184 |
| Deferred income tax assets | 2,129 | 2,460 |
| Property, plant and equipment – net | 9,920 | 10,777 |
| Trademarks with indefinite lives | 14,465 | 10,395 |
| Goodwill | 19,363 | 17,506 |
| Other intangible assets | 785 | 649 |
| **Total assets** | **$ 94,354** | **$ 87,296** |
| **LIABILITIES AND EQUITY** | | |
| **CURRENT LIABILITIES** | | |
| Accounts payable and accrued expenses | $ 14,619 | $ 11,145 |
| Loans and notes payable | 3,307 | 2,183 |
| Current maturities of long-term debt | 1,338 | 485 |
| Accrued income taxes | 686 | 788 |
| **Total current liabilities** | **19,950** | **14,601** |
| Long-term debt | 38,116 | 40,125 |
| Other non-current liabilities | 8,607 | 9,453 |
| Deferred income tax liabilities | 2,821 | 1,833 |
| **SHAREOWNERS' EQUITY** | | |
| Common stock, $0.25 par value; authorized – 11,200 shares; issued – 7,040 shares | 1,760 | 1,760 |
| Capital surplus | 18,116 | 17,601 |
| Reinvested earnings | 69,094 | 66,555 |
| Accumulated other comprehensive income (loss) | (14,330) | (14,601) |
| Treasury stock, at cost – 2,715 and 2,738 shares, respectively | (51,641) | (52,016) |
| **Equity attributable to shareowners of The Coca-Cola Company** | **22,999** | **19,299** |
| Equity attributable to non-controlling interests | 1,861 | 1,985 |
| **Total equity** | **24,860** | **21,284** |
| **Total liabilities and equity** | **$ 94,354** | **$ 87,296** |

## 2.2 The income statement

The income statement shows the income, expenses and profits of a company for a particular period. Whereas a balance sheet is a cumulative statement, the income statement is focused on one period of fixed length, such as one year or one quarter. We can see from the Coca-Cola example in Table 2.2 that the income statement begins with revenues and then shows a range of deductions for a variety of costs, some of which are operating (selling, general and administrative costs – SG&A) and some of which are financing (for example, interest expense). This leads to a range of profit measures – gross profit (after manufacturing costs only, i.e. after cost of goods sold), operating income (after all operating costs, i.e. SG&A and other operating charges) and consolidated net income (after all costs including interest and taxes).

At the end of this income statement the profit is divided by the number of shares to produce an 'earnings per share' (EPS) figure. As we shall see later, EPS is used for valuation especially in the price to earnings (P/E) multiple.

TABLE 2.2 STATEMENT OF FINANCIAL PERFORMANCE (INCOME STATEMENT) – COCA-COLA

| **CONSOLIDATED STATEMENTS OF INCOME** – (in millions except per share data) | | | |
|---|---|---|---|
| Year ended December 31 | 2021 | 2020 | 2019 |
| **Net operating revenues** | $ 38,655 | $ 33,014 | $ 37,266 |
| Cost of goods sold | (15,357) | (13,433) | (14,619) |
| **Gross profit** | 23,298 | 19,581 | 22,647 |
| Selling, general and administrative expenses | (12,144) | (9,731) | (12,103) |
| Other operating charges | (846) | (853) | (458) |
| **Operating income** | 10,308 | 8,997 | 10,086 |
| Interest income | 276 | 370 | 563 |
| Interest expense | (1,597) | (1,437) | (946) |
| Equity income (loss) – net | 1,438 | 978 | 1,049 |
| Other income (loss) – net | 2,000 | 841 | 34 |
| **Income before income taxes** | 12,425 | 9,749 | 10,786 |
| Income taxes | 2,621 | 1,981 | 1,801 |
| **Consolidated net income** | 9,804 | 7,768 | 8,985 |
| Less: net income (loss) attributable to non-controlling interests | (33) | (21) | (65) |
| **Net income attributable to shareowners of The Coca-Cola Company** | $ 9,771 | $ 7,747 | $ 8,920 |
| Basic net income per share 1 | $ 2.26 | $ 1.80 | $ 2.09 |
| Diluted net income per share 1 | $ 2.25 | $ 1.79 | $ 2.07 |
| Average shares outstanding – basic | 4,315 | 4,295 | 4,276 |
| Effect of dilutive securities | 25 | 28 | 38 |
| Average shares outstanding – diluted | 4,340 | 4,323 | 4,314 |

## 2.3 The cash flow statement

The cash flow statement is the last of the critical (often called 'primary') accounting statements for valuation purposes.[7] This statement classifies the cash flowing through a company in a particular period into three categories. The first category is operating cash flows. It provides cash flow statement information about items that relate to the operating performance of the company. It is normally the cash equivalent of items going through the income statement. We shall explore the difference between profit and cash flow in more detail in Chapter 3. We can see from the Coca-Cola cash flow statement (Table 2.3) that the statement starts with consolidated net income of $9,804, which can be traced back to the income statement in Table 2.2. Various adjustments are made to this net income number to convert it into cash flows. The second category is investing cash flows. It shows cash flows that relate to buying and selling of non-current (long-term) assets. The last category is cash flows from financing activities. It shows cash movements relating to debt and equity. For example, borrowing from a bank would be shown as a cash inflow (and the payment of dividends to shareholders would be shown as an outflow) in this section of the cash flow statement.

---

7   Technically, the primary statements include the statement of financial position (balance sheet), statement of financial performance (income statement), statement of cash flows and the statement of shareholders' equity. The latter, while technically important and useful disclosure, rarely plays a major role in valuations.

## TABLE 2.3 STATEMENT OF CASH FLOWS – COCA-COLA

| CONSOLIDATED STATEMENTS OF CASH FLOWS – (in millions) | | | |
|---|---|---|---|
| Year ended December 31 | 2021 | 2020 | 2019 |
| **OPERATING ACTIVITIES** | | | |
| Consolidated net income | $ 9,804 | $ 7,768 | $ 8,985 |
| Depreciation and amortisation | 1,452 | 1,536 | 1,365 |
| Stock-based compensation expense | 337 | 126 | 201 |
| Deferred income taxes | 894 | (18) | (280) |
| Equity (income) loss – net of dividends | (615) | (511) | (421) |
| Foreign currency adjustments | 86 | (88) | 91 |
| Significant (gains) losses – net | (1,365) | (914) | (67) |
| Other operating charges | 506 | 556 | 127 |
| Other items | 201 | 699 | 504 |
| Net change in operating assets and liabilities | 1,325 | 690 | 366 |
| **Net cash provided by operating activities** | **12,625** | **9,844** | **10,471** |
| **INVESTING ACTIVITIES** | | | |
| Purchases of investments | (6,030) | (13,583) | (4,704) |
| Proceeds from disposals of investments | 7,059 | 13,835 | 6,973 |
| Acquisitions of businesses, equity method investments and nonmarketable securities | (4,766) | (1,052) | (5,542) |
| Proceeds from disposals of businesses, equity method investments and nonmarketable securities | 2,180 | 189 | 429 |
| Purchases of property, plant and equipment | (1,367) | (1,177) | (2,054) |
| Proceeds from disposals of property, plant and equipment | 108 | 189 | 978 |
| Other investing activities | 51 | 122 | (56) |
| **Net cash provided by (used in) investing activities** | **(2,765)** | **(1,477)** | **(3,976)** |
| **FINANCING ACTIVITIES** | | | |
| Issuances of debt | 13,094 | 26,934 | 23,009 |
| Payments of debt | (12,866) | (28,796) | (24,850) |
| Issuances of stock | 702 | 647 | 1,012 |
| Purchases of stock for treasury | (111) | (118) | (1,103) |
| Dividends | (7,252) | (7,047) | (6,845) |
| Other financing activities | (353) | 310 | (227) |
| **Net cash provided by (used in) financing activities** | **(6,786)** | **(8,070)** | **(9,0040** |
| Effect of exchange rate changes on cash, cash equivalents, restricted cash and restricted cash equivalents | (159) | 76 | (72) |
| **CASH AND CASH EQUIVALENTS** | | | |
| Net increase (decrease) in cash, cash equivalents, restricted cash and restricted cash equivalents during the year | 2,915 | 373 | −2,581 |
| Cash, cash equivalents, restricted cash and restricted cash equivalents at beginning of year | 7,110 | 6,737 | 9,318 |
| Cash, cash equivalents, restricted cash and restricted cash equivalents at end of year | 10,025 | 7,110 | 6,737 |
| Restricted cash and restricted cash equivalents at end of year | 341 | 315 | 257 |
| **Cash and cash equivalents at end of year** | **$ 9,684** | **$ 6,795** | **$ 6,480** |

## 2.4. Statement of changes in shareholders' equity

This statement helps a user reconcile the opening and closing equity on a balance sheet. For many companies it would be very difficult, if not impossible, to undertake this task without further information and this note provides that. However, it is not a widely used statement and most users will focus much more on the income statement, balance sheet and cash flow statements.

## 2.5. Notes to the financial statements

These notes are included after the main financial statements and provide critical detailed information on balance sheet, income statement and cash flow numbers as well as other disclosures. For those undertaking valuations, consulting the detail in the notes will almost always be required to produce forecasts with robust values.

# 3. Fundamental accounting concepts

Accounting has, in essence, developed as a pragmatic activity. Unlike science or mathematics, it has no universal set of theoretical principles. Therefore, for many years accounting practice has developed in a piecemeal and fragmented fashion. However, attempts have been made to address this and the reporting standard-setter, International Accounting Standards Board (IASB), has set out an objective of financial statements:

> *"The objective of general purpose financial reporting is to provide financial information about the reporting entity that is useful to existing and potential investors, lenders and other creditors in making decisions relating to providing resources to the entity."*
>
> (IASB Conceptual Framework, p.A19)

This view of accounting puts forward the decision utility paradigm, i.e. accounting information exists to help economic decision-making, such as undertaking valuations. Also, note the wide range of users that are within this definition, e.g. shareholders, analysts, employees, government bodies (including tax collection bodies). This objective is supplemented by a number of 'fundamental concepts' that all valuers should be aware of.

## 3.1. Conservatism

Essentially this means prudence, i.e. when preparing financial statements, it is acceptable to anticipate losses, but gains should, in general, not be recognised until they are reasonably certain to occur. The application of this concept encourages the recognition of a lower profit figure.

For example, a publishing house signs a new musical band to its record label for a three-year contract for a fee of $3m. One view is that this transaction has created an asset that the business will enjoy over the next three years, and the publisher could spread the cost over this three-year period. This is an accruals or matching approach, which is considered further below. However, adopting a prudent or conservative approach to accounting for this transaction would in theory entail the entire $3m being recognised as an immediate cost. It should be noted that accounting now places less emphasis on this principle than was historically the case.

## 3.2. Accruals

Expenses (and items of income) are included in the income statement in the period to which they relate. This may or may not be the period in which such expenses are paid in cash. Another way of thinking about this is to imagine that we are trying to link or match sales for the period with all the costs of making these sales. This concept attempts to calculate a 'fair' profit figure.

For example, the phone bill for the last quarter of a specific accounting period may not have been paid by the cut-off date (i.e. end of the accounting year). The accruals concept would still require this cost to be estimated and included in the financial statements for the previous year as that is the period to which it relates. This is irrespective of the fact that it is paid in the following year. The means of recording the expense in the correct period is called 'an accrual'. This is a critical concept and one we shall return to a number of times.

## 3.3. Going concern

When drawing up financial statements we assume that the business will continue in operational existence for the foreseeable future. Historical cost is therefore the accepted accounting convention for recording transactions in financial statements. Where going concern is in doubt, the balance sheet of an entity is prepared on a 'break-up' basis instead. For example, assets are reflected at their realisable value (i.e. the value that can be realised upon a sale of the assets) rather than historical cost.

## 3.4. Consistency

Similar items should be treated in a similar manner from year to year. This aids comparability of the performance of the entity. Any changes in the methods used to prepare financial statements should be disclosed separately so that users can clearly see what has happened.

### 3.5. Separate entity

When preparing the accounts of a business, the business is treated separately from the owners. This means that it will exclude the personal assets and personal transactions of the owners. Thus, if a company was set up with €100,000 cash from the key shareholder, then this would be reflected in the company's balance sheet as:

TABLE 2.4. BALANCE SHEET AFTER INVESTMENT OF EQUITY

| Assets | € | Liabilities & equity | € |
|---|---|---|---|
| Cash | 100,000 | Shareholders' equity | 100,000 |

Shareholders' equity here refers to the investment made by the owners of the business. It is their stake in the business at book value.

# Stretch yourself

We have already alluded to the difference between cash flow and profit, a topic we shall return to repeatedly in the text. To illustrate this difference and the accruals concept, further consider the following example:

A firm uses substantial amounts of telecommunication services in the year to 31 December 2022. On 25 January 2023 the firm receives the bill for these services, amounting to £5m. The firm's revenue for the year is £25m and other cash costs are £8m. Calculate and compare the firm's performance on a cash basis and on an accruals (earnings) basis for 2022.

**Solution:**

TABLE 2.5. ACCRUALS VERSUS CASH CALCULATION

|  | Earnings (£m) | Cash flow (£m) |
|---|---|---|
| Revenues | 25 | 25 |
| Cash costs | −8 | −8 |
| Telecommunications bill | −5 | 0 |
| Profit or cash flow | 12 | 17 |

We can see in this calculation that the company has accrued the telecommunications bill in the year. Even though it has not been paid in cash it is nonetheless included in the income statement. In many ways this seems reasonable – the cost does relate to the year in question and so profit would be overstated if we followed a cash approach. The problem is that if we had not received the bill by the time the financial statements were being prepared then we would need to make an estimate of the amount. In fact, the accruals concept means that, in practice, there are many estimates that flow through the accounts.

# CHAPTER 3

# Earnings versus cash flows

## Bite size

Even those unfamiliar with valuation methods will be aware of the central role that cash flows play in estimating value. Therefore, we need to understand how we go from accounting numbers, in the form of earnings, to cash flows useful for valuation. In this chapter we shall focus on the relationship between the two in some detail. This is a critical foundation to the valuation methodologies we will employ as we go through the text.

## Practitioner focus

The approach to valuation used in practice is to analyse and forecast earnings before proceeding to convert these to cash flows and ultimately to an estimate of intrinsic value. The content of this chapter will provide essential concepts to apply in this process.

## Core content

### 1. Why both cash flows and earnings are important

You might hear analysts or investors say something like the following:

> *"Accounting earnings do not matter – only cash flow is important."*

What matters is not just that this proposition is completely false, it is also symptomatic of an approach to the analysis and valuation of companies that is entirely misguided. It is generally based on the idea that if it is true that the value of a company is the present value of the future cash flows that it will generate between now and infinity, we should not care about anything other than cash flows. This misses the point that, to capture these future streams of cash flows, we need to use financial statement information in the first place. Why? First, the information set we are presented with by the various components of financial statements (that we summarised in Chapter 2) is hugely detailed, whereas there is very limited cash flow disclosure. Second, it turns out that forecasting earnings first, and subsequently converting these into forecasts of free cash flow, is a much more effective valuation process than forecasting cash flows directly.

## 2. The accruals concept

Accounting is based on what is known as the accruals concept. This concept requires that we recognise items in the income statement in the period when they are incurred ('enjoyed') rather than when they are paid. For example, if we pay the rent for the year 2022 in January 2023 then the accruals concept holds that even though it was paid in 2023 the rent was incurred for 2022. It relates to 2022, we enjoyed the benefit of the rented premises in 2022 and not 2023. Therefore, when we calculate an earnings number, we would include the rent cost in 2022. For cash flow purposes it would appear as an outflow in 2023. This encapsulates the difference between the earnings and cash flows.

## 3. Converting profits to cash flow – the cash flow statement

Accountants realise the strong interest from users in cash flow-based information, as well as earnings, and so financial statements include a cash flow statement, which we introduced in Chapter 2. Table 3.1 represents an extract from the cash flow statement from Netflix Inc. for 2021, showing the cash flow generated by operations. This is the part of the cash flow statement that 'converts' profit into cash flows.

## TABLE 3.1 STATEMENT OF CASH FLOWS – NETFLIX

| Netflix Inc. Consolidated Statements of Cash Flows (in thousands) | | | |
|---|---|---|---|
| Year ended December 31 | 2019 | 2020 | 2021 |
| Cash flows from operating activities: | | | |
| Net income | $ 1,866,916 | $ 2,761,395 | $ 5,116,228 |
| Adjustments to reconcile net income to net cash provided by (used in) operating activities: | | | |
| Additions to content assets | (13,916,683) | (11,779,284) | (17,702,202) |
| Change in content liabilities | (694,011) | (757,433) | 232,898 |
| Amortisation of content assets | 9,216,247 | 10,806,912 | 12,230,367 |
| Depreciation and amortisation of property, equipment and intangibles | 103,579 | 115,710 | 208,412 |
| Stock-based compensation expense | 405,376 | 415,180 | 403,220 |
| Foreign currency remeasurement loss (gain) on debt | (5,576) | 533278 | (430,661) |
| Other non-cash items | 228,230 | 293,126 | 376,777 |
| Deferred income taxes | (94,443) | 70,066 | 199,548 |
| Changes in operating assets and liabilities: | | | |
| Other current assets | (252,113) | (187,623) | (369,681) |
| Accounts payable | 96,063 | (41,605) | 145,115 |
| Accrued expenses and other liabilities | 157,778 | 198,183 | 180,338 |
| Deferred revenue | 163,846 | 193,247 | 91,350 |
| Other non-current assets and liabilities | (122,531) | (194,075) | (289,099) |
| Net cash provided by (used in) operating activities | **(2,887322)** | **2,427,077** | **392,610** |

The statement begins with net income, an accounting-based measure of profit. We must now adjust this number to convert it into a cash flow-based number. Like any real set of financials, Netflix's cash flow includes a number of complex items. For the moment we will focus on the more basic fundamental items and ignore the more advanced issues, as they require more advanced accounting knowledge. Readers might like to come back to this section later as their accounting knowledge develops.

- *Depreciation and amortisation of property, plant, equipment and intangibles*: When a company acquires assets that it will use over many years, it does not expense[8] the entire cost of these assets all in one charge. Instead, it spreads the cost over the useful life of the assets. This makes sense given the accruals concept asks us to 'match-up' costs with the years to which they relate. The cost which results from this spreading is called depreciation (in the case of tangible non-current assets) or amortisation (in the case of intangible long-lived assets). However, in the year of

---

[8] Expensing a cost means that it is charged to the income statement, i.e. subtracted from revenue to determine profit for the given period.

the actual depreciation or amortisation charge there is no cash outflow. The cash outflow happened only once – when the asset was acquired. To 'convert' accounting net income to cash flows, this cost is 'added back' in the cash flow statement.

- *Changes in operating assets and liabilities*: Here we employ what is often referred to as the rules of cash. These are the easiest way to understand the cash flow statement deductions:

| Assets | • An increase in an asset is a USE of cash<br>• A decrease in an asset is a SOURCE of cash |
|---|---|
| Liabilities | • An increase in a liability is a SOURCE of cash<br>• A decrease in a liability is a USE of cash |
| Revenues and expenses | • Revenues are a SOURCE of cash<br>• Expenses are a USE of cash |

An increase in an asset represents an outflow. Here we are only concerned with current assets, such as inventory. Non-current assets are dealt with in the investing cash flows section of the cash flow statement although the same principles apply. It makes sense that if we acquire inventory then it will lead to an outflow of cash.

In the same way, if a liability goes up that is a source of cash. The easiest example here is a bank loan. If debt liabilities go up it must be because we borrowed more. In current liabilities terms, which is what we are looking at when converting net income into operating cash flows, an increase in accounts payable means we have received credit from our suppliers and so we have more cash as we have not yet settled our supplier balances. In the Netflix cash flow statement there are a number of other lines:

- *Other current assets*: For example, this might reflect an increase in prepaid costs. Hence, there is a deduction from net income because if we have higher prepaid costs it is an increase in an asset and hence a cash outflow based on our rules of cash above.

- *Accounts payable*: The increase in payables is an addition because if payables are not being settled then cash has increased. In other words, drawing from our rules of cash, a liability has increased, which is an inflow. Note that in year 2020 there is a deduction for accounts payable. This must be because it had reduced cash flow in that year. Netflix had paid down their supplier balances, hence a cash outflow.

- *Accrued expenses*: These are expenses that have been incurred but have not yet been settled in cash and are consequently reversed. They have reduced profit but not cash flow.

## 4. Cash conversion

One way of relating cash flow information to accruals- (or earnings-) based measures is through the calculation of a suitable 'cash conversion' ratio. There are a variety of approaches to calculating such a measure. For example, one approach is as follows:

$$\text{Cash conversion (\%)} = \frac{\text{Operating cash flow}}{\text{EBIT}}$$

Imagine we have an operating cash flow of $50m in comparison to an operating profit (EBIT) number for the same period of $100m. This would mean the amount of operating profit that we have converted into operating cash flow is 50%. On its own this does not mean much but you could compare this to historical cash conversion rates and look for abnormal movements. In this case, if the long run average was 75%, we would want to investigate as to why the rate produced in the year under investigation was 50%. What might this deteriorating cash conversion rate indicate?

You will recall from an earlier chapter, and reaffirmed in this one, that the difference between profit and cash flow is a result of the accruals concept. If the gap between profit (earnings) and cash flow is widening, then this would indicate that earnings contain more accruals. Accruals involve lots of managerial judgement and so this is telling users that the earnings contain more managerial judgement. In a famous piece of research published in 1996, Richard Sloan[9] established that accruals are less persistent than cash flows. By persistent we mean how likely it is that the current level of profits or cash flows will continue into the future. Sloan established that cash flows are more persistent than accruals. Consequently, if profits have large amounts of accruals, then they are, on average, likely to be less persistent. We use the term 'earnings quality' to describe this idea – so high earnings quality emerges from profits with low accruals and vice versa. We describe this further in the 'Stretch yourself' section below.

# Stretch yourself

We address two issues relevant to the focus of this chapter. The first introduces the idea of high accruals as a warning sign. The second addresses margins analysis, a critical analytical tool for forecasting.

---

9   Sloan, R. G. (1996). Do stock prices fully reflect information in accruals and cash flows about future earnings? *The Accounting Review*, 71(3), 289–315.

# 1. Accruals as an accounting quality measure

In this chapter we mentioned an area of accounting-based research around accruals. Here we delve into this a little more deeply.

The accruals concept requires financial statement preparers to use significant judgements rather than to follow a simple 'cash in less cash out' model. The accruals anomaly was formally documented by Sloan in a seminal paper that suggested that firms with high (low) reported accruals tend to have abnormally low (high) future earnings and stock returns. Sloan's thinking can be broken down as follows:

a.  Investors attempt to forecast a firm's earnings using both cash flow and accrual information.

b.  However, certain components of income are less persistent than others. In particular, accruals tend to reverse in future periods.

c.  Investors fail to weight the cash flow and earnings components properly based on this divergent persistency as they "*naively fixate on bottom line income and they do not appear to understand that the cash flow and accrual components of earnings have different abilities to predict future earnings*".[10]

d.  This leads to a biased forecast of future earnings, and the current price is then incorrect.

It is also worth reaffirming the concept of earnings quality. High earnings quality is consistent with earnings that contain a low level of accruals. If we consider accruals to be management estimates, and that these are vulnerable to bias, then this makes sense. On the other hand, low quality earnings contain a high level of accruals. Management estimates are much more vulnerable to bias and so, if profits contain a higher level of accruals, then they are (arguably and empirically) less persistent.

# 2. Key elements of accounting needed for the forecasting phase – margins analysis

When valuing companies, particularly in the forecasting phase, we need estimates of a number of items, such as profit margins. Here we provide some detail on margins analysis, which is often integral to valuation. All profit margin calculations express an earnings number as a percentage of sales. The result informs users of how much profit is earned for every dollar of sales. Although there are a wide range of profit

---

10  Scott Richardson S., Tun I. and Wysocki P. (2010) Accounting anomalies and fundamental analysis: A review of recent research advances, Journal of Accounting and Economics, 2010, vol. 50, issue 2-3, 410-454

margin calculations that can be undertaken, there are two profit margin variants that are particularly important: gross profit margin and operating profit margin. We also consider net income margin below.

## Gross profit margin

$$\frac{Gross\ profit}{Turnover} \times 100\%$$

Gross profit is the profit a company makes after deducting cost of sales. These are costs that are directly related to the core activity of the business. For example, for a food retailer, cost of sales would include the cost of food that has been sold, the salary costs of employees working in the stores and costs associated with the stores themselves. Gross profit margin is a particularly important metric in those sectors where costs of sales is a very significant cost component and so the ability of the company to control this cost is crucial.

## Operating profit margin

$$\frac{Operating\ profit}{Turnover} \times 100\%$$

Operating profit is derived from gross profit by deducting all other operating costs that are ancillary to the core business activity (these are often referred to as overhead costs), such as marketing and administrative expenses. These costs are essential to the successful operation of a business but are less directly related to the sale of food in the supermarket in the food retail example. Operating profit margin is a more complete measure of profitability than gross profit margin. However, exploring both and looking at the relationship between the two over time can be revealing. For example, if in Year 1 a company had a gross margin of 20% and an operating margin of 6%, but in Year 2 this changed to a gross margin of 21% with an operating margin of 6%, then we might be concerned about cost control. In Year 1, 14% of the gross profit margin was consumed by overhead costs, but in Year 2 this expanded to 15%. This would be the starting point for some interesting analysis.

## Net profit margin

$$\frac{Net\ income}{Turnover} \times 100\%$$

The final margin calculation is based on net income, which is profit after all costs have been deducted. Given that the objective of analysing margins is to understand relationships among turnover, costs and profits, then net margin is the least logical of our three margin calculations. This is because net income will include items that do not necessarily vary with sales. For example, it will often include items such as income in the form of interest, which bears no relationship to turnover. For these reasons, the operating profit margin and gross margin are more logical calculations for our purposes.

# CHAPTER 4

# Assets and capital structure

## Bite size

We have now explored the income statement and how earnings can be converted into cash flow. There are two more accounting building blocks we need before we can focus on valuation. The first, addressed here, is the resources and financing disclosed on balance sheets. The second brings all three financial statements aspects together in the form of accounting ratios.

## Practitioner focus

Understanding the resources available to management, and how they are financed, feeds directly into how we assess and value companies. How can we possibly understand the opportunities facing management if we do not have knowledge of the resources available to them? Balance sheets are a key source of information in this regard.

## Core content

### 1. Assets on the balance sheet

Expenditure incurred by a business will either result in the recognition of an asset on the balance sheet or an expense in the income statement. When expenditure is treated as an investment in an asset, and the asset is recognised on the balance sheet, we refer to it as 'capitalisation' of expenditure.

## FIGURE 4.1 CAPITAL VERSUS REVENUE EXPENDITURE

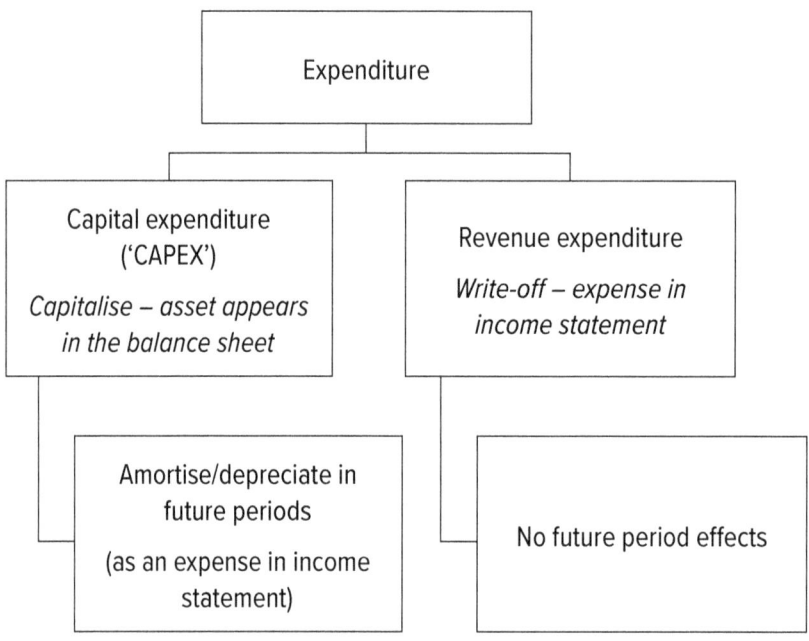

Once expenditure is capitalised and an asset is recognised in the balance sheet, the cost of the asset is then (usually) spread over future accounting periods and charged to the income statement as a depreciation and amortisation expense.[11] When expenditure is not treated as an investment in an asset, it is 'written off', that is, the full amount is recognised as an expense in the income statement. It is therefore essential to identify whether expenditure should be capitalised in the balance sheet as 'capex' (i.e. capital expenditure, building up assets) or written off as revenue expenditure. As we saw in Chapter 2 assets can be current (i.e. benefits that are expected to be used up in one accounting period) or non-current (i.e. assets that are expected to benefit the organisation over more than one accounting period).

There is a large amount of information and detailed accounting rules on assets. For the purposes of valuation, we will restrict ourselves to the necessary fundamentals.

---

11  Note that under the current accounting standards not all capitalised expenditure (i.e. assets) are required to be depreciated or amortised. For example, an asset such as land is not depreciable.

## TABLE 4.1 NETFLIX CONSOLIDATED BALANCE SHEETS

| Netflix Inc. Consolidated Balance Sheets (in thousands) | | |
|---|---:|---:|
| As of December 31 | 2020 | 2021 |
| **ASSETS** | | |
| Current assets: | | |
| Cash and cash equivalents | $ 8,205,550 | $ 6,027,804 |
| Other current assets | 1,556,030 | 2,042,021 |
| **Total current assets** | **9,761,580** | **8,069,825** |
| Content assets, net | 25,383,950 | 30,919,539 |
| Property and equipment, net | 960,183 | 1,323,453 |
| Other non-current assets | 3,174,646 | 4,271,846 |
| **Total assets** | **$ 39,280,359** | **$ 44,584,663** |
| **LIABILITIES AND STOCKHOLDERS' EQUITY** | | |
| Current liabilities: | | |
| Current content liabilities | $ 4,429,536 | $ 4,292,967 |
| Accounts payable | 656,183 | 837,483 |
| Accrued expenses and other liabilities | 1,102,196 | 1,449,351 |
| Deferred revenue | 1,117,992 | 1,209,342 |
| Short-term debt | 499,878 | 699,823 |
| **Total current liabilities** | **7,805,785** | **8,488,966** |
| Non-current content liabilities | 2,618,084 | 3,094,213 |
| Long-term debt | 15,809,095 | 14,693,072 |
| Other non-current liabilities | 1,982,155 | 2,459,164 |
| **Total liabilities** | **28,215,119** | **28,735,415** |
| **Total stockholders' equity** | **11,065,240** | **15,849,248** |
| **Total liabilities and stockholders' equity** | **$ 39,280,359** | **$ 44,584,663** |

In the Netflix Inc. balance sheet in Table 4.1 we can see current assets (cash and 'other') and non-current assets (content assets, property and equipment, and 'other'). Content assets represent the media assets of the company from which they expect to benefit over future years. Other current assets could represent a wide range of assets and so valuers should delve into the notes to the financial statements to establish precisely what these are.

# 2. Current assets, current liabilities and working capital

Working capital is a key component of the investment in any business and represents the capital needed for the day-to-day operations of the business. The formal definition is explained below but let us take the example of a furniture company. Imagine the company buys raw materials and employs skilled labour to construct the pieces of furniture. It must make this investment before receiving any cash from customers. Only after selling the furniture and receiving payment from customers will any cash inflow take place. In order to survive, a company needs to fill any gap between the time when suppliers demand payment and labour requires salary and when cash will arrive from customers.

Working capital in accounting is formally defined and calculated as:

*Current Assets less Current Liabilities*

In valuation we are focused on operating working capital rather than total working capital. Why? Because in finance and valuation we like to separate operating analysis from financing analysis as it provides useful analytical advantages that we will address in later chapters.[12] Some working capital items may relate to financing and so we would like to consider those separately. The most obvious example would be short-term borrowings included in current liabilities. We would consider these as financing items and would therefore leave them out of an analysis of operating working capital.

Operating working capital is calculated as:

*Operating Current Assets less Operating Current Liabilities*

Details about specific accounting rules of recognition and measurement of these items are outside the scope of this textbook but a high-level overview of key categories of current assets and current liabilities is summarised in Table 4.2, indicating which are operating and which are financing.

---

12   One simple reason that we can mention now is the fundamental difference between analysing the operations of a company against analysing how those operations are financed. Imagine it is an airline, an analysis of operations would require details of, for example, fleet management and airport hub optimisation. These are very different from considering the levels of debt-equity mix that would produce the most appropriate capital structure.

## TABLE 4.2 KEY CATEGORIES OF CURRENT ASSETS AND CURRENT LIABILITIES

| Item | What is it? | How it is recognised in balance sheet | Operating/non-operating classification |
|---|---|---|---|
| **Current assets** | | | |
| Accounts receivable | The amounts owed to the firm by customers | Recognise at the amount expected to be recovered | Operating |
| Inventory | Goods held for (re)sale | Recognise at the lower of cost and net realisable value (i.e. net sales price) | Operating |
| Pre payments | Costs not yet recognised in the income statement but already settled in cash | Recognise at costs paid in advance | Operating |
| Cash | Balances from bank accounts which are rapidly accessible | No specific recognition criteria. Recognised at face value. | Surplus cash is generally considered to be financing. If needed for the operations of the business, then some of it will be operating |
| **Current liabilities** | | | |
| Accounts payable | Amounts owed by the firm to suppliers | Recognise at the amount expected to be paid | Operating |
| Accruals (i.e. accrued expenses) | Costs of goods or service that the firm used/consumed and recognised in the income statement but not yet settled in cash | Recognise at estimated costs to settle when due | Operating |
| Debt repayable in less than one year | Interest bearing debt due within 12 months | Recognise at amount to settle when due | Financing |

Operating current assets are mainly accounts receivable, inventory and prepayments, and operating current liabilities are represented by accounts payable and accruals. Generally, as stated above, cash is excluded from operating working capital as it is non-operational in nature. This is considered further below.

## 3. Non-current assets

Non-current assets can be tangible (they have a physical form) and intangible (non-physical). Examples of tangible non-current assets include vehicles, buildings and computer equipment, and intangible non-current assets include goodwill, patents and software. Generally, tangible and intangible non-current assets are recognised at cost less depreciation (for tangible assets) and less amortisation (for intangibles). Let us look at a simple example to explain the fundamentals.

Fire PLC purchased an industrial processing machine for €100,000. Installation costs were €16,000. The expected useful life is eight years. The residual value at the end of Year 8 is expected to be €8,000.

### Required

Calculate the annual depreciation charge and book value for each year of its useful life on the assumption that straight line depreciation is being used.

### Solution:

$$\text{Annual depreciation charge} = \frac{(100,000+16,000)-8,000}{8 \text{ years}} = €13,500$$

*Net book value = Original cost of asset − Accumulated depreciation*

| Year | Annual depreciation charge (income statement) (1) | Accumulated depreciation (2) | Original cost of asset (3) | Net book value (balance sheet) (3) − (2) |
|---|---|---|---|---|
|  | € | € | € | € |
| 1 | 13,500 | 13,500 | 116,000 | 102,500 |
| 2 | 13,500 | 27,000 | 116,000 | 89,000 |
| 3 | 13,500 | 40,500 | 116,000 | 75,500 |
| 4 | 13,500 | 54,000 | 116,000 | 62,000 |
| 5 | 13,500 | 67,500 | 116,000 | 48,500 |
| 6 | 13,500 | 81,000 | 116,000 | 35,000 |
| 7 | 13,500 | 94,500 | 116,000 | 21,500 |
| 8 | 13,500 | 108,000 | 116,000 | 8,000 |

If we look at this calculation, we can also view it as (taking Year 4 as an example):

| Year 4 | |
|---|---|
| Opening balance of net book value | €75,500 |
| Add: Capital expenditure in Year 4 | 0 |
| Subtract: Annual depreciation charge | 13,500 |
| Closing balance of net book value | €62,000 |

Amortisation works in a very similar way and is deducted each year over the useful economic life of the intangible asset.

# 4. Capital structure

Capital structure refers to the mix of financing that a company has used to finance its activities. In simple terms, this would be a mix of debt type finance and equity finance. In practice, there is a broad range of financing alternatives available to firms but at this stage we shall focus on straightforward debt (raised from a bank or on bond markets) and common stock.

Below we address a number of relevant basic aspects of capital structure.

***Debt equity ratios.*** Debt equity ratios can be used to express the mix of debt and equity a company uses. One of the most common ratios is the debt/equity ratio:

$$Debt\text{-}to\text{-}equity\ ratio = \frac{Debt\ finance}{Equity\ finance}$$

This expresses the amount of debt finance for every $ of equity finance. Another version expresses debt as a percentage of the total financing:

$$Debt\text{-}to\text{-}capital\ ratio = \frac{Debt\ finance}{Debt\ finance\ +\ Equity\ finance}$$

***Debt finance and industry.*** Different industries can support different levels of debt finance. In broad terms, industries with predictable cash flows can support higher levels of debt finance. These firms can be more confident of having sufficient cash to satisfy principal and interest repayments. The utilities sector, with its relatively predictable and constant demand, would be an example of such an industry. Industries that are highly cyclical or those with volatile (unpredictable) cash flows may not be suitable for very high levels of debt finance. The airlines sector is one such example.

***Debt finance and firm maturity.*** Younger firms generally cannot support significant levels of debt. These firms need to invest and often have low or volatile cash inflows as they become established over time. They cannot commit to very strict interest and debt principal repayment schedules. Conversely, in more mature firms, the patterns of cash inflows are better established. Consequently, there is much more potential to support the cash flow demands of debt.

***Net debt.*** Often, for the purposes of valuation, we will use net debt. Technically speaking this is debt less surplus cash. Surplus cash is a difficult concept to define and indeed there is no widely accepted definition. The most useful way to think about the concept is that some cash a company retains is needed to support its operations. Any excess of cash held by a company over these operational needs is considered 'surplus'. Surplus cash is considered to be finance related. It is not needed for operating activities and so we subtract surplus cash from debt as this better reflects the 'indebtedness' of the company. It is also consistent with treating surplus cash as finance related.

# Stretch yourself

Investment in intangible assets has become much more important over recent decades, as illustrated in Figure 4.2. As we can see, the percentage of intangibles relative to total assets in companies' balance sheets has been steadily increasing over the past decades. Therefore, we need to spend a little more time on the relevant accounting.

FIGURE 4.2 THE CHANGING PATTERN OF INTANGIBLE ASSETS AS A PERCENTAGE OF TOTAL ASSETS

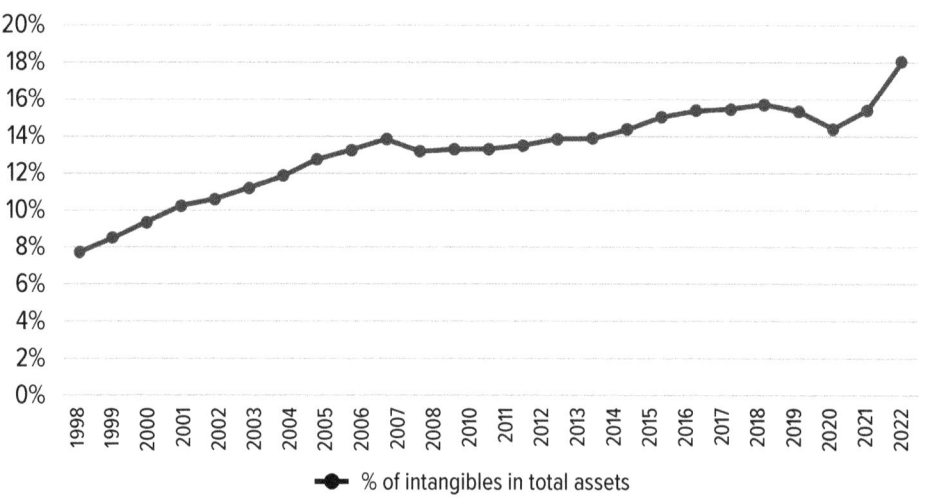

Data source: Compustat. Based on data of US-listed companies, excluding financials and utilities.

We have already established that an intangible asset is an asset with no physical presence. These assets pose difficulties for accountants and analysts for a number of reasons, such as the difficulty in measuring existing value in the market and the need for subjective inputs to amortisation calculations (e.g. useful economic life). These matters are so significant that they call into question whether such assets have any value. To address this, accounting standard-setters have tended to hold users' needs in abeyance on intangibles and instead adopt a highly conservative approach whereby only acquired intangibles are recognised.

The general model for intangible asset recognition is set out in Figure 4.3. In essence, the accounting recognition criteria boil down to whether the asset was purchased or not. Purchased intangibles are capitalised[13] as assets on the balance sheet, but those arising without a purchase are essentially written off as costs. This means that the value of internally generated intangibles is not generally recognised. The general model is then adapted somewhat to cope with certain specific intangibles, as explained in Figure 4.3. Research and development is a special case and we have set out the accounting treatment below.

FIGURE 4.3 THE GENERAL MODEL FOR ACCOUNTING FOR INTANGIBLES

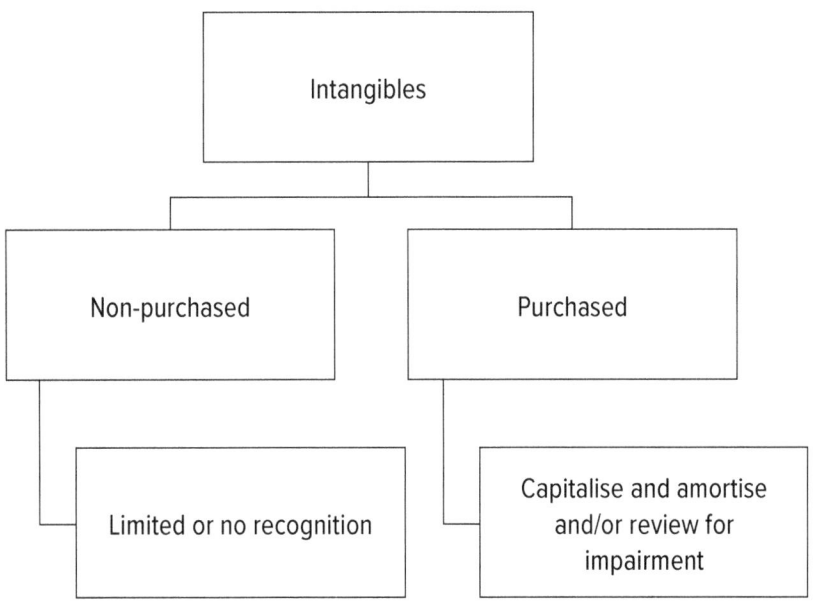

---

13  In a similar way to tangibles, which are depreciated, intangibles which are capitalised are amortised. In other words the cost of the asset (e.g. an acquired patent) is spread over its economic life (e.g. the life of the patent) as a cost that flows through the income statement. The cost is referred to as amortisation.

The result of this emphasis on expensing rather than capitalisation is a highly restrictive regime for intangible expenditure recognition. There are specific rules for certain intangibles, such as research and development (R&D) and goodwill, some of which we will address in later chapters, but overall, the result is that existing GAAP tends to materially understate intangible assets.

# SECTION B
# Forecasting

## CHAPTER 5

# Forecasting earnings

## Bite size

In this chapter we focus on the essential elements of the income statement that need to be forecast in order to feed into our valuations. These key items are sales, operating expenses, interest and taxes. We discuss which analytical tools are best used to analyse and then drive the forecasts of each of these items and how to do this in practice.

## Practitioner focus

We need sensible bases for our forecasts. This requires us to use a variety of data sources. Historical data is usually important on the basis that the past performance of a company may well be a useful guide to its future performance. We can also use peer company comparisons on the assumption that what impacts one company in a sector is likely to impact other similar companies in the same sector in a similar way. Guidance from management can also be helpful, assuming that we trust what they are saying and have confidence in their ability to execute their plans.

Buy-side analysts at investment management firms and sell-side analysts at research houses will follow public companies closely and produce their own forecasts. It is very useful for us to consult these if and when they are available. Even if individual analyst forecasts are not available, we can potentially take advantage of consensus estimates from traditional data providers like Bloomberg, FactSet and London Stock Exchange Group's I/B/E/S Estimates (Institutional Brokers' Estimate System) and from newer services such as Visible Alpha.[14]

---

14   Consensus estimates represent an average of the forecasts published by analysts who cover and research the company in question. We call these analysts sell-side analysts, and they generally work in large investment banks. Their research and forecasts are typically only available to paying clients and are often disseminated on data aggregators such as the ones mentioned above (Bloomberg, FactSet, etc.).

# Core content

## 1. Sales

The forecasting process almost always begins with sales and sales are almost always analysed and forecast using sales growth rates. We compare the sales figures from one period to the next to see whether they are growing or declining and at what rate:

$$Period\text{-}on\text{-}period\ sales\ growth\ rate\ (\%) = \left(\frac{Current\ period\ sales}{Previous\ period\ sales} - 1\right) \times 100\%$$

For example, if the company has sales in the current period of $105m and sales in the previous period of $100m, then it will have a period-on-period sales growth rate of 5%:

$$5\% = \left(\frac{\$105m}{\$100m} - 1\right) \times 100\%$$

Depending on how much time and data we have available, we can perform our analysis and forecasting at very different levels of detail. If we lack detailed data or do not wish to devote too much time to this particular valuation, we can analyse and forecast sales (and sales growth rates) at the total or group sales level. There is nothing wrong with this approach but when time and data allow, we can break total sales down into its component parts and gain a richer understanding of the business.

To start with we could disaggregate sales by division/product type or by different geographical regions. We will usually be guided by the primary segments that the company divides itself into in its segmental reporting, most likely in the notes to its financial statements. This approach will be particularly useful if we expect the different parts of the business to grow at different rates in the future.

Once we have begun this process, we can continue it further. For each segment we could consider whether growth was inorganic, arising from merger and acquisition (M&A) activity, or organic, arising from underlying sales growth in the business itself. M&A activity will be broken down into sales-positive acquisitions and sales-negative disposals. Underlying sales growth will often be broken down into price and volume components, i.e. can the company increase sales by increasing its selling price and/or by increasing the amount of product it sells? M&A activity can be difficult to predict, as we do not know which businesses the company might buy or sell in the future or when and what impact these acquisitions and disposals might have on sales. Therefore,

Chapter 5 – Forecasting earnings

in practice, sales forecasting tends to focus on organic underlying sales growth and the impact of changes in price and/or volume.

FIGURE 5.1 AN EXAMPLE OF THE BREAKDOWN OF TOTAL SALES GROWTH RATES INTO ITS KEY COMPONENT PARTS

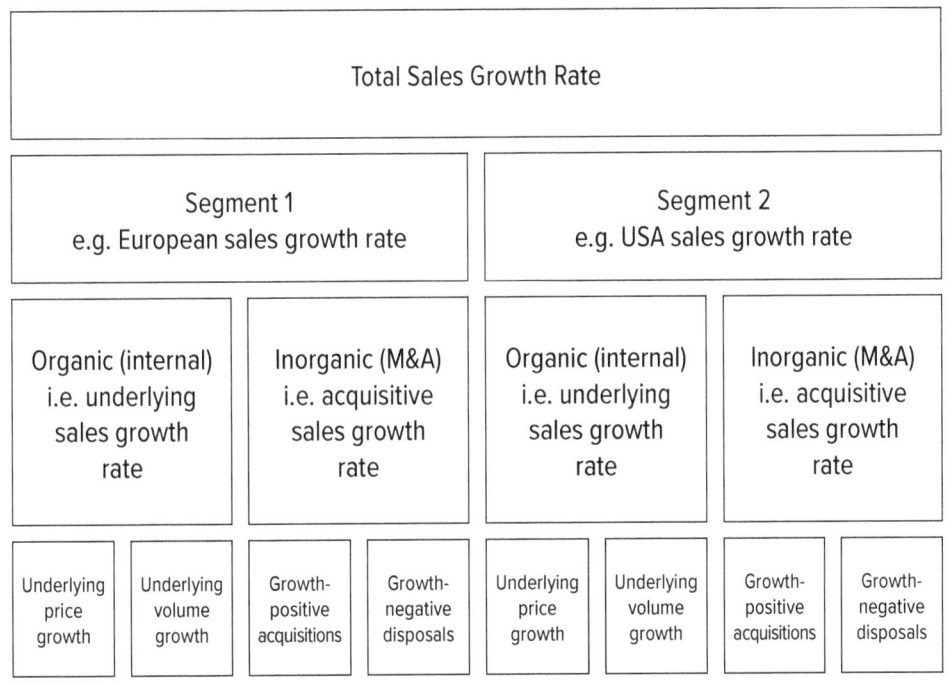

Using the various data sources outlined above we can analyse the company's historical sales growth rates and those of its peers; we can factor in management strategy with regards to sales (for example planned product launches and/or geographical expansion); and any other relevant information and form our own view. We can then use our sales growth forecasts to produce sales forecasts by rearranging the formula above:

$$\textit{Next period sales} = \textit{Current period sales} \times (100\% + \textit{Next period sales growth rate}\ \%)$$

For example, if the company has sales in the current period of $105m and we forecast a period-on-period sales growth rate of 10%, then the next period's forecast sales will be $115.5m:

$$\$115.5m = \$105m \times (100\% + 10\%)$$

## 2. Operating expenses

Once we have dealt with sales, we can logically move on to operating expenses. These are commonly analysed and forecast using margins. We compare the operating expenses for a period with sales for the same period to see what percentage of sales is being consumed by that cost:

$$Current\ operating\ expense\ margin\ (\%) = \left(\frac{Current\ operating\ expenses}{Current\ sales}\right) \times 100\%$$

For example, if the company has operating expenses in the current period of $84m and sales in the current period of $105m, then it will have a current operating expense margin of 80%:

$$80\% = \left(\frac{\$84m}{\$105m} - 1\right) \times 100\%$$

Once again, we can choose to analyse and forecast total operating expenses and margins. Alternatively, we can break these down into sensible component parts. Rather than disaggregating by division/product type/geographical regions as we might with sales, we are more likely to break operating expenses down into more common categories, such as cost of goods sold (CoGS) and selling, general and admin expenses (SG&A). This approach will be particularly useful if we expect the relationship between the different elements of operating expenses and sales to evolve differently over time.

Again, we can continue this process further. For a manufacturing business, for example, CoGS could be broken down into material and labour costs. SG&A could be broken down into advertising and marketing costs and other overheads. We could go further still and separate out the 'cash' operating expenses, i.e. those that are more-or-less paid in cash each year, and the non-cash operating expenses that are definitely not paid in cash each year, such as the depreciation expense on tangible assets and the amortisation expense on intangible assets. This will be quite a useful distinction to draw as we move from analysis and forecasting into valuation.

FIGURE 5.2 AN EXAMPLE OF THE BREAKDOWN OF OPERATING EXPENSE MARGINS INTO KEY COMPONENT PARTS

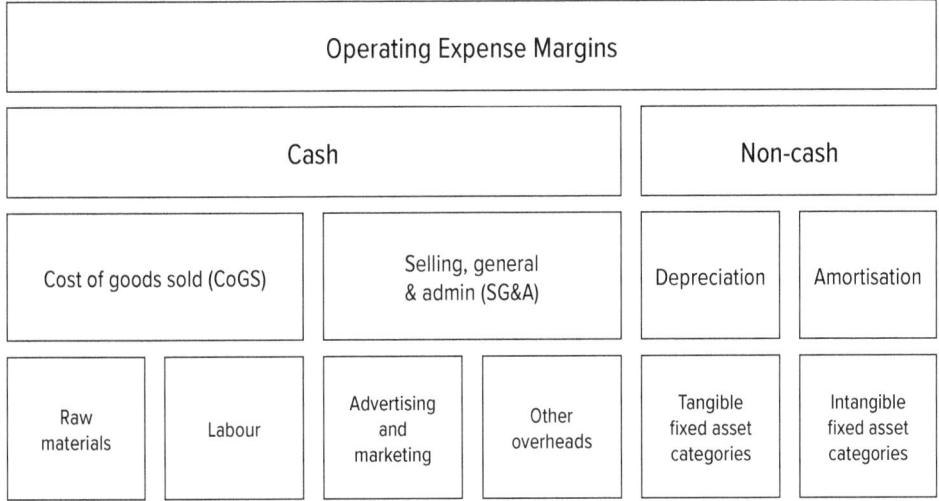

Using similar data sources as for sales, we can form our own view with regards to future operating expense margins (for example, do we expect commodity prices and labour costs to rise or fall) and then use these to produce operating expense forecasts by rearranging the formula above:

*Next period operating expense*
    *= Next period sales × Next period operating expense margin (%)*

For example, if the company has forecast sales in the next period of $115.5m and we forecast an operating expense margin of 82%, then the next period's forecast operating expenses will be $94.7m:

$$\$94.7m = \$115.5m \times 82\%$$

# 3. Interest

Once we have dealt with sales and operating expenses we will have arrived at operating profit or earnings before interest and taxes (EBIT), so we can then sensibly move away from the operational focus of the income statement to the non-operating elements, such as the cost of debt financing, i.e. interest expenses.

We can attempt to understand the cost of debt financing for the business in a number of ways. We can compare the interest expense for a particular period from the income statement with the average debt balance over the same period using balance sheet data to discern the effective interest rate the company appears to be suffering:

$$Current\ effective\ interest\ rate\ (\%) = \frac{Current\ interest\ expense}{Current\ average\ debt\ balance} \times 100\%$$

For example, if the company has interest expenses in the current period of $3m and an average debt balance in the current period of $40m, then it will have a current effective interest rate of 7.5%:

$$7.5\% = \frac{\$3m}{\$40m} \times 100\%$$

We can cross-check this analysis by looking at the notes to the financial statements to see if there are any disclosures regarding the interest rates the company suffers on any bank loans, bonds or leases. Also, if the company has any publicly traded debt we can use market data sources to find the yield-to-maturity (i.e. expected return on the bond/debt if held until maturity) on any outstanding bonds. Our analysis and cross-checking should give us a reasonable idea of the cost of the company's debt.

However, there is still more to do. We will need to regard the general macroeconomic environment and form a view as to whether we think interest rates will rise or fall or remain stable. We will also have to consider the company's financial strategy – if they plan to lever up (i.e. increase the level of debt) then it is likely that their credit rating[15] will deteriorate, and their cost of debt financing will increase, whereas if they plan to de-lever then the opposite may well be the case.

Once we have formed a view with regard to future effective interest rates, we can then use these to produce interest expense forecasts by rearranging the formula above:

$$Next\ period\ interest\ expense \\ = Next\ period\ average\ debt\ balance \\ \times Next\ period\ effective\ interest\ rate\ (\%)$$

---

[15] A credit rating is an assessment of the quality of debt instruments issued by companies. The largest credit rating agencies are Standard and Poor's, Moody's and Fitch.

For example, if the company has a forecast average debt balance in the next period of $42m and we forecast an effective interest rate of 8%, then the next period's forecast interest expenses will be $3.4m:

$$\$3.4m = \$42m \times 8\%$$

## 4. Taxes

After dealing with the interest expense, we will have arrived at pre-tax profits or earnings before taxes (EBT), so we can then move on to consider tax expenses.

We can attempt to understand the tax expenses for the business in a number of ways. We can compare the tax expense with profit before tax from the same income statement to discern the effective tax rate the company appears to be suffering:

$$Current\ effective\ tax\ rate\ (\%) = \frac{Current\ tax\ expense}{Current\ profit\ before\ tax}$$

For example, if the company has tax expenses in the current period of $4m and profit before tax in the current period of $18m, then it will have a current effective tax rate of 22.2%:

$$22.2\% = \frac{\$4m}{\$18m}$$

We can cross-check this analysis by finding the statutory corporate tax rate(s) in the country or countries in which the company operates. If the company's effective tax rate appears lower than the official rates, we may need to investigate further to discern whether this is a temporary or permanent phenomenon.

The company's effective tax rate may appear low if it has previously suffered losses that it is now carrying forward to offset against profits and reduce its tax bill. However, such losses will eventually either run out or will no longer be able to be carried forward and the company will return to paying tax on its full profits and its effective tax rate will return to a more normal level. Also, if the company has been investing in new assets to fuel its growth it may well have been receiving generous tax deductions from the government. If we expect growth and investment in new assets to decline, then so will these generous deductions and again the effective tax rate will return to a more normal level. Since the global financial crisis and the work of the OECD and

G20 on Base Erosion and Profit Shifting, tax planning has become more difficult. So, again, if a low effective tax rate is a result of such activity, it may prove more difficult to maintain this going forward.

Once we have formed a view on future effective tax rates, we can use these to produce tax expense forecasts by rearranging the formula above:

*Next period tax expense*
$= Next\ period\ profit\ before\ tax \times Next\ period\ effective\ tax\ rate$ (%)

For example, if the company has a forecast profit before tax in the next period of $17.4m and we forecast an effective tax rate of 25%, then the next period's forecast tax expenses will be $4.4m:

$$\$4.4m = \$17.4m \times 25\%$$

Once we have forecast tax expenses, we arrive at post-tax profits, i.e. net income or earnings.

At this stage we have now forecast revenues and all of the key expense captions down to and including tax. This means we have completed the income statement forecast down to profit after tax and this is the vast bulk of the income statement forecasting we will need for our valuation.

# Stretch yourself

### 1. Normalisation

We analyse historical and peer data in order to help us forecast. When we forecast, we do so on what's called a normal or 'normalised' basis, that is we ignore any abnormal events. We know such abnormalities will happen, but we cannot forecast what they will be, when they will happen or what their financial impact (positive or negative) might be.

So, when we analyse historical and peer income statements, we must be careful to normalise them by removing the impact of any abnormal items. These may be variously referred to as exceptional, non-recurring or non-underlying items. An example might be an accounting gain or loss on the disposal of an asset or business unit. This may have happened in the past and must be reported by the company but is not an ongoing source of income or expense and should be excluded from our forecasts.

However, we must also be careful not to blindly accept any item that the company describes as exceptional. A company might try to persuade us that restructuring costs are exceptional but further investigation might show that they recur most years and we might conclude that they are quite normal.

## 2. Sales

Forecasting revenues or sales represents a hugely important part of the overall forecasting process. Many of the other items that need to be forecasted derive directly or indirectly from our expectations of future sales. It is therefore vital that they are sensible and as such they need to be sanity checked. This can be done in simpler ways such as calculating sales per square foot or sales per staff member to see if the forecasts appear reasonable in historical/peer context.

It can also be done in more complicated ways. The sales forecasting process outlined above could be described as bottom-up, i.e. building upwards by looking at the different parts of the business in order to arrive at total sales forecasts. These can be sense checked using a top-down approach, i.e. looking at the size of the market or markets the company is involved in and the company's market share. This can be easier said than done but if the two sets of numbers arrived at are reasonably close then this gives a degree of comfort that the forecasts are reasonable; if they are far apart then it casts doubts on the quality of the forecasts.

Also, as well as using period-on-period growth rates as seen above, you could consider using compound annual growth rates (or CAGRs) to calculate and compare historical and forecast growth rates over longer periods of time:

$$CAGR\ \%\ (over\ 'n'\ periods) = \left(\sqrt[(n-1)]{\frac{'n'th\ period\ sales}{1st\ period\ sales}} - 1\right) \times 100\%$$

For example, if the company has sales of $100m in Year 1 and sales of $150m in Year 10, then it has a compound annual sales growth rate of 4.6%:

$$4.6\%\ CAGR\ (over\ 10\ periods) = \left(\sqrt[(10-1)]{\frac{\$150m}{\$100m}} - 1\right) \times 100\%$$

## 3. Operating expenses

The process above uses margins to analyse and forecast operating expenses. This is very common, but it implies that we expect these expenses to move up and down broadly in line with movements in sales, i.e. they are essentially variable costs. That may well be the case but for some businesses in some sectors it may not be; they may have a more fixed cost base. A good example of this would be property costs such as rent for a bricks-and-mortar retailer. Their sales can go up and down from one quarter to the next, but their quarterly rent payment does not. This is worth bearing in mind at the very least and considering whether the margin approach is genuinely appropriate or not.

# CHAPTER 6
# Forecasting balance sheets

## Bite size

In this chapter we focus on the essential elements of the balance sheet that need to be forecast in order to feed into our valuations. On the operating side, these key items are the shorter-term working capital assets and liabilities and the longer-term tangible and intangible assets. On the non-operating (or financing) side, the key item is the debt funding of the business. We discuss which analytical tools are best used to analyse and then drive the forecasts of each of these items and how to do this in practice.

## Practitioner focus

In practice, analysts will use common frameworks such as Porter's five forces (shown below) to aid in their analysis and forecasting. For example, in relation to the working capital discussion below, considering the power of buyers can help us understand what credit periods the company might offer and therefore what its level of accounts receivable might be. Similarly, considering the power of suppliers can help us understand what credit periods a company might receive and therefore what its level of accounts payable might be.

FIGURE 6.1 PORTER'S FIVE FORCES

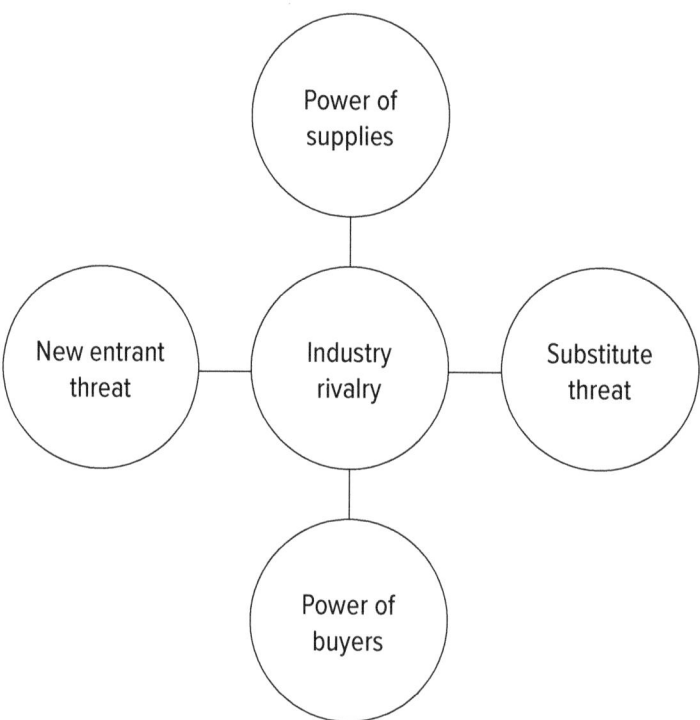

# Core content

## 1. Working capital

As explained in Chapter 4, working capital is an accounting concept that brings together **all** of the company's shorter-term assets and liabilities:

| Current assets | X |
|---|---|
| Current liabilities | (X) |
| Net working capital | X/(X) |

It is the net of **all** of these current assets and liabilities but the word 'net' is usually dropped and it is referred to as working capital. In forecasting and valuation, we usually separate the operating and non-operating elements of the business, but the above version captures both of these. For our purposes, we will focus primarily on the operating items and so we will be looking at the net **operating** working capital (NOWC) of the business:

| Current **operating** assets | X |
|---|---|
| Current **operating** liabilities | (X) |
| **Net operating working capital** | X/(X) |

Without trying to be comprehensive, we will focus on the common current operating assets (i.e. inventories and accounts receivable) and liabilities (i.e. accounts payable). Once we understand how to analyse and forecast these items, the same logic can be applied to other working capital items (for example, prepayments and accruals).

## 1.1 Inventories

NOWC items, such as inventories, are best analysed and forecast using working capital days ratios. Linkages between different items in the financial statements are important. Inventories are simply cost of goods sold (CoGS) that are waiting to be recognised as expenses. So, there is a link between inventories in the balance sheet and CoGS in the income statement. In the first instance, we can analyse inventories by calculating inventory turnover ratio. The ratio shows how many times during the period the company churns through its average inventory level:

$$Inventory\ turnover\ (x) = \frac{Current\ period\ CoGS}{Current\ period\ inventory\ balance}$$

For example, if the company has CoGS in the current period of $45m and current period inventory balance of $3m, then it will have inventory turnover of 15.0x:

$$15.0x = \frac{\$45m}{\$3m}$$

If we know how many days the company operates during a period then we can calculate how long on average each of those inventory turnover cycles lasts:

$$Inventory\ days = \frac{Period\ length\ (days)}{Inventory\ turnover\ (x)}$$

The Valuation Book

For example, if the company has a 365-day year and inventory turnover of 15.0x, then it will have inventory days of 24.3 days:

$$24.3\ days = \frac{365\ days}{15.0x}$$

Inventory days (which are sometimes also called the 'inventory holding period') is a measure of efficiency, because it shows how long a firm holds on to goods between buying them in and selling them on to customers. In an ideal world we would like it to be lower rather than higher. However, it cannot be zero as then the company would have no inventory. So, there is a sweet spot – we do not want it to be too high as there might be unused or wasted inventory, but we do not want it to be too low as inventory might run out.

To forecast inventory, we would again start off by looking at historical data for the company, benchmarking against sector peers and considering management guidance. For example, we may find out that management is planning to invest in 'just-in-time' software so that they do not buy in more products than they have customers for at any given point in time. Once we have formed a view with regard to the impact of management plans on future inventory days, we can then use these to project inventory levels by rearranging the formulae above:

$$Next\ period\ inventory\ balance = \frac{Next\ period\ inventory\ days}{Period\ length\ (days)} \times Next\ period\ CoGS$$

For example, if we forecast inventory days of 24 days, the company has a 365-day year and next period forecast CoGS of $50m, then it will have a forecast inventory balance of $3.3m:

$$\$3.3m = \frac{24\ days}{365\ days} \times \$50m$$

## 1.2 Accounts receivable

As mentioned earlier, there are important linkages between different items in the financial statements. Accounts receivable arise as a result of the company making sales on credit to customers. So, there is a clear link between accounts receivable in the balance sheet and sales in the income statement. In the same vein as with inventory turnover, we can calculate receivables turnover to see how many times during the period the company churns through its receivables:

$$Receivables\ turnover\ (x) = \frac{Current\ period\ sales}{Current\ period\ receivables\ balance}$$

For example, if the company has sales in the current period of $105m and current period receivables balance of $9m, then it will have receivables turnover of 11.7x:

$$11.7x = \frac{\$105m}{\$9m}$$

We can also calculate how long on average each of these receivables cycles lasts:

$$Receivables\ days = \frac{Period\ length\ (days)}{Receivables\ turnover\ (x)}$$

For example, if the company has a 365-day year and receivables turnover of 11.7x, then it will have receivables days of 31.2 days:

$$31.2\ days = \frac{365\ days}{11.7x}$$

This measure shows how long, on average, the company waits for customers to pay, or what credit period the company gives to its customers. This is sometimes also called the 'customer collection period'. We would also like this efficiency measure to be lower rather than higher. However, it cannot be zero as then the company would be making no credit sales.[16] So, again, there is a sweet spot – we do not want it to be too high as the company might be providing overly generous credit, and we do not want it to be too low as the company might lose out on sales to competitors that offer customers more generous credit terms.

In practice, when generating forecasts, we would again look at historical data for the company, benchmark against sector peers and consider management guidance. Management may, for example, be planning to increase credit to attract more

---

16  Of course, in certain sectors, accounts receivable may be virtually nil as customers pay immediately on receipt of goods such as in the food retail sector.

sales. Alternatively, they may be planning to reduce credit if they feel they can in their competitive environment. Once we have formed a view with regard to future receivables days, we can then use these to project future receivables by rearranging the formulae above:

$$\text{Next period receivables} = \frac{\text{Next period receivables days}}{\text{Period length (days)}} \times \text{Next period sales}$$

For example, if we forecast receivables days of 30 days, the company has a 365-day year and next period forecast sales of $115.5m, then it will have a forecast receivables balance of $9.5m:

$$\$9.5m = \frac{30 \text{ days}}{365 \text{ days}} \times \$115.5m$$

## 1.3 Accounts payable

Accounts payable arise as a result of the company making purchases (e.g. of goods to resell) on credit from suppliers. There is a clear link between accounts payable in the balance sheet and CoGS in the income statement. We can calculate the payables turnover ratio that shows how many times during the period the company churns through its average payables:

$$\text{Payables turnover } (x) = \frac{\text{Current period CoGS}}{\text{Current period payables balance}}$$

For example, if the company has CoGS in the current period of $45m and current period payables balance of $5m, then it will have payables turnover of 9.0x:

$$9.0x = \frac{\$45m}{\$5m}$$

We can then calculate how long on average each of those payables cycles lasts:

$$\text{Payables days} = \frac{\text{Period length (days)}}{\text{Payables turnover } (x)}$$

For example, if the company has a 365-day year and payables turnover of 9.0x, then it will have payables days of 40.6 days:

$$40.6 \: days = \frac{365 \: days}{9.0x}$$

This measure shows how long on average the company waits to pay suppliers, or what credit period the company is 'granted' by its suppliers. This is sometimes also called the 'supplier payment period'. We would like this to be higher rather than lower. However, it cannot be infinite as then the company would be making no payments to suppliers. So, there is a sweet spot – we do not want it to be too low as the company might not be taking advantage of free credit, but we do not want it to be too high as this might damage their relationships with their key suppliers.

In the process of forecasting, we would again look at historical data for the company, benchmark against sector peers and consider management guidance. Once we have formed a view with regard to future payables days, we can then use these to project future payables by rearranging the formulae above:

$$Next \: period \: payables = \frac{Next \: period \: payables \: days}{Period \: length \: (days)} \times Next \: period \: CoGS$$

For example, if we forecast payables days of 40 days, the company has a 365-day year and next period forecast CoGS of $48.0m, then it will have a forecast payables balance of $5.3m:

$$\$5.3m = \frac{40 \: days}{365 \: days} \times \$48.0m$$

## 2. Non-current assets

We have already considered the cost of tangible and intangible assets, i.e. the depreciation and amortisation expenses that hit the income statement each period, in Chapter 4. These also reduce the net book value (or NBV) of these assets in the balance sheet, which effectively reflects the wearing out or using up of these assets. These physical (e.g. machinery) and non-physical (e.g. licences to use the intellectual property of others) assets will need to be replaced or renewed if the company is to continue in business.

When forecasting non-current assets, we are looking at the additions to tangible and intangible assets, which will increase the net book value of these assets in the balance sheet. This capital expenditure (or 'capex') on longer-term assets can be split into two important categories – replacement (or maintenance) capex and growth (or expansionary) capex (see Figure 6.2).

FIGURE 6.2 THE SPLIT OF TOTAL CAPITAL EXPENDITURE INTO ITS TWO KEY CATEGORIES

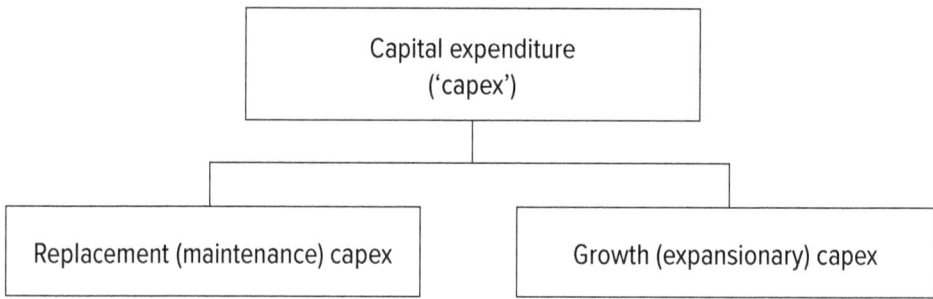

If the company wants to maintain its existing level of operating capacity, then over time it will need to replace the assets which it is wearing out or using up. Companies do not generally disclose the breakdown of their capex into replacement and growth elements and so analysts often use depreciation and amortisation expenses as a proxy for the replacement element, i.e. an accounting measure of the value of assets used up or worn out over the period. This is not ideal as companies can calculate their depreciation and amortisation expenses in different ways, but sometimes we have to be pragmatic.

One way we can analyse total capex is by comparing it to the depreciation and amortisation (D&A) expenses:

$$Capex\text{-}to\text{-}D\&A\ multiple\ (x) = \frac{Total\ capex\ for\ period}{D\&A\ expenses\ for\ period}$$

For example, if the company has total capex in the current period of $10m and depreciation and amortisation expenses of $8m, then it will have a capex-to-D&A multiple of 1.25x:

$$1.25x = \frac{\$10m}{\$8m}$$

The capex-to-D&A multiple of up to 1.00x signals a situation of no growth in the net book value of non-current assets, i.e. no growth in its existing productive capacity. In contrast, a capex-to-D&A multiple of over 1.00x is a 'growth' capex, and in this case the company is expanding its operating asset base (i.e. its net book value of non-current assets).

As ever, when generating forecasts, we should consider the historical data, sector comparisons and management guidance as to their capex plans but we will have to make sure that we maintain consistency within our forecasts between the growth assumptions driving our sales forecasts and the capex assumptions driving our asset forecasts. The higher the growth, the greater the investment will need to be to drive it. Once we have formed a view with regards to future capex-to-D&A multiples, we can then use these to produce capex forecasts by rearranging the formula above:

$$Next\ period\ capex = Next\ period\ D\&A \times Next\ period\ capex\text{-}to\text{-}D\&A\ (x)$$

For example, if the company has next period forecast depreciation and amortisation expenses of $8.5m and we forecast next period capex-to-D&A multiple of 1.5x, then it will have a forecast capex of $12.75m:

$$\$12.75m = \$8.5m \times 1.5x$$

## 3. Debt

The capex, and in particular the growth capex, described above will need to be funded and it may well be funded at least in part by additional debt finance. If the company is not in financial distress, then we may well just look at the overall debt financing of the business and its general debt capacity.

There are a number of leverage or gearing ratios that we could use to analyse historical and sector capital structure data, such as debt-to-equity (x) or debt-to-total capital (%) ratios. In theory, we could then use these to forecast the company's capital structure and the amount of debt required to fund the net operating asset base forecast above. However, while very sound in theory, this can be rather difficult to model in practice. So, we are going to use a measure that has moved from the world of private equity and leveraged buyouts into more mainstream use – the debt-to-EBITDA multiple:

$$Current\ debt\text{-}to\text{-}EBITDA\ (x) = \frac{Current\ period\ debt\ balance}{Current\ period\ EBITDA}$$

For example, if the company has a current period debt balance of $40m and current period EBITDA of $20m, then it will have a current debt-to-EBITDA multiple of 2.0x:

$$2.0x = \frac{\$40m}{\$20m}$$

EBITDA can be thought of as some sort of proxy for operating cash flow.[17] It is part way between smoother accruals-based operating profit (EBIT) and lumpier cash-based operating cash flow. The debt-to-EBITDA multiple measures how many times the company's annual EBITDA (or smoothed operating cash flow) lenders are willing to lend.

As ever, we will consider the historical data, sector comparisons and management guidance as to their financing strategy. They may be planning to lever up or de-lever, depending on their current financial position, their growth plans and the availability and cost of debt financing. Once we have formed a view with regard to future debt-to-EBITDA multiples, we can then use these to produce debt forecasts by rearranging the formula above:

$$Next\ period\ debt = Next\ period\ EBITDA \times Next\ period\ debt\text{-}to\text{-}EBITDA\ (x)$$

For example, if the company has next period forecast EBITDA of $21.0m and we forecast next period debt-to-EBITDA multiple of 2.1x, then it will have a forecast debt balance of $44.1m:

$$\$44.1m = \$21.0m \times 2.1x$$

# Stretch yourself

### 1. Working capital

Historical working capital numbers can be quite volatile. To manage this problem, rather than using numbers from one period-end at a time, you might consider averaging numbers over a period (i.e. [beginning of period balance + end of period

---

[17] Please beware that EBITDA does not actually equal operating cashflow. It still includes the impact of accruals, including sales on credit for example, in the EBITDA number. But it is closer to cash as two large non-cash items have been reversed out of EBITDA, namely depreciation and amortisation.

balance]/2). For particularly volatile data, you could even extend this idea to averaging over several periods rather than just one. This should help to smooth out the volatility and make it easier to discern any underlying trends over time.

## 2. Non-current assets

For convenience above, we have analysed and forecast additions to tangible and intangible assets combined. For a richer understanding of the company under review you could separate this analysis and forecasting into the tangible and intangible components and again you could go even deeper into the separate categories of tangible assets and intangible assets, as shown in Figure 6.3.

FIGURE 6.3 AN EXAMPLE OF THE BREAKDOWN OF NON-CURRENT ASSETS INTO SUB-CATEGORIES

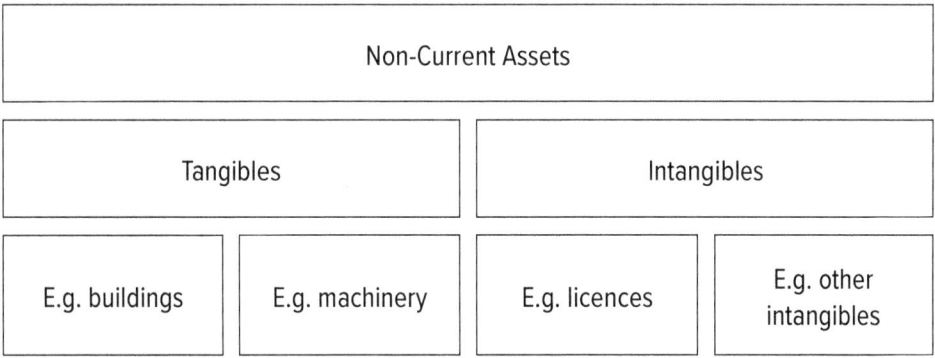

Also, we mentioned above the importance of maintaining consistency between our sales forecasts and our asset forecasts. We can perform some analysis to act as a sanity check on our forecasts:

$$Asset\ turnover\ (x) = \frac{Current\ sales}{Current\ net\ operating\ asset\ base}$$

For example, if the company has current sales of $105m and a current net operating asset base of $80m, then it will have a current asset turnover ratio of 1.3x:

$$1.3x = \frac{\$105m}{\$80m}$$

This measures the number of dollars of sales made per dollar of assets. You could compare what is implied by your forecasts with historical and peer company data to check whether your forecasts are reasonable. Forecasts are often overly optimistic, assuming too much growth for too little investment and need to be corrected by dialling down the growth assumptions and/or dialling up the investment assumptions to restore consistency.

For some sectors we may also have to consider whether there will be a time lag between investment being made and the benefits feeding through in terms of sales growth. For example, in the utilities sector, it will take time for a new hydroelectric power station to be built before it can generate and sell electricity.

## 3. Debt

If the company under review is in financial distress, then we will need to analyse its financial position in more detail. So, rather than looking at the debt overall as we did above, we will want to break it down into its component parts (see Figure 6.4).

FIGURE 6.4 AN EXAMPLE OF THE BREAKDOWN OF A COMPANY'S DEBT INTO ITS COMPONENT PARTS

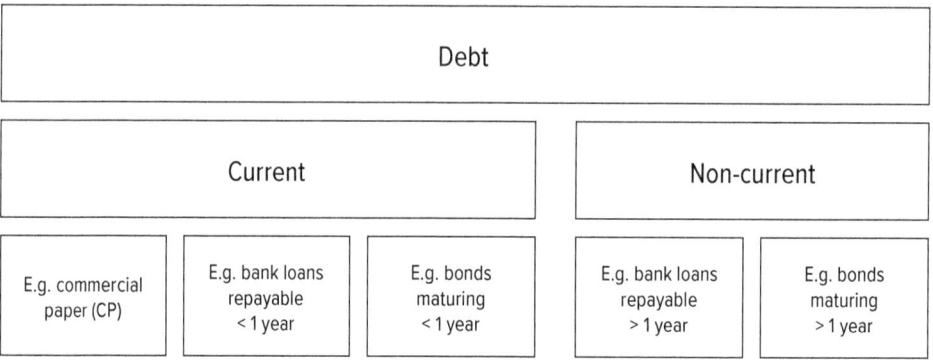

We will be particularly interested to see the maturity profile of the company's debt to see if there are any high repayments due, especially in the nearer term.

# CHAPTER 7

# Forecasting – completing cash flows

## Bite size

In this chapter we focus on pulling together and completing the essential elements of the cash flow statement that need to be forecast in order to feed into our valuations. Some of these were dealt with when we forecast earnings in Chapter 5 (e.g. net income, depreciation and amortisation expenses, interest and taxes). Some were dealt with when we forecast balance sheets in Chapter 6 (e.g. capex). Some have been partially dealt with but require further adjustment for cash flow purposes, e.g. net operating working capital (NOWC) and debt. And some have not yet been covered, e.g. dividends and equity capital movements. For these, we discuss which analytical tools are best used to analyse and then drive the forecasts of each of these items and how to do this in practice.

## Practitioner focus

Analysts will use the NOWC cycle to pull together the separate days ratios we calculated in Chapter 6 to gain a deeper understanding of the cash flow impact of the day-to-day operating activities of the business.

FIGURE 7.1 AN EXAMPLE OF THE NOWC CYCLE

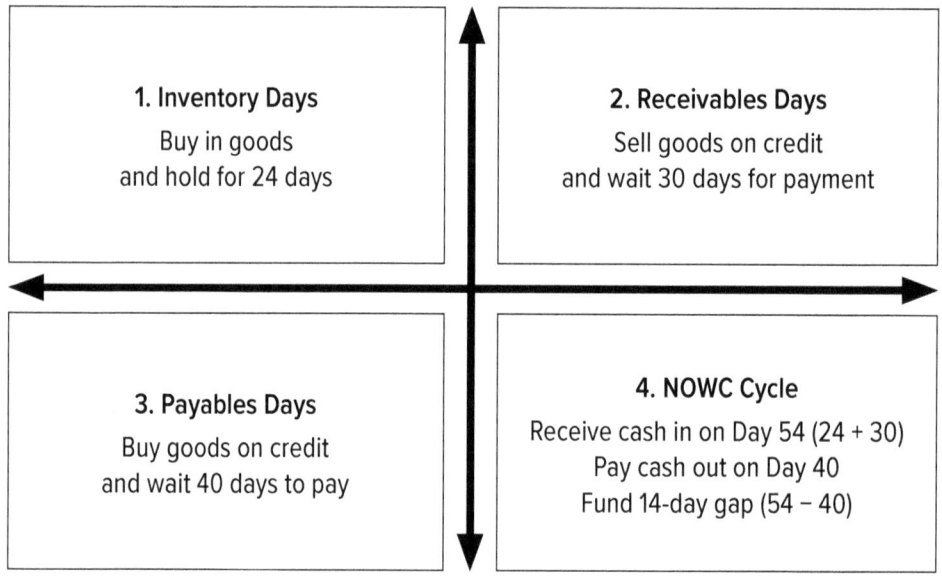

In the example in Figure 7.1, the company buys in goods and holds them for 24 days, then sells them on credit and waits a further 30 days before receiving payment. Having bought the goods in on credit, they wait 40 days to pay, which means they pay out cash on Day 40 of the cycle but do not receive cash in until Day 54. This leaves a 14-day gap that has to be funded by the company. This uses cash that could be used for other purposes and has to be raised in debt and equity capital, which has a cost. This is why it is important that the company is efficient in its management of its working capital.

# Core content

## 1. Cash flows relating to operations (CFO)

We begin our cash flow statements in the usual way, using the indirect method to turn accruals-based profits into cash-based cash flows.[18]

---

[18] There are two methods for putting together the operating cash flow calculation in the cash flow statement – direct and indirect. The vast majority of companies use the indirect method so we focus on that throughout the text.

## 1.1 Net income

We can bring the net income we arrived at when we forecast earnings in Chapter 5 from the bottom of our income statements through to the top of our cash flow statements. So, we can see whether the company is profitable overall or not.

## 1.2 Depreciation and amortisation expenses

In arriving at net income, we deducted depreciation and amortisation expenses, but we know that these are only this period's non-cash share of the total cost of tangible and intangible assets and not the actual cash payments made to acquire these assets. So, we will add these forecast expenses back in order to reverse the accruals-based accounting and move closer to cash flow.

## 1.3 Increases/decreases in NOWC items

Increases and decreases in the NOWC items that we saw in Chapter 6 have a real cash flow impact on the business. Having already forecast these items in the balance sheet, all we have to do to calculate the increase or decrease over a period is compare the balance sheet figure at the end of the period with that at the beginning of the period, as in the expression below:

$$\textit{Increase or (decrease) in NOWC item} = \textit{Next period balance} - \textit{Current period balance}$$

For example, if the current period inventory is $3.0m and the company has forecast next period inventory of $3.3m, then the next period's forecast increase in inventory will be $0.3m:

$$\$0.3m = \$3.3m - \$3.0m$$

It is important to be clear on the logic of these adjustments and to get the cash flow impact the right way round as this is a common area of confusion in practice.

### 1.3.1 Inventory

Put simply, if inventory increases over the period, then the company has bought more inventory that has to be paid for and so this will be cash-flow negative and vice versa. More technically, if inventory increases over the period, the company has made purchases that have to be paid for, but which have not yet been accounted for as cost of goods sold (CoGS) in the income statement. So, net income understates the cash outflows related to purchasing goods and we need to make a downward adjustment to account for this in the cash flow statement. The opposite would be the case if inventory decreased during the period.

### 1.3.2 Accounts receivable

Again, put simply, if accounts receivable increase over the period, the company has allowed customers to delay paying for goods and so this will be cash-flow negative and vice versa. More technically, if accounts receivable increase over the period, the company has made sales that have yet to be paid for (by customers) but which have been accounted for in the income statement. So, net income overstates the cash inflows related to selling goods and we need to make a downward adjustment to account for this in the cash flow statement. The opposite would be the case if receivables decreased during the period.

### 1.3.3 Accounts payable

Again, put simply, if accounts payable increase over the period, the company has delayed paying suppliers for goods and so this will be cash-flow positive and vice versa. More technically, if accounts payable increase over the period, the company has made purchases that have yet to be paid for but which have been accounted for as CoGS in the income statement. So, net income overstates the cash outflows related to purchasing goods and we need to make an upward adjustment to account for this in the cash flow statement. The opposite would be the case if payables decreased during the period.

## 1.4 Interest

In real financial statements there will often be a small difference between the interest expense that hits the income statement and the interest paid that hits the cash flow statement. This is often due to small timing differences between the period to which the interest cost relates and the period in which it is actually paid. For forecasting purposes, if we have good reason to believe that there may be a significant difference between the interest expense and the interest paid (for example because the company has issued zero coupon bonds, where there is an interest charge in the income statement but there is no actual interest paid in the cash flow statement) then we may well make an adjustment. However, more often than not we will simplify reality and assume that the interest expense and the interest paid will be the same and so no cash flow adjustment is required.

In Chapter 5 we forecasted the interest expense for the income statement, which has already hit net income. We will assume that this is more or less the same as the interest paid and so we need make no adjustment in the cash flow statement.

## 1.5 Taxes

In real financial statements there will often be a significant difference between the tax expense that hits the income statement and the tax paid that hits the cash flow statement. This is usually partly due to simple timing differences between the period to which the tax cost relates and the period in which it is actually paid (taxes are generally paid in arrears, i.e. with a time lag). It is also partly due to the more complex accounting issue of deferred taxes. For forecasting purposes, there are a number of ways we can manage this issue. However, the simplest solution can be to assume that over the longer term, the tax expense and the tax paid will even out and so not adjust cash flows. Again, this is a significant simplification of reality.

In Chapter 5 we forecasted the tax expense for the income statement, which has already hit net income. For our purposes, we will assume that this is a reasonable long-term proxy for the tax paid and so we will make no adjustment in the cash flow statement.

## 1.6 CFO summary

Using some of the numbers from Chapters 5 and 6, we can pull together the CFO section of our forecast cash flow statement (see Example 7.1).

EXAMPLE 7.1 HOW TO CALCULATE CFO FROM NET INCOME

|  | $m |
| --- | --- |
| Net income | 13.0 |
| Depreciation and amortisation expenses | 8.5 |
| (**Increase**)/decrease in inventories (3.3 – 3.0) | (0.3) |
| (**Increase**)/decrease in account receivable (9.5 – 9.0) | (0.5) |
| **Increase**/(decrease) in accounts payable (5.3 – 5.0) | 0.3 |
| **Net cash flow relating to operations** | **21.0** |

We can see that, as far as our forecasts are concerned, not only is the company profitable but it is also cash-generative (at least at the net operating level). They are succeeding in converting profits into cash flow.

## 2. Cash flows relating to investing (CFI)

Within CFI the key item we will be interested in forecasting is capital expenditure (capex). In Chapter 6 we forecasted the additions to tangible and intangible (non-current) assets in the balance sheet. Capex is just the other side of the same coin. Here we are simply seeing double-entry bookkeeping in action. Once we have forecast the additions to the non-current assets, the dual effect is that the tangible and intangible assets in the balance sheet increase, as they did in Chapter 6, and the payment for the acquisition of these assets is reflected as a capex cash outflow within CFI in the cash flow statement. This capex cash outflow ultimately flows through and decreases cash in the balance sheet. So, we can bring the additions to the non-current assets in the balance sheet that we forecast in Chapter 6 through to our forecast cash flow statement as capex.

## 3. Cash flows relating to financing (CFF)

Within CFF the key items we will be interested in forecasting are dividends, movements in equity finance (i.e. issuing stock to raise additional equity finance or engaging in stock buybacks to return surplus equity capital to shareholders) and movements in debt financing (i.e. raising new loans or issuing bonds to raise more debt finance or repaying old loans/bonds).

### 3.1 Dividends

Dividends are an important part of the forecasting and valuation process. Often, but not always, they will be analysed using dividend payout ratios, comparing the dividends paid to net income or earnings:

$$Dividend\ payout\ ratio\ (\%) = \frac{Current\ period\ dividends}{Current\ period\ net\ income} \times 100\%$$

For example, if the company has dividends in the current period of $7.7m and net income of $14m, then it will have a current period dividend payout ratio of 55.0%:

$$55.0\% = \frac{\$7.7m}{\$14m} \times 100\%$$

In the earlier years of its life cycle, we might expect a company to pay no or very low dividends as it will likely want to retain and reinvest most of its profits back into the business in order to fund its growth. However, as the company matures and meaningful growth opportunities become harder to find, it is likely that the company will increase its dividend payout. Rather than hold on to cash earning a relatively low return, the company can return it to shareholders who can put it to more productive use.

As ever, we look at historical data for the company, benchmark against peers and consider management guidance. The company may, for example, have a stated dividend payment policy. Once we have formed a view with regard to future dividend payout ratios, we can then use these to project future dividends by rearranging the formula above:

*Next period dividends*
$$= \text{Next period net income} \times \text{Next period dividend payout ratio (\%)}$$

For example, if the company has forecast net income of $13m and we forecast a dividend payout ratio of 60%, then the next period's forecast dividends will be $7.8m:

$$\$7.8m = \$13m \times 60.0\%$$

It is worth considering if the company will have sufficient profits to pay its dividends. However, a dividend payout ratio of over 100% is possible, as the company can pay out of previous profits, i.e. retained earnings. Arguably, it is more important to check if the company will have enough cash to pay the forecast dividends. Although again, the company could simply borrow money to cover the dividend payments. In some jurisdictions, we have to assess whether the company will be legally able to pay a dividend, i.e. whether it has sufficient distributable reserves.

## 3.2 Equity

In practice, forecasting share issues can be difficult unless we have clear guidance from the company with regard to their equity raising plans. But if we are forecasting that the company is going to grow and is going to invest in operating assets to achieve that growth, then, for the sake of consistency, we will have to make sure the investment is funded, which will likely be through a mixture of equity and debt. However, do not forget that if we are forecasting a dividend payout ratio of less than 100% then the remainder of the net income will inevitably be retained and reinvested in the business and is in effect additional equity finance.

Also problematic is the issue of forecasting stock buybacks. Again, if management provides clear guidance on the amount and timing of any such returns of capital to shareholders then we can build these into our forecasts. However, in the absence of such clarity it will prove rather more difficult.

## 3.3 Debt

As with the NOWC items, increases and decreases in the debt capital we saw in Chapter 6 have a real cash flow impact on the business. Having already forecast this item in the balance sheet, all we have to do to calculate the increase or decrease over a period is compare the balance sheet figure at the end of the period with that at the beginning:

*Increase or (decrease) in debt = Next period debt − current period debt*

For example, if the company has forecast debt of $44.1m and current period debt of $40.0m, then the next period's forecast increase in debt will be $4.1m:

$$\$4.1m = \$44.1m - \$40.0m$$

It is this increase or decrease in debt that will flow through the debt raised/repaid line in the CFF section of the cash flow statement and effectively through into cash in the balance sheet.

# Stretch yourself

Rather than building cash flow statements in the traditional accounting way with three separate sub-totals for CFO, CFI and CFF, analysts will sometimes build cumulative cash flow statements that flow from top to bottom, just like an income statement. The main reason for this is that it can help to tell the story and build the narrative.

A mature, stable company will likely be profitable and converting these profits into cash flows, some of which will be reinvested to maintain and grow the business, after which dividends will be paid out (and possibly share buybacks too) and there may even be some repayment of debt. Fundamentally, cash will flow from the top to the bottom of this cumulative cash flow statement, which tells that particular story.

On the other hand, a young start-up business will be raising equity (and possibly, although less likely, debt capital), which it will then invest into non-current assets to grow the business. It may also spend some of the capital raised on activities such as advertising and marketing, R&D and even day-to-day running costs. Fundamentally, cash will flow from the bottom to the top of this cumulative cash flow statement, telling a rather different story.

EXAMPLE 7.2 CUMULATIVE CASH FLOW STATEMENT FORECAST

|  | $m |
|---|---|
| Net income | 13.00 |
| Depreciation and amortisation expenses | 8.50 |
| (**Increase**)/decrease in inventories (3.3 – 3.0) | (0.30) |
| (**Increase**)/decrease in account receivable (9.5 – 9.0) | (0.50) |
| **Increase**/(decrease) in accounts payable (5.3 – 5.0) | 0.30 |
| **Net cash flow relating to operations** | **21.00** |
| Capex | (12.75) |
| **Cash flows before dividends** | **8.25** |
| Dividends paid | (7.80) |
| **Cash flows before financing** | **0.45** |
| Debt raised (44.1 – 40.0) | 4.10 |
| **Net increase/(decrease) in cash & cash equivalents** | **4.55** |

In Example 7.2, cash flows mostly from the top to the bottom of the cumulative cash flow statement. The business is profitable and cash-generative at the operating level. A significant portion of these cash flows are being reinvested back into non-current assets (i.e. capex) after which the company is just about able to cover the dividend it plans to pay. It has then raised additional debt finance, possibly to provide some extra breathing space and potentially for further growth investment.

# SECTION C
## Discount Rates

# CHAPTER 8
# The impact of risk

## Bite size

Risk is a core aspect of every business valuation. It describes the uncertainty about the future development of the company to be valued, which is due to the fact that nobody has a crystal ball to foretell exactly what the future will bring. Risk can have different origins – it could be due to the inherent fluctuations of the company's earnings, dividends, cash flows, etc., but it could also be due to an individual's inability to perfectly forecast or understand the core drivers of the company's performance. In reality, we are all risk averse (some more, some less), i.e. we always prefer a situation of low risk as compared to a situation of higher risk. This leads to a generally value-reducing effect of risk. The good news is that a) we can measure risk and b) the impact of risk can be incorporated into our time-value-of-money (TVM) concept.

## Practitioner focus

In our description of the TVM concept we show that future cash flows matter in valuation. However, the future is unknown today. In some cases we are better able to predict the future, in others we are less able to do so. As human beings are generally risk averse (i.e. they do not like risk) it is important to properly deal with the impact of risk (or uncertainty) about the future cash flows in our valuation models. We describe the main aspects of this challenge in this chapter, in particular how to adjust discount rates for the impact of risk. However, it is important to understand that beyond the pure technicalities, the identification and measurement of risk can be quite tricky in some cases.

# Core content

## 1. What is risk anyway?

Risk comes necessarily along with the general TVM concept. We need future cash flows as an input into our valuation model to get to today's value – the present value. But the future is always uncertain. We do not have a crystal ball that tells us what happens tomorrow, in one week, in one year, in one decade, etc.

However, we can do fundamental research to narrow down the range of possible future outcomes or at least to assign probabilities to different outcomes. Doing research always stands at the beginning of every valuation process. But even after conducting research we are still left with some level of uncertainty about the future. This uncertainty could be due to the simple fact that the world is uncertain per se, which means that with the best research we cannot precisely predict the quantity of a company's products that customers will buy in the future. But it could also be due to our individual inability, in certain cases, to perfectly understand the drivers of a company's performance in the first place. Imagine a start-up company that does research in pre-clinical oncology and may or may not come up with a marketable product in some years. For many of us it would be almost impossible to perfectly quantify all relevant risk aspects.

Hence, there is always risk in every valuation case – sometimes more, sometimes less – but we can never bring it down to zero.

## 2. Why risk/uncertainty matters in valuation

The relevance of risk in valuation stems from an empirically well-observable attitude of human beings: risk aversion! If it comes down to important decisions, all individuals are risk averse, i.e. they do not like risk. Or better: they always prefer a situation of certainty over a situation of risk, even if the economic benefit of the latter situation is equal to, or higher than, that of the more certain situation. This is due to evolutionary habits. In the ancient past, it was clearly more comfortable and better for survival to walk on a plain field where one could oversee everything that happens than in a forest where a dangerous animal could jump at you just because you did not see it hiding behind a tree.

Of course, today's risk aversion is not so much about animals attacking but rather about more modern life problems. It is about not knowing whether resigning from your current job and going for a certain education programme can get you a better job or whether you would be better to stay where you are. Similarly, whether you should invest your money in a risky asset with a potentially high but highly uncertain return or keep the funds in your bank account and earn a low, but almost certain, return.

Risk aversion, however, does not mean that we do not take risks. However, if we do take risks, we want to gain some compensation for it. This compensation might be the expectation of a much better job than the existing one, or the expectation of a better living situation once you have taken out the loan for buying the house, or the expectation of a better return on your money invested if you do go for the risky investment. But if we do not expect an improvement in the situation, we usually do not take on additional risks. This is basic human behaviour.

If you ask people whether they would rather choose a) a certain payment of $100, or b) an uncertain payment of either €0 (with 50% probability) or $200 (with 50% probability) they will almost always prefer option a), although the expected value is the same in both situations.

FIGURE 8.1 A BIRD IN THE HAND IS WORTH TWO IN THE BUSH

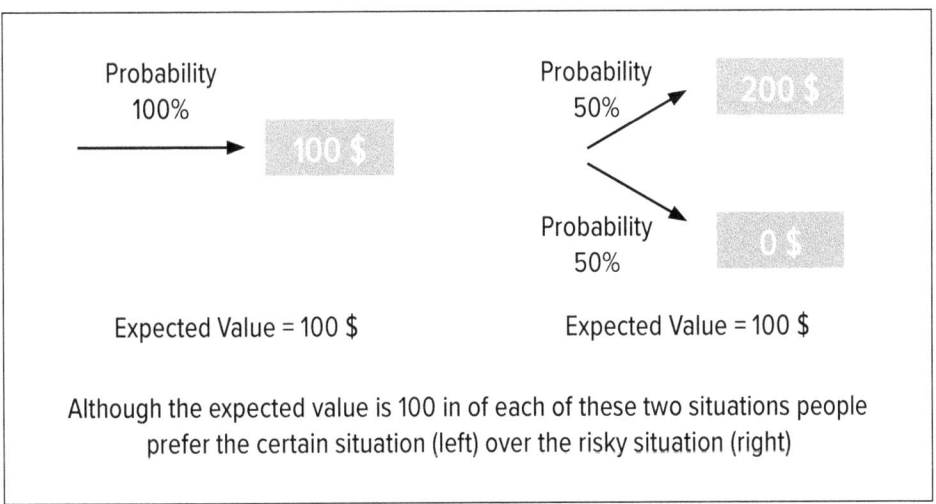

Admittedly, we know certain situations where individuals do not exhibit risk averse (i.e. economically rational) behaviour, such as playing the lottery. Here the amount paid for participating in the lottery is regularly much too high to justify the expected (low probability) gain. But if we look beyond the pure economics, and include behavioural aspects, it all makes perfect sense. Participating in the lottery allows us to dream away with a multi-million gain for some days. The money we spend for the lottery is often not material. Hence our dreaming is a perfect compensation for the big risk we take.

For reasons of completeness, it is important to understand that not everybody has the same degree of risk aversion. Although we are all risk averse, some are more and some are less. You know this from your friends: some of them are very cautious, others less cautious in life and this extends also to making investments.

Coming back to the bird-in-the-hand example from above. If people prefer the certain situation over the uncertain situation they obviously see less value in the uncertain situation than in the certain situation. For valuation purposes the same is true: higher uncertainty means lower value, all other things being equal. Putting it differently: if we go for higher-risk investment we would require a higher compensation (higher expected cash flows or return) to get to the same value. This is a basic principle of valuation, and a whole lot of empirical evidence supports it. This is why risk matters in valuation.

FIGURE 8.2 MAKING CERTAINTY AND RISK EQUIVALENT

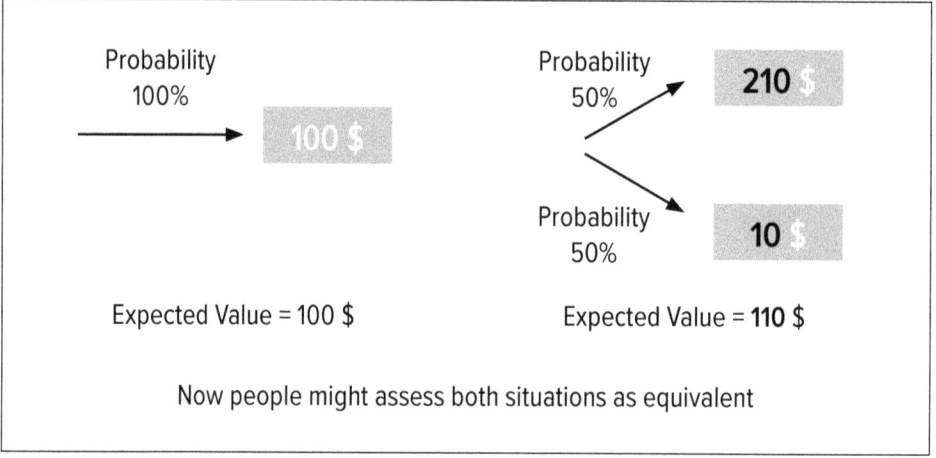

## 3. What is risk in the context of valuation?

A very general problem is that it is not easy to measure risk. Already the definition of risk is a tricky one. If we ask people what the term 'risk' means for them, they usually answer that it is some sort of downward measure, i.e. the downward deviation from an expected event. Risk has a negative connotation in our language. If we talk about upward deviations we prefer to use words like 'chances' or 'opportunities'.

Admittedly, there is a long dispute about what risk really means. In the context of valuation, we understand risk rather as a two-sided measure: it is the sheer possibility of deviations from an expected event, e.g. deviation from an expected level of cash flow. This deviation could be to the upside or to the downside of our expectations. But this is just a definition. In many cases we fare well with this symmetric definition but not in all cases. Be aware that for reasons of valuation, the question of what risk really means is often not resolved until the very end.

# 4. The TVM concept and the calculation of present values

At the core of our cash flow-based valuation approaches is the concept of TVM. This concept allows us to transform expected future cash flows into today's value. It is based on the idea that interest rates make cash flows of different periods comparable because an investor can invest a cash flow in $t=0$ for one year, receive interest payments (or any other rate of return $r$ on his investments) and hence will have a different amount of money in $t=1$.

$$cash\ flow_1 = cash\ flow_0 \times (1+r)$$

However, in valuation we rarely want to know what the future cash flow is but rather what the value equivalent of this future cash flow is today. By rearranging the above equation and labelling today's cash flow as $Value_0$ we get a so-called present value formula:

$$Value_0 = \frac{cash\ flow_1}{1+r}$$

If the future cash flow is not expected in period 1 but in period 2, we have to use a comparable basis of investing a cash flow for two years at the rate $r$, which gives a factor of $(1 + r)^2$. The resulting present value formula is:

$$Value_0 = \frac{cash\ flow_2}{(1+r)^2}$$

If more than one future cash flow has to be transformed into today's value, we can add up the single present value calculations:

$$Value_0 = \frac{cash\ flow_1}{1+r} + \frac{cash\ flow_2}{(1+r)^2} + \ldots$$

If we assume that we receive the same cash flow every period until eternity (i.e. *cash low₁* = *cash flow₂* = *cash flow₃* , and so on), we get the so-called perpetuity formula:

$$Value_0 = \sum_{t=1}^{\infty} \frac{cash\ flow_t}{(1+r)^t} = \frac{cash\ flow}{r}$$

The perpetuity is often a helpful valuation formula as we always try to look until eternity in valuation. We will learn more about valuation formulae for long-term cash flow streams in Chapters 20–29. It is worth noting here that usually risk is covered in the discount rate $r$. The basic rule is: the higher the risk, the higher the discount rate. This is shown in the following example.

## 5. A simple example of risk consideration in valuation

Imagine Company A is operating in a mature market and offers commodity products to end-customers for their everyday use. The company has existed for a long time and has shown very stable earnings and cash flow patterns in the past. It is not expected that something changes materially in the future. The company is expected to generate a constant stream of cash flow (of $100 per year) that lasts forever. In other words, we assume a perpetuity. Let us further assume that a low-risk discount rate is at 5%. Using the present value of perpetuity technique this would lead to the following valuation model:

$$Value_{A,0} = \frac{\$100}{5\%} = \$2{,}000$$

Now imagine Company B. This company is operating in a high-tech industry under very dynamic circumstances. Technological advances and new product developments happen regularly. The degree of competition is high. The visibility of what happens next is very low for the whole industry and even lower for single companies. Company B is also expected to generate a constant stream of cash flows of $100 per year. A risk averse investor – despite the same expected cash flows for Companies A and B – would not attribute the same value to both companies. She would attribute a much lower value to the second company due to the inherently higher risk. From a technical point of view this value adjustment is performed by applying a higher discount rate for Company B than for Company A. Assuming a discount rate of 15%, the valuation of Company B is:

$$Value_{B,0} = \frac{\$100}{15\%} = \$667$$

As we can see, risk has a value-reducing effect (all other things being equal). We can address this effect in our valuation models by adjusting the discount rates for risk. However, from the descriptions in this chapter it is not clear how much is a fair adjustment of discount rates for risk. Putting it differently, where do the 5% and 15% in our examples come from? And why not take 10% and 20% instead? We will address this issue in future chapters.

# Stretch yourself

Even if we can master the technical challenges of dealing with risk in valuation, we still face a lot of practical problems in many valuation cases. One of them relates to the fact that risk could be due to operating issues or financial issues, i.e. the same business model can have different risk characteristics from the viewpoint of an equity investor if it is financed by equity only versus if it is financed by a combination of equity and debt.

The reason for this is that debt serves as a lever on the fluctuations of cash flows to equity investors. This is also why we call this effect 'financial leverage', as illustrated in Figure 8.3.

FIGURE 8.3 FINANCIAL LEVERAGE AND RISK

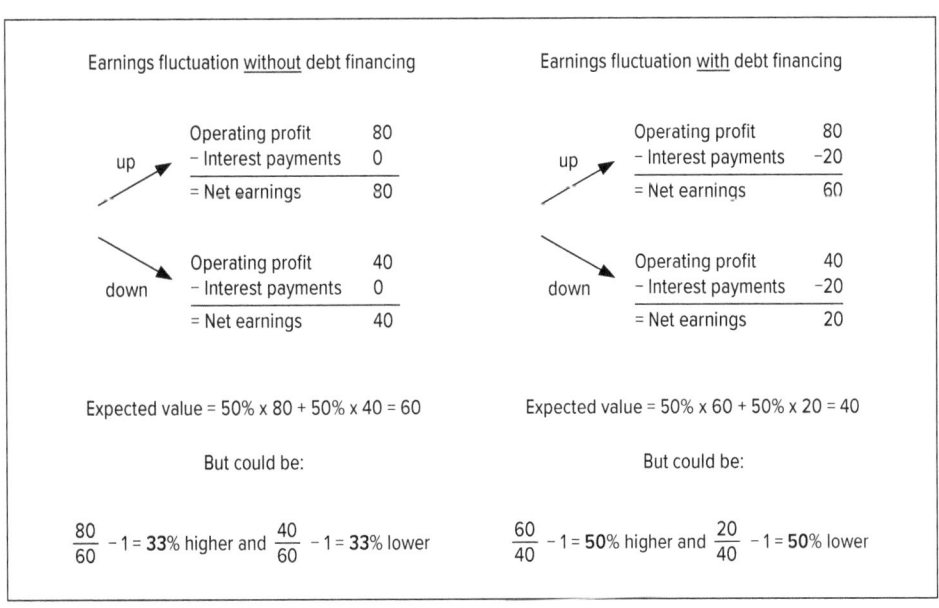

We can see that due to the fact that debt has to be serviced (i.e. interests have to be paid) before equity investors have a claim on the company's cash flows, the fluctuations of net earnings are stronger for a partially debt-financed company than for a purely equity-financed company. This leverage effect – as a factor affecting risk – can be taken into consideration by adjusting our discount rate further (see Chapter 9). Moreover, certain costs, such as fixed costs (e.g. personnel or overhead costs, or rents that show up independently of the revenues generated) have a similar leverage effect, the so-called operating leverage, as financial indebtedness.

Finally, it is worth highlighting that risk measurement is always an individual process and requires in-depth analysis of the revenue and cash flow generation process of the company. Some revenue streams might be backed by long-term contracts (and are hence less uncertain than those without a contract). Some revenue streams might be recurring by nature – e.g. because the customer needs the products or services continuously (pet or human food, certain subscription-based business models, etc.) – and are hence more predictable than revenue streams that are characterised by one-off customer purchases (e.g. special machines for certain industrial businesses). Additionally, variable costs, such as the costs of material, move more in line with revenues than fixed costs. Make sure that you analyse the business model, the revenue-generating process and the cost situation of the company properly to come up with a proper risk assessment.

# CHAPTER 9

# Standard approaches to determine risk-adjusted discount rates

## Bite size

The main approach to account for risk in a present value valuation model is the consideration of risk as part of the discount rate. There are different models that allow including the effect of risk into the determination of discount rates. The core model is called the Capital Asset Pricing Model (CAPM), which has its roots in capital market theory and derives its parameters using data from capital markets. The CAPM models the risk-adjusted discount rate as a combination of a risk-free rate plus a company-specific risk component. However, there are also other models (or combinations of models) to determine the appropriate discount rate.

## Practitioner focus

As we know from the previous chapter, risk is an important aspect in any business valuation and it has to be properly accounted for when setting up a valuation model. Risk is in most cases considered as part of the discount rate, as is the case with CAPM, which is one of the most commonly used models in practice. The main form of the CAPM is very straightforward and applicable for practitioners. Depending on the concrete valuation setting there are also some other, more heuristic models, that can be applied – such as the so-called build-up model. All models have in common that they form a combination of a risk-free component plus one or more risk factors.

# Core content

## 1. Why do we need models to account for risk in the discount rate?

In the previous chapter we learned that risk usually has an increasing impact on discount rates. However, the quantitative impact of risk on business values in general, or on discount rates in particular, cannot be observed directly in most cases. Therefore, we need an explanatory function that allows us to translate our risk measurement into an appropriate risk component to be included in our valuation models.

## 2. The basic framework of every risk-adjusted discount rate model

The framework for every model for risk-adjusted discount rates is basically the same. We start with the risk-free rate. This is the fair discount rate for an investment that is without risk. As increasing risk means lower valuation outcomes (all other things being equal) and higher discount rates we now build up components of risk measurement on top of this risk-free rate ($r_f$) to account for the specific risk of the company to be valued.

$$r = r_f + Risk\ premium(s)$$

Models differ in a) how they translate risks into the specific risk factor; and b) which specific risks should be accounted for. An appropriate model can be a one-factor model, i.e. only taking one risk factor into account, or a multi-factor model that considers different risk factors. However, in all cases it is a combination of the risk-free rate plus risk premium for the risk factor(s).

## 3. The CAPM as the core model

Today, the most common model for determining risk-adjusted discount rates is the CAPM. It has its original roots in the 1950s when academics found out that investment risk can be reduced when investing in more than one asset, i.e. into a portfolio of assets. This risk reduction – called diversification – is the result of spreading the money over different assets. For example, the risk of being exposed to a bad management of a particular company can be significantly reduced when you invest (i.e. diversify) into a bigger number of companies. A well-diversified portfolio might contain some companies with poor management and also some with exceptional management teams, but differences in the quality will even out and you will end up with an average company management quality in your portfolio. Hence, diversification helps to get rid of the management quality uncertainty. We call these diversifiable risks non-systematic or idiosyncratic risks.

However, there are other risks that you cannot get rid of by building bigger portfolios. Imagine the risk in macroeconomic developments (boom or bust) or interest rate movements or pandemics, such as that related to Covid-19. While not every company is exposed to the same degree of risk to these events, even those with a well-diversified portfolio will retain some exposure. You cannot get rid of those risks by diversification. We call these non-diversifiable or systematic risks.

The idea of the CAPM – which was first published in academic literature in 1965 – is that rational investors will strive to eliminate as much risk as possible by diversification. They can get rid of all the non-systematic risks and hence will only be left with the systematic risks. For an investor, according to the CAPM, it is only the systematic risk that matters. Figure 9.1 highlights how increasing the number of assets in a portfolio reduces the total risk (thick shaded line) down to only the systematic risk.

FIGURE 9.1 THE EFFECT OF DIVERSIFICATION

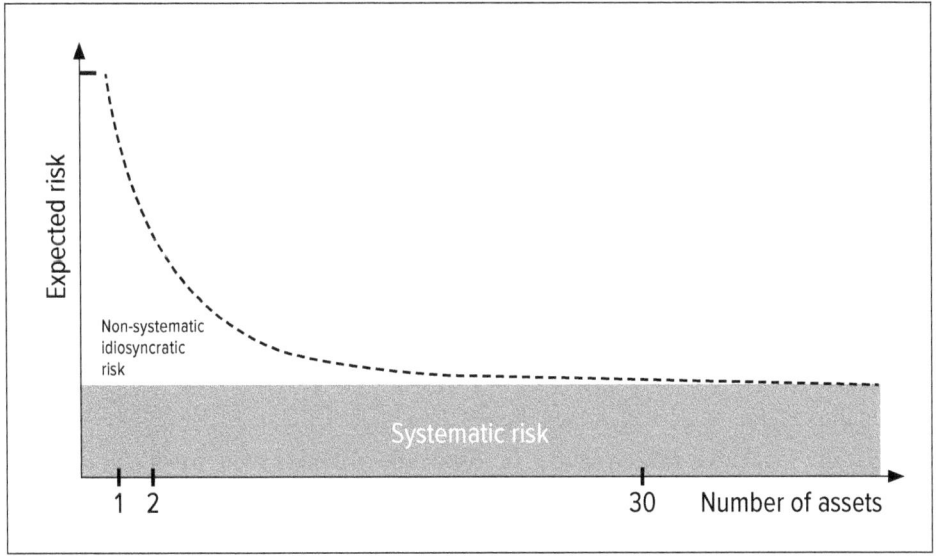

In such a well-diversified portfolio (often called market portfolio) it is possible to measure the systematic risk of a particular asset, as long as the asset is a traded stock. It is the sensitivity of the particular stock price movements to the movements of the market portfolio. In practice, we can apply statistical regression analysis to determine this risk parameter. In such a regression analysis the estimated risk coefficient (we call this risk 'beta coefficient') is represented by the slope of the line of best fit. This line of best fit represents the assumed linear relationship between the returns of the stock of the company (for which we want to determine the beta) and the returns of the market portfolio, which is typically proxied by the return of a broad equity index (e.g. S&P 500), illustrated below.

FIGURE 9.2 USING REGRESSION ANALYSIS TO DERIVE BETAS FOR THE CAPM

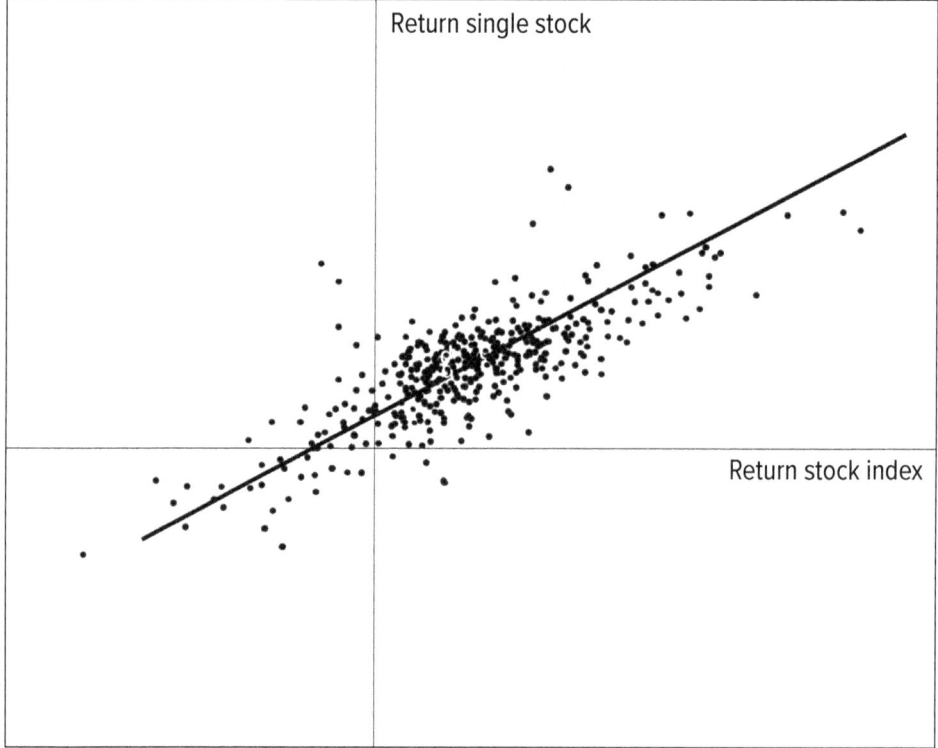

Beta is just a relative risk measure. It shows the riskiness of a particular asset in comparison to the market portfolio risk. A beta of 1 (i.e. a slope of the line of best fit of 45°) means that the asset has the same risk as the market portfolio; a beta lower than 1 (slope lower than 45°) indicates a lower risk than the market; and a beta higher than 1 (slope greater than 45°) indicates a higher risk than the market. Companies with betas lower than 1 typically have more stable (or less fluctuating) business models and performance, and/or operate in relatively stable sectors, such as companies in basic consumer goods, regulated utilities and infrastructure industries. Companies with betas higher than one have more volatile business models and performance, and/or operate in sectors that are more susceptible to external market shocks and economic boom or bust cycles, such as companies operating in high-tech, luxury goods, entertainment and leisure industries, etc.

| Beta | Interpretation |
|---|---|
| >1 | More volatile/risky than average |
| =1 | Market/Average |
| <1 | Less volatile/risky than average |

In order to translate beta into a risk component we now have to multiply it with the market-risk premium (MRP), i.e. the risk premium that an investor would require over and above the risk-free rate if he or she invests in a broad market portfolio.

$$Risk\ premium = \beta \times MRP$$

Hence, for a beta of 1 we would get a risk premium of one times the MRP, which makes sense as a beta of 1 indicates the same risk as the market, and for a beta lower than 1 we would get a risk premium of lower than the MRP.

The ultimate equation for deriving the risk-adjusted discount rate (or the cost of equity) for a particular equity investment, $r$, is:

$$r = r_f + \beta \times MRP$$

Where $r$ is the risk-free rate.

As you can see, what we need to apply the CAPM are just three variables:

- The risk-free rate (usually proxied by government bond yields of high-quality issuing countries; can be determined based on observations).
- The beta of the stock (can be determined based on own statistical analysis, or can use ready-made estimates from data vendors, e.g. Bloomberg).
- The MRP (can be determined based on historical evidence or certain explanatory models).

Many valuation experts are looking for these variables, and hence, you can find them in different data sources. It is also worth noting that the only company-specific measure is beta, while the risk-free rate and the MRP can be used as an input parameter for all valuation cases.

## 4. From cost of equity to WACC

The relevant discount rate for free cash flows to the firm is called the 'weighted average cost of capital' (WACC). As the free cash flow to the firm belongs to debt and equity providers, WACC reflects the risks perceived by, and returns required for, both capital provides, i.e. lenders and shareholders.

FIGURE 9.3 THE ELEMENTS OF WACC

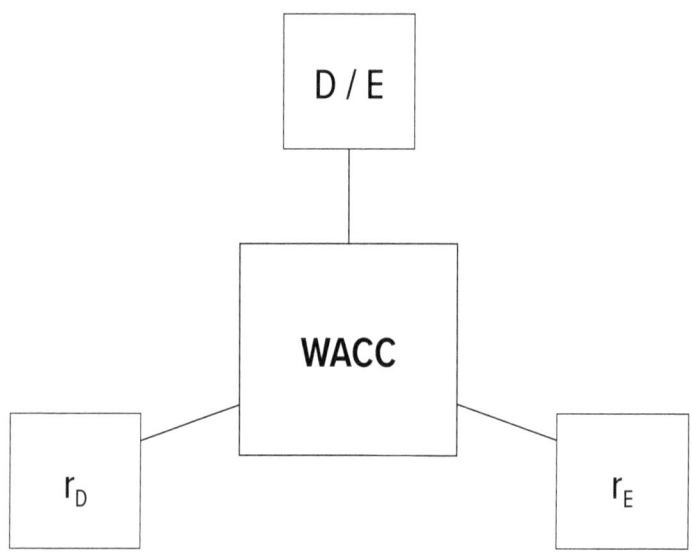

Additionally, WACC takes into account the tax shield, i.e. the tax advantage of the partial debt financing of the company. This tax advantage stems from interest payments on debt being (at least partially) deductible from the tax base.

The WACC formula looks as follows:

$$WACC = r_E \times \frac{E}{EV} + r_D \times \frac{D}{EV} \times (1 - T)$$

Where $T$ is the tax rate of the company.

# Stretch yourself

Financial theory provides a lot of different models to determine risk-adjusted discount rates. Most of the modern academic models are quite complicated. Sometimes we operate with consumption-based models, sometimes with multi-period models, etc. So far none of these models has matched the practical applicability and theoretical soundness of the CAPM. This is why none of these models plays a major role in today's valuation practice, nor in this text. But keep your eyes open. This might change at some point in the future.

The CAPM might be a good model in many valuation situations but it loses quality and relevance the further you move away from the basic assumptions that underpin the model. For example, if you need to value a company with illiquid stock (e.g. if the company is very small or it is not traded on a public market) you might not be able to generate an estimate of the stock's beta. Also, the expected return of the market portfolio cannot be assumed as an appropriate risk benchmark if the stock is only held by investors who do not maintain a well-diversified (market) portfolio. Always keep an eye on whether the basic assumptions still fit the valuation setting in which you want to use the model.

Finally, be aware that all models are only simplifications of the reality. They might explain a lot of what we are interested in, but they can never explain everything. This means you always have to interpret the results of all models carefully. A risk-adjusted discount rate of 10% that was determined by, for example, the CAPM might still be higher or lower than the 'true' value.

# CHAPTER 10

# Practical perspectives on risk-adjusted discount rates

## Bite size

Breathing life into the models for risk-adjusted discount rates – i.e. assigning values to the relevant parameters – is essential when performing business valuation. There are different methods of determining these parameters. In most cases, one can rely on public data sources. In this section, building on the theoretical content of the previous chapter, we provide examples of how to determine the cost of equity and the WACC.

## Practitioner focus

Using cost of capital theory in practice requires access to data to determine the key parameters. For example, the risk-free rate and the market-risk premium are available from several websites. Furthermore, several free web-based courses provide estimates of industry-level betas, i.e. average betas for companies of certain industries. If one wants to go deeper here, it is necessary to rely on non-public sources or, if you are very confident, run your own regression analyses.

## Core content

### 1. Cost of capital in practice

Imagine that we are interested in determining the risk-adjusted discount rate, i.e. the cost of equity and the WACC, of Allianz SE for 31 January 2024. For application of

Chapter 10 – Practical perspectives on risk-adjusted discount rates

the CAPM we only need three parameters: the risk-free rate, the market-risk premium and the stock's beta. For the WACC we additionally need the cost of debt.

Below we derive these parameters from public sources.

## 2. Risk-free rate

The risk-free rate for Germany is based on the yield curve for German government bonds of different maturities. On average we get a present value weighted risk-free rate of roughly 2.5%.

FIGURE 10.1 DERIVING THE RISK-FREE RATE

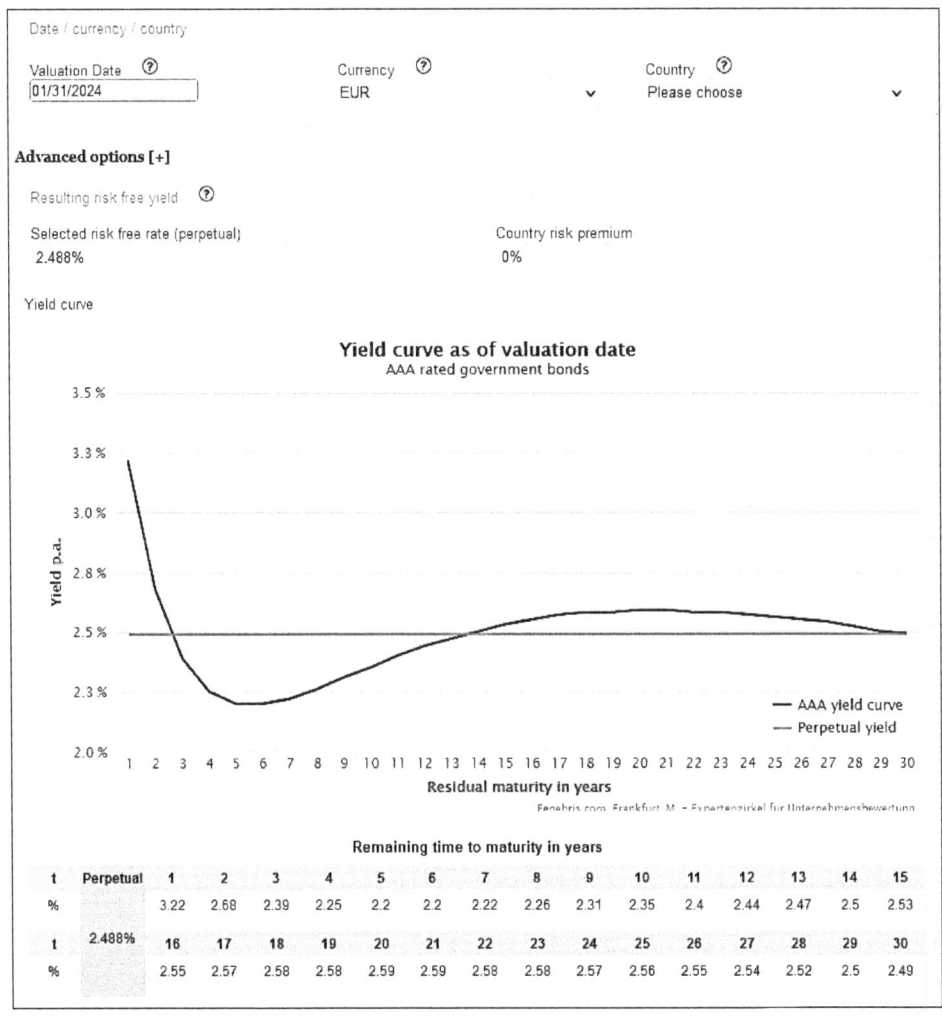

Source: www.basiszinskurve.de/basiszinssatz-gemaess-idw.html

## 3. Market-risk premium

The market-risk premium can be derived in different ways. The first is through long-term historical analyses. These compare the risk-free rate with the return on equity markets each year over periods of sometimes 100 years or more. Such analyses are always problematic. The answer you get will depend on when you start and end the study, which government bond you choose as the risk-free proxy, which equity index you choose and whether you calculate the average differential over time on an arithmetic or geometric basis. It is also backward looking!

The second approach applies the Gordon Growth model (the Gordon Growth model is introduced in Chapter 21) to an equity market rather than an individual equity. Below we show the results of such a model-based derivation of the market-risk premium, i.e. a market-risk premium that is implied in actual stock prices. Under this approach the market-risk premium is extracted from a valuation model that uses actual stock price data. For example, on 31 January 2024, the implied market-risk premium in Germany stood at 6.7%.

FIGURE 10.2 DERIVING THE MARKET-RISK PREMIUM

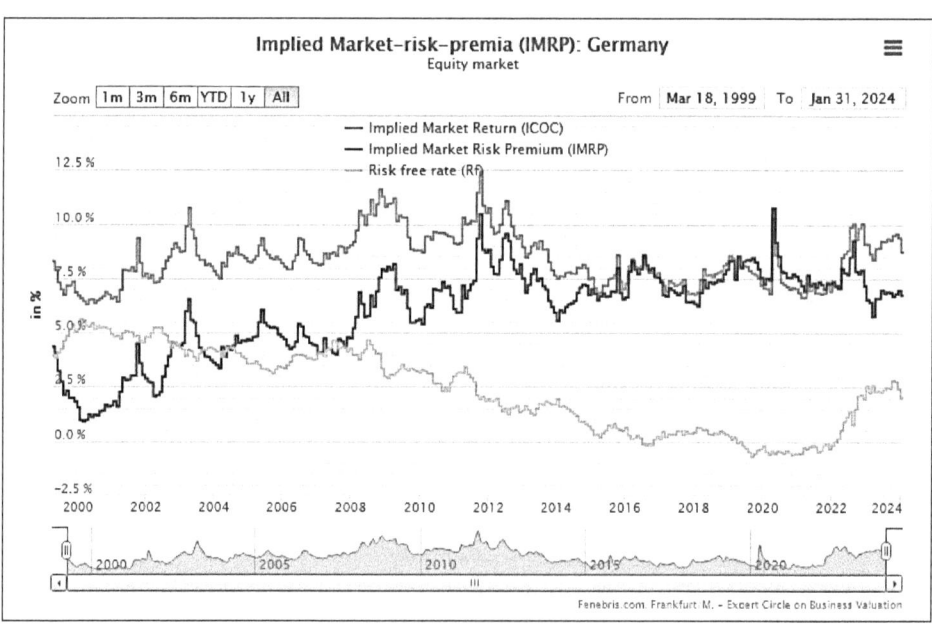

Source: www.market-risk-premia.com/market-risk-premia.html

This market-risk premium model works as follows. First, a typical valuation equation (e.g. a Gordon Growth model) is set up where the market value of a broad equity index equals expected future dividends (or cash flows) from the stocks of this index discounted at the index discount rate. As the value of the index is known and estimates for dividends (cash flows) can be drawn from equity analysts' analyses, the only unknown is the index discount rate. Solving the equation for this index cost of equity (Step 1) and deducting the risk-free rate (Step 2) leads to the market-risk premium that is implied in analysts' estimates and actual stock prices.

**Step 1:**

$$Index\ value = \frac{Forecast\ dividends\ (CASH)}{Cost\ of\ equity\ of\ the\ index\ (RISK) - Growth\ rate\ (GROWTH)}$$

**Step 2:**

$$Implied\ market\ risk\ premium = Cost\ of\ equity\ of\ the\ index - Risk\ free\ rate$$

Readers can use this website www.market-risk-premia.com/market-risk-premia.html to search for current and historical market-risk premium estimates for a range of countries.

## 4. Beta

We further determined the beta of Allianz SE by using data from Refinitiv Eikon (now LSEG). For 31 January 2024 we have the following picture (for a historical observation period of one year, daily return measurement, against the German DAX index):

## FIGURE 10.3 DERIVING THE BETA OF ALLIANZ SE

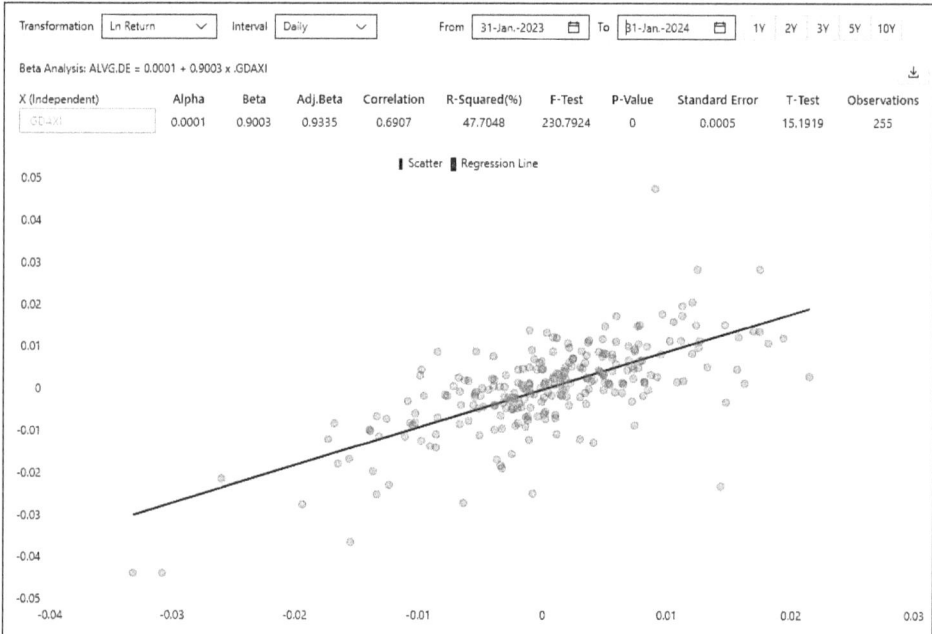

Source: Refinitiv Eikon

The beta of Allianz SE is at 0.90 on 31 January 2024. Admittedly, this might differ for different observation periods and different return intervals but for this introductory example we can use this number.

Alternatively, one can visit the website of Professor Damodaran and go to the section on industry betas.[19] Here it is possible to at least search for average betas of companies of a certain industry. For insurance we can find beta values of 1.23 for general insurance, 0.94 for life insurance, and 0.80 for property and casualty insurance. Allianz SE is a mixture of all three sub-segments and hence using the mean value is a reasonable approach in a first step, which results in a beta of 0.99. As Allianz SE has a relatively strong life insurance business, fine-tuning of the sub-segment weightings would ultimately lead to a slightly lower beta. This final result will not be very different from the 0.90 derived via Refinitiv Eikon (now LSEG). It is worth noting that not only the industry but also the capital structure has a meaningful impact on beta. However, in the case of insurance companies it is often not a big mistake to make a comparison without adjusting for capital structure.

---

19  See: https://pages.stern.nyu.edu/~adamodar/New_Home_Page/datafile/Betas.html

With all this information we can now apply the CAPM:

$$r = r_f + \beta \times MRP$$

$$r = 2.5\% + 0.90 \times 6.7\% = 8.5\%$$

Hence, according to the CAPM the risk-adjusted discount rate (i.e. the discount rate that is used in our present value model as a cost of equity) of Allianz SE is 8.5%.

## 5. Cost of debt

In practice, analysts will often arrive at a cost of debt by analysing the company's financial statements and calculating an effective interest rate (EIR), investigating the notes to the financial statements to see what rate of interest the company suffers on its bank loans and bonds and if the company has publicly traded debt looking up the yield-to-maturity (YTM) on these bonds. They can then work backwards and derive the credit spread:

$$\mathit{Credit\ risk\ premium\ (CRP) = Cost\ of\ debt\ (r_D) - Risk\ free\ rate\ (r_f)}$$

Either way, we arrive at the pre-tax cost of debt, i.e. the interest rate the company pays on average to lenders.

For Allianz SE we could observe at the end of 2023 a YTM for long-term bonds of ca. 3.1%, i.e. a credit risk premium of about 0.6% over the risk-free rate, which is in line with the company's high-quality credit rating.

## 6. Capital structure

When determining the capital structure of the business, essential for the weighting calculation within WACC, we must be wary of using balance sheet numbers. We are performing a valuation exercise, and accounting book values (for equity in particular) will not reflect genuine economic values. We should instead use market values. We are building a WACC for the longer term. If the company is already mature and has a settled capital structure, then current market values of debt and equity may well be appropriate. However, if that is not the case, we may need to look at other more mature companies in the same sector to see what capital structure they have settled into in order to form a sensible long-term view.

For Allianz SE we could see in public sources that the market capitalisation was at about €98bn and the net debt was at approximately €6bn at the end of January 2024. This leads to a debt-to-enterprise value ($\frac{D}{EV}$) ratio of about 5.8%.

With a tax rate ($T$) of Allianz SE of about 30% (based on the information given in the annual report) we get to a WACC of:

$$WACC = r_E \times \frac{E}{EV} + r_D \times \frac{D}{EV} \times (1 - T)$$

$$WACC = 8.5\% \times (1 - 5.8\%) + 3.1\% \times 5.8\% \times (1 - 30\%)$$

$$WACC = 8.13\%$$

# Stretch yourself

Deriving an accurate beta in practice can be quite tricky. We only performed a hands-on approach in this section.

We have shown a regression-derived beta using daily returns and one year of observation period but we can also apply a two-year weekly-return basis or a five-year monthly-return basis. Additionally, if we change that basis or the market against which we regress the stock (i.e. if we chose another equity index in our regression) we get different answers.

Also, our approach is backward looking, and some might prefer a forward-looking perspective in their valuation. Therefore, some data providers also provide the following so-called adjusted betas:

$$Adjusted\ beta = Raw\ beta \times 2/3 + Market\ beta \times 1/3$$

And finally, to translate betas from one company to the other (or industry betas available from a public source to one for a specific target company) it is often necessary to adjust the betas for the differences in capital structure risk between the comparable and the target. This procedure is called unlevering and relevering beta.

# SECTION D
# What Are You Valuing?

# CHAPTER 11

# What is enterprise value?

## Bite size

We introduced the idea of enterprise value (EV) in Chapter 1 and showed that there are two ways to conceptualise the value of a business:

1. Equity value
2. Enterprise value.

In this chapter we explore in more detail the concept of EV. In essence, EV captures the value of the entire operations of the company, irrespective of how they are financed. As we shall see in this chapter, if you want to calculate EV you can approach the valuation by ascertaining the market value of debt and the market value of equity or, alternatively, by valuing the operating assets that these forms of finance support. The EV bridge links the value of equity and EV together.

## Practitioner focus

EV is widely used in valuation. As we shall see, it has a number of advantages over valuing equity directly, particularly when it comes to controlling for capital structure differentials. We address the question of when to use equity and when to use EV in Chapter 13. It is always important to remember that valuations are undertaken for a variety of reasons. One reason may be to compare the operations of different peers within a particular industry. This is where EV is very useful – it ignores capital structure differences between businesses and allows the user to focus on the operations of the business.

# Core content

## 1. Moving from equity value to EV

Imagine, as part of building up the property portfolio within a real estate business, you decided that you wanted to buy a rental property on a particular street in the suburbs of a large city. You arrive at the street to survey the area having already undertaken some research into the market value of properties in the location. Let us assume that all houses in the area are more or less identical. You have established that the houses could be rented out at £50,000 per year, and your required rate of return is 5%. Assuming that the annual amount of rental income does not change in future years, this is a perpetuity that has a present value of:

$$Present\ value\ of\ perpetuity = \frac{£50,000}{0.05} = £1,000,000$$

This present value of perpetuity is essentially the value of the house 'asset'. It could also be thought of as the value of the rental operation if you can acquire a house. We have already heard that EV represents the value of the operations of the business, so here, ignoring any other properties the company might have, we would say the operations have an EV of £1,000,000.

We then proceed to walk down the street and knock on doors to ask owners about the value of their ownership in the properties. Imagine we knocked on one door and asked the owner what equity (ownership) they had in the house, and they replied that they had a mortgage (i.e. debt) of £800,000.

We can quickly calculate that the portion that they own (that is, their equity) is £200,000 (see Figure 11.1).

## FIGURE 11.1 EQUITY OWNERSHIP VERSUS ASSET VALUE

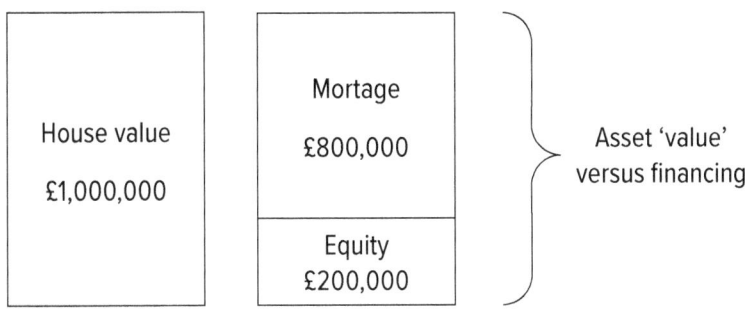

We could repeat this process, knocking on lots of doors and getting different values for equity depending on the mortgage (debt) levels of the owner. We can see that despite the asset having a consistent value (£1,000,000, also known as EV), the equity value varies widely dependent upon the mortgage of the owner. The question is, which approach to valuation is more useful?

Should we value the asset irrespective of the debt levels of the existing owners (in the case of our example in Figure 11.1, the value of the houses is £1m)? Or should we value the equity by deducting debt from the value of the asset (in our example, the value of this person's equity is £200,000)?

It should be reasonably clear that the value of the asset is a more useful approach. If we were to purchase the property, we could decide what mortgage (if any) was needed irrespective of the mortgages of other owners, or the person we buy the house from. Therefore, the particular levels of debt that they have are less important. The EV approach allows us to value the asset irrespective of the amount of debt used to finance the purchase of the asset.

We can now take this conclusion – that EV is often a more useful way to think about valuation – and translate it into a corporate valuation perspective (as illustrated in Figure 11.2).

Firstly, we shall replace the asset value in our example with EV, which is also often referred to as 'firm value'. This is the market value of the firm's operations, or operating assets. For example, if we are valuing an airline then we speak of its operations as its airline business. Such operations consist of operating assets (for example airplanes) and operating liabilities (for example deferred income from ticket sales). Consequently, we can think of the value of the airline as the value of these net operating assets (operating assets less operating liabilities).

In our simple property example, and assuming there are no other properties in the portfolio and no operating liabilities, our simple rental business is valued at an EV of £1,000,000. This represents the value of the operating assets (£1,000,000) less the value of the operating liabilities (£0 in our simple example).

Let us assume we require £800,000 from a bank to support the purchase of this property. Instead of a mortgage, we now refer to such finance as debt, and equity now becomes shareholders' equity. Importantly, both debt and equity are at market value.

We can now see a simple relationship between these various elements:

*Enterprise value = Value of operations = Value of net operating assets*

*Enterprise value = Market value of (Net debt + equity)*

FIGURE 11.2 ENTERPRISE VALUE EQUALS THE VALUE OF THE OPERATIONS

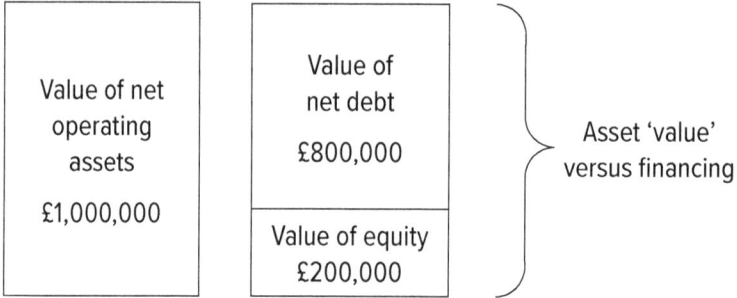

## 2. Different pathways to EV

In our basic example of a rental company, we reached the value of £1,000,000 by taking the rental stream from the asset (£50,000 per year) and dividing it by the required rate of return (5%) to bring us to a value of £1,000,000. In other words, EV – the value of the operations of a business (in this case a simple rental company) – can be calculated as the present value of the future cash flows from those operations. This is consistent with one of the building blocks of valuation that valuations are based on future forecasts.

But we also know from the figure and discussion above that this equals the market value of net debt plus the market value of equity. These relationships allow us to follow two approaches to the calculation of EV:

1. The first is to calculate EV based on the present value of cash flows from operations, as we did for our rental business above.
2. The alternative approach is to calculate EV through the prism of financing, i.e. calculate the market value of equity and add on the market value of net debt.

*Enterprise value = Market value of net operating assets*

*Enterprise value = Market value of net debt + Market value of equity*

From the above relationship it also follows that the market value of the business less the market value of net debt equals the market value of equity.

*Enterprise value − Market value of net debt = Market value of equity*

For example, if my business has a market value of £1m and the market value of net debt is £600,000, then the market value of the remaining ownership (equity) must be £400,000. Consequently, even if we calculate EV we can still determine the implied value of equity. This is critical as often we will want to use EV to compare the value of operations but also equity value as it allows us to compare our calculation of intrinsic value of equity with the actual value of shares trading in the market. This is fundamental to deciding whether there is an investment opportunity. For example, if your estimate of intrinsic value of equity is above the market value of equity then this might represent a buying opportunity.

## 3. EV and balance sheet values

It is easy to confuse concepts that are used in accounting convention and concepts that are used for the calculation of EV. Figure 11.3 explores these relationships.

The most important difference is that accounting uses book value, which represents a mix of fair values and historical cost-based measures. In other words, accounting uses a hybrid valuation model. In contrast, for EV, we always use market values.

If we approach EV through a financing lens, we require the market value of debt and the market value of equity. Companies' financial statements provide us with the book value of both of these measures. As book values will often diverge materially from market values, accounting numbers do not provide us with EV. If we adopt the asset approach to EV, then again EV demands that we ascertain the market value of net operating assets (i.e. the operations), whereas once again the financial statements provide us with, in the main, book values of these assets, which will often be very different.

FIGURE 11.3 RELATIONSHIP BETWEEN BALANCE SHEETS AND EV

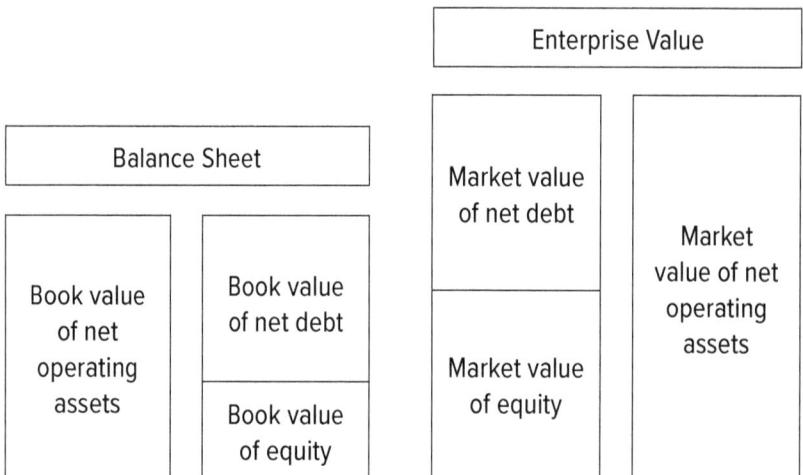

## 4. Advantages of using EV

There are two critical but interwoven reasons why practitioners are attracted to using an EV approach.

- **Capital structure neutrality:** EV is based on the value of the operations irrespective of how they are financed (i.e. the mix of supporting debt and equity financing). So, two identical companies, one with 50% debt and one with no debt, will have the same EV. An unusual, or temporary, capital structure will not distract us from our analysis of the value of the operations.

- **Separating operating and financing decisions:** Related to the previous point is that EV separates financing and operating decisions within a business. This feature of EV allows a user to consider the quality and value of a company's operations and analyse capital structure later. This can be important as the two (operations and financing) have very different characteristics. For example, if we consider the example of an airline, financing decisions about the appropriate mix of debt and equity for the business are very different from decisions about which airplane model to construct a fleet around. It is often much easier to refinance and reconfigure an unsuitable capital structure than it is to reconstruct weak operating structures.

Most practitioners will use EV where possible. However, there are some circumstances where it cannot be used. We consider this question, of when to use EV and when it may not be suitable, in Chapter 14.

## 5. From EV to equity value: the EV bridge

FIGURE 11.4 VALUATION APPROACHES: ENTERPRISE VALUE OR EQUITY VALUE

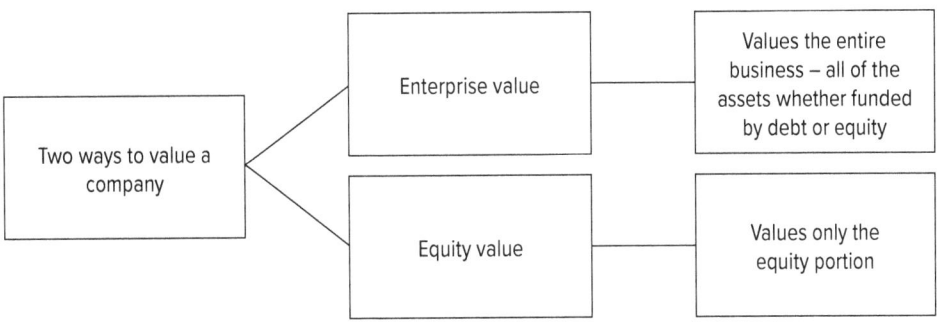

You can see in Figure 11.4 the essential difference in choice when valuing a company. However, even if the decision is made to adopt an EV approach, valuers will still wish to calculate equity value as well. Fortunately, we have a straightforward 'bridge' which links the two. If a valuer adopts an EV approach, then we can use this bridge to calculate equity value. If we have the equity number, then we can use the bridge to calculate EV.

The basic version of the EV bridge is based on what we have already seen:

*Enterprise value − Market value of net debt = Market value of equity*

Continuing with our earlier example of a business with an asset worth £1,000,000 and a mortgage of £800,000 we can see that equity is valued at £200,000:

| Enterprise value | £ 1,000,000 |
|---|---|
| Net debt | (800,000) |
| Equity value | **£ 200,000** |

If we are moving from EV to equity value, the required adjustment is to deduct net debt. If we are moving from equity value to EV, we do the opposite and add on net debt:

*Market value of equity + Market value of net debt = Enterprise value*

| | |
|---|---|
| Equity value | £ 200,000 |
| Net debt | + 800,000 |
| **Enterprise value** | **£ 1,000,000** |

# Stretch yourself

In this chapter we addressed the very important issue of EV and why it is used so widely in practice. In this section we delve deeper into the definition of EV.

There are actually two different versions of EV – operating EV and total EV.

Operating EV represents the value of the operations of a business and is consistent with the version of EV that we addressed earlier in the chapter. We also refer to it as 'firm' value.

However, what if a company has some non-operating assets? For example, imagine a company has a 5% investment in equity of another company, which operates in an entirely different business and so is not part of 'core' operations. And yet such an investment is financed by the debt and equity of the business and is owned by the equity investors. Therefore, when we say the value of debt and value of equity is equal to EV we need to be careful with our terminology. In effect, debt and equity finance refers to Total Enterprise Value (TEV). This is the value of core operations *and* the value of non-core investments: debt and equity finance TEV rather than just the core operations. It is different from operating enterprise value (OEV), which is limited to core operations only. Let us write these out in simple equation form:

*OEV = Value of operations*

*TEV = OEV + Non-operating assets*

*TEV = Value of equity + Value of net debt*

It is worth noting that many practitioners do not use the term 'operating EV' nor distinguish OEV from TEV. However, it is useful for us to be as disciplined as possible as we develop our knowledge. Note that in this textbook going forward, where we refer to EV, we mean operating enterprise value (OEV).

# CHAPTER 12

# What is equity value?

## Bite size

In this chapter we explore equity value, including the nature of book value of equity (and its associated accounting) and the market value of equity. Equity represents the residual asset class, and so equity owners (who own ordinary shares, also often called common stock) only earn a return once other providers of finance have been serviced. Book value of equity is an accounting measure that can be ascertained from companies' financial statements. It consists of share capital plus reserves, the latter representing the retained earnings of the business. To ascertain the market value of equity we can observe it from stock prices quoted on the stock market or calculate our estimate of its intrinsic value.

## Practitioner focus

When practitioners think about the value of a company it is often the equity value they are thinking of. In this chapter we clarify the difference between the book value of equity and its market value equivalent, an understanding of which is critical to valuation.

# Core content

## 1. The nature of book equity capital

Equity represents the ownership interest in a business. It is defined in International Accounting Standard (IAS) 1 as:

> *"The residual interest in the net assets of an entity that remains after deducting its liabilities. In a business enterprise, the equity is the ownership interest."*

In accounting (i.e. in companies' financial statements), equity consists of three major components: **called-up capital, share premium** and **reserves**. For example, see the extract below from the financials of AstraZeneca:

FIGURE 12.1 EXTRACT FROM THE BALANCE SHEET OF ASTRAZENECA

|  | Notes | 2022 $m | 2021 $m | 2020 $m |
|---|---|---|---|---|
| **Equity** | | | | |
| Capital and reserves attributable to equity holders of the Company | | | | |
| Share capital | 24 | 387 | 387 | 328 |
| Share premium account | | 35,155 | 35,126 | 7,971 |
| Capital redemption reserve | | 153 | 153 | 153 |
| Merger reserve | | 448 | 448 | 448 |
| Other reserves | 23 | 1,468 | 1,444 | 1,423 |
| Retained earnings | 23 | (574) | 1,710 | 5,299 |
| | | 37,037 | 39,268 | 15,622 |
| Non-controlling interests | 26 | 21 | 19 | 16 |
| Total equity | | 37,058 | 39,287 | 15,638 |

We can see these elements in the above extract although there are also a number of more complex items such as a capital redemption reserve and a merger reserve. These are beyond the scope of an introductory text, but it is worth noting that even experienced practitioners would treat all of these reserves simply as sources of equity.

## 1.1 Share capital and share premium

These are the shares that have been issued by the company to raise equity capital and so it is called share capital or called-up share capital. This capital represents the actual number of shares in issue. Note that there is also authorised share capital, which refers to the maximum number of shares a company can issue. The terminology in this area can be confusing and so for clarity it is also worth noting that common stock is the same as ordinary share capital.

When shares are issued, they are 'assigned' a par or nominal value. However, the actual price at which shares are issued to investors is usually higher than the par or nominal value. The difference between the par value and the actual price the shares are issued at is referred to as share premium or additional paid in capital. From a valuation perspective, this distinction is not especially significant but is worth being aware of.

In order to illustrate the basics of accounting for equity in financial statements we can take a hypothetical company, RockBlack PLC, which issues 250,000 ordinary shares with the par value per share of €1. Let us assume that the shares are issued at the actual price per share of €1. In this case, the called-up common stock will equal €250,000. Let us now assume that RockBlack PLC issues further units of common stock some years later. This new issue consists of 200,000 ordinary shares with a par value of €1 per share, but the shares are issued at the actual price per share of €1.50. In other words, the shares are issued at a premium of €0.50 per share. We would record the excess of the issue price over the nominal (par) value as share premium. In this case, called-up share capital would increase by €200,000 and additional paid in capital (also known as share premium) would increase by €100,000 (i.e. 200,000 × €0.50).

In this section we have focused on the fundamentals of accounting for ordinary shares as it represents the ownership interest and is most relevant for our analysis. However, another form of shares are sometimes issued and, although much less important for our valuation work, it is useful to distinguish between the two, as we do in Table 12.1.

TABLE 12.1 COMMON STOCK VERSUS PREFERRED STOCK – KEY DIFFERENCES

| Issue | Common stock | Preferred stock |
|---|---|---|
| Who gets priority repayment in a liquidation? | Subordinated to preferred stock | Paid in preference to common stock |
| Dividend priority | Paid after preference dividend | Paid in preference to common stock |
| Can the shares be converted into common stock? | N/A | Potentially |
| Can the shares be repurchased (redeemable)? | May be repurchased | May be repurchased/ redeemed |

## 1.2 Retained earnings

Retained earnings represent the total accumulated profits of the company that have been retained rather than distributed to shareholders as dividends. In essence, the ordinary shareholders own the retained earnings and so by leaving the profits within the business they represent an investment in (the book equity of) that business. This is why retained earnings increase the recognised book equity in the financial statements.

## 1.3 Reserves

There may also be other reserves, such as a revaluation reserve, and these also represent investments made and owned by the common stockholders. These can be thought of as undistributed gains a company has recognised in the financial statements.

## 2. The market value of equity

The first section of this chapter has focused on the accounting for equity as it represents a clear component of company balance sheets. From a valuation perspective, even though a knowledge of the accounting for equity is important, we are much more interested in the market value of equity.

The most familiar approach to the market value of equity is simply to calculate it from prices quoted on the stock market. This is referred to as market capitalisation as illustrated below:

*Ordinary share outstanding × Share price = Market capitalisation*

This is the market value we could calculate if we opened up a Bloomberg or Reuters terminal. It is relevant for valuation in two senses. First, we may need to compare our intrinsic value calculation of equity with this current market value to decide whether to buy, sell or hold a security. Second, for a number of valuation multiples we need a market price. For example, if we want to calculate a P/E ratio, comparing the market price with earnings per share, then we need the market capitalisation to calculate it.

However, importantly, from a valuation perspective this is not the end of the story. We want to produce our own model of the intrinsic value of the equity. This will come from a careful process of analysing the company's business (e.g. its strategy, competitive position, value drivers, prospects, etc.), its financial statements, producing forecasts, and then converting these into a valuation. We cannot just observe the intrinsic value from looking at the stock market prices, we have to estimate it. As explained in Chapter 11, we can estimate equity directly or we can first estimate enterprise value and then calculate equity value from this. Where possible we recommend estimating enterprise value first and then solving for equity value. This approach has several advantages, such as the use of a more stable suite of inputs to our valuation process. For example, we use earnings before interest and taxes (EBIT) level inputs, or their equivalent for enterprise value. If we are valuing equity, we use net income level inputs which are post-interest and tax. These items can introduce significant volatility into our estimates. Additionally, enterprise value of itself is a very useful value that can be used in a number of valuation multiples and comparisons important to sophisticated analysis.

# Stretch yourself

This chapter has addressed a number of straightforward aspects of equity. However, one area of interest to valuers is to delve more deeply into the determination of the market value of equity (or market capitalisation). As we saw earlier in the chapter, the market value of equity is the product of share price and the number of shares outstanding. The share price is straightforward and so we shall focus on the second element, the number of shares outstanding. We already explored the most basic example where a company simply issues shares, and this is used to determine the market value of equity. However, for most sophisticated companies there are a number of complications with determining an accurate share count number.

The first complication relates to companies that repurchase some of the shares that they had previously issued, often referred to as treasury stock. This is permitted by company law in many countries, though not all. We should deduct the amount of treasury shares when calculating the ordinary shares outstanding. The logic of this exclusion is that these shares are no longer outstanding. Whether they have been cancelled or remain 'in treasury' on a balance sheet is irrelevant from an economic or valuation context.

The second complication is regarding potentially dilutive securities. These consist of instruments such as employee share options and convertible bonds. Before suggesting how these items should be dealt with it is worth thinking about what is reflected in the share price that we are using. Imagine we have two companies, Dilute PLC and Simple PLC, which are identical with the exception that Dilute PLC has significant stock options and convertible bonds whereas Simple PLC has a much simpler capital structure, consisting of nothing beyond shares issued. Assuming the convertible bonds and options are likely to be converted (i.e. are 'in-the-money'), the share price of Dilute PLC will be lower. To the extent that shareholders anticipate the likely future dilution to their ownership, their expectations will be impounded in the stock price of Dilute PLC. If we want the most economically meaningful measure of equity value then we should include diluted securities in our share count once the convertible bonds and options are in the money. To adjust the share count we can use an approach known as the 'Treasury Stock Method'. This method calculates how many additional shares would be generated if all in-the-money options are 'exercised'. The number of additional shares that would be generated can be calculated using this formula:

$$\text{Additional shares} = \text{Number of shares from options} \times \frac{\text{Share price} - \text{Exercise price}}{\text{Share price}}$$

The method assumes that the money obtained by the company from the exercising of all in-the-money options is used for stock repurchases. As noted earlier, repurchased shares are called treasury stock, hence the name of the method. The following example illustrates how to apply this method.

## Example 1

Box Inc. common stock has traded at an average market price of €40 per share during the year. The company has 20,000 stock options, each of which gives the holder the right to buy one share in Box Inc. at €30 per share. What would be the adjusted share count for equity value purposes if the company has 40,000 shares outstanding?

## Solution

Using the above formula, the number of additional shares can be calculated as:

$$\text{Additional shares} = 20,000 \times \frac{40 - 30}{40} = 5,000$$

The intuition behind this calculation can be explained as follows:

## Step 1:

Calculate the proceeds that would be received if options were exercised, i.e. €600,000 (20,000 × €30).

## Step 2:

Calculate how much stock at the average market price could be repurchased by the company from these proceeds (and converted into treasury stock), i.e. €600,000 / €40 = 15,000

## Step 3:

| | |
|---|---|
| Number of shares issued if exercised | 20,000 |
| Less number of shares that could be bought at average price | 15,000 |
| **= Additional shares** | **5,000** |

It works out that the company will end up with 5,000 more shares. Therefore, the equity value would be based on a count of 45,000 – the original 40,000 shares outstanding plus the additional shares' adjustment.

# CHAPTER 13

# The enterprise value bridge

## Bite size

In Chapters 11 and 12 we explored enterprise value (EV) and equity value and the importance of each. In this chapter we address the linkages between the two. This is very important as even if we accept the advantages of using EV, often investors will want to value a share. You cannot trade EVs as they do not exist on the stock market. Instead, you need to convert these into equity values. Explaining the mechanics of how to achieve this transition (from EV to equity value or vice versa) is the objective of this chapter.

## Practitioner focus

One of the cornerstones of modern valuation is the use of EV. Practitioners want to go beyond just conceptualising value as equity value and so, in most sectors, extensive use is made of EV as well as equity value. Consequently, practitioners need to have a robust knowledge of both, and this is why we have dedicated two separate chapters to address these critical concepts.

## Core content

Let us remind ourselves of the definition of EV that we have used so far:

*Enterprise value = Market value of equity + Market value of net debt*

# Chapter 13 – The enterprise value bridge

We can rearrange this to show that:

*Enterprise value − Market value of net debt = Market value of equity*

This last equation shows how we get from EV to equity: we simply deduct net debt from EV. We call the adjustment of enterprise value for the purpose of calculating equity value (or vice versa) as the EV bridge. This is the simplest form of EV bridge as it only involves one adjusting item – net debt. It is often presented as:

|                  | $   |
|------------------|-----|
| Enterprise value | X   |
| Less: Net debt   | (X) |
| Equity value     | X   |

Although debt is the most common and important adjustment, in a real-world model we would expect to have a number of other adjustments, some of which can cause confusion. Therefore, we want to address a range of adjusting items.

Consider the following example:

|                                    | £          |
|------------------------------------|------------|
| Enterprise value                   | 867,322.00 |
| Cash balance at the valuation date | 2,256.40   |
| Non-operating assets               | 885.80     |
| Long-term debt balance             | 51,122.50  |
| Short-term debt balance            | 22,376.30  |
| Non-controlling interest           | 8,033.90   |

What is the equity value of this company?

To establish the equity value requires us to use the EV bridge. Here the EV bridge goes beyond only a debt adjustment and includes additional adjustments for cash, non-operating assets and non-controlling interests. Remember our objective is to calculate an estimate of equity value based on going from EV to equity across the enterprise value bridge.

The main adjustments in the EV bridge (see calculation below) are consistent with the debt adjustment we have seen above – debt is deducted from EV as a step towards calculating equity. Note we could have deducted net debt, i.e. debt (short-term debt and long-term debt) less surplus cash. This is considered further in the 'Stretch yourself' section at the end of this chapter. In terms of extending our knowledge of the EV bridge, our main interest lies with the two other adjustments that we have not yet addressed.

# 1. Non-operating assets

These assets are not part of the core operations of the business and hence have not been included in EV. Remember, EV is the value of the operations, so if some assets are outside of this 'operational' definition they will not be included. This might represent, for example, a small (say 1%) investment in a distribution company undertaken for strategic reasons, to strengthen relations between the two entities. This is therefore not part of ongoing operations, so it is excluded from EV. However, it is owned by the shareholders and has value. Hence the market value of these shares must be added in our journey from EV to equity value.

# 2. Non-controlling interests

If Company A owns 80% of Company B, then Company A is clearly in control. However, it does not *own* all of company B – 20% of that company is owned by third parties, whom we call 'non-controlling interests' (often called minority interests). In accounting, even though Company A only owns 80% of Company B, we consolidate 100% of Company B into almost all of the balance sheet and income statement numbers. Therefore, when we calculate Company A's enterprise-level cash flows, we are unable to strip out the 20% we do not own. We simply do not have sufficient information. Concurrently, it is clear that the equity shareholders of Company A do not own this 20% slice that has been included in EV (as valuers cannot extract it in most cases). Therefore, in the EV bridge we deduct this non-controlling interest (i.e. market value of the 20% third-party holding) to ensure we only include 80% of the value of Company B in our equity value. This represents the real ownership of the equity holders of Company A.

The workings of these calculations are shown below:

|  | £ |
|---|---|
| Enterprise value | 867,322.00 |
| Long-term debt balance | (51,122.50) |
| Short-term debt balance | (22,376.30) |
| Non-controlling interest | (8,033.90) |
| Cash balance at the valuation date | 2,256.40 |
| Non-operating assets | 885.50 |
| Equity value | **788,931.50** |

The process we have completed can be illustrated in different ways. For example, Figure 13.1 comprises a waterfall chart showing how we got from one side of the EV bridge to the other.

FIGURE 13.1 ENTERPRISE VALUE 'WATERFALL'

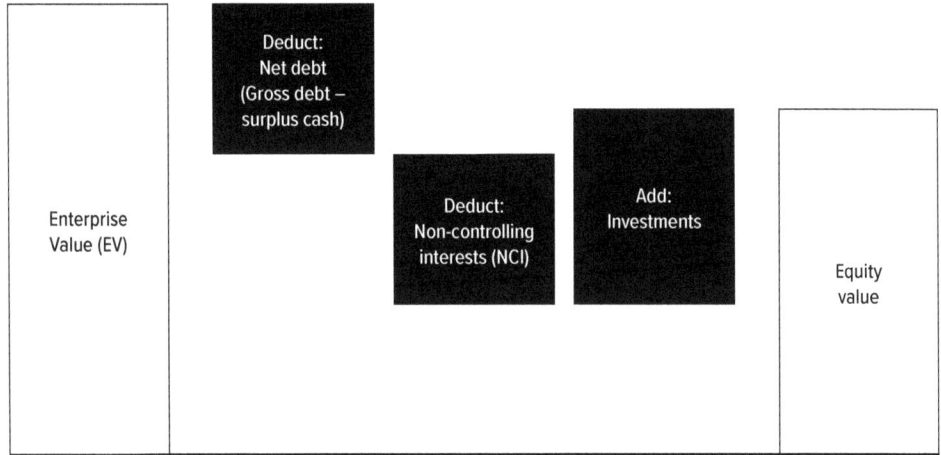

# Stretch yourself

In the EV bridge calculation above, rather than deducting debt and adding surplus cash, we deducted 'net debt' from EV. More formally, net debt equals:

$$Net\ debt = Gross\ short\ term\ debt + Gross\ long\ term\ debt - Surplus\ cash$$

Net debt is widely used as it represents a more economically literate depiction of leverage. If a company has surplus cash that could be used to promptly pay down debt then its underlying levels of leverage are in reality lower than they might appear. There are two key assumptions being made here. Firstly, we are assuming that all of the cash is surplus and is not needed for operations. This means that it is essentially financing in nature as it plays no operating role and merely generates a low-interest income stream. This is a simplifying assumption and, if some of this cash was needed in the business for working capital purposes, then it would not be appropriate to consider it all as 'surplus'. Secondly, we are also assuming the cash is available and not materially restricted. This might occur for tax reasons or if countries implement exchange controls to limit cash leaving a particular jurisdiction. In these cases, the surplus cash may not be available to promptly pay down debt if needed.

# CHAPTER 14

# When to use enterprise value and when to use equity value

## Bite size

In the previous three chapters we explored equity value, enterprise value (EV) and the EV bridge. In this chapter we bring these concepts together and consider when to use EV or equity value. In general, valuers will use EV where they can. This is because it has several advantages, including that it helps us to value the operations of a firm without considering the mix of debt and equity used for financing. Furthermore, it uses less volatile earnings inputs – numbers such as earnings before interest and tax (EBIT) rather than net income. However, as we shall see, it is unsuitable for banks and other financial services companies where it is problematic to separate financing and operating flows.

## Practitioner focus

Many practitioners are mostly interested in the valuation of equity. This might be to determine whether there is a buying or selling opportunity on a stock or to analyse an appropriate bid price in the context of an acquisition. However, even though the objective is to value equity, the most suitable approach may not be to value equity 'directly' and instead calculate it 'indirectly', by valuing EV first and then using the EV bridge to establish an equity value.

# Core content

## 1. Refresh on EV and equity

In the preceding chapters we have explored this in some detail, but it is worth refreshing the fundamentals again before identifying specific use parameters:

- There are two major notions of value used within valuation theory – EV and equity value.
- EV is the value of the operations of the business irrespective of their financing. It can also be valued, and conceptualised, through the financing of these operations. In other words, it represents the market value of net debt plus the market value of equity.
- Equity value represents the residual ownership in the business. It is the value most relevant to shareholders at it represents their investment in the business.
- Intrinsic or relative valuation: we can estimate value by exploring the cash flow generation fundamentals of a business (intrinsic value) or by looking at how the market is valuing other similar assets (relative value).

To help with our discussion it is worth introducing valuation multiples at this point. Although we have a full chapter on valuation multiples later in the book, they are very useful for explaining the use of EV.

Multiples are a form of relative valuation. So, for example, if we want to value an aerospace company and we know that companies in that sector are valued at approximately 12x earnings then we could value our company based on multiplying the company's earnings by a factor of 12. There are two types of multiples – equity and EV multiples. The most common equity multiple is the well-known price-to-earnings (or P/E) ratio, which is the share price divided by earnings per share. Earnings per share is net income divided by shares outstanding. Recall that net income is the 'bottom-line' earnings attributable to equity shareholders. In contrast, enterprise multiples use earnings numbers 'higher up' the income statement such as EBIT or earnings before interest, tax, depreciation and amortisation (EBITDA). This measure captures earnings attributable to equity shareholders and providers of debt. For example, a popular enterprise value multiple is EV/EBITDA, which relates enterprise value to EBITDA. We shall use this basic description of multiples in our discussion below but for a more comprehensive discussion of valuation multiples please refer to Chapters 16–19.

# 2. When to use which?

As we have mentioned already, most valuers prefer using EV wherever possible rather than valuing equity directly. As we shall see, in certain circumstances it may not be possible to use an EV approach and so we are left with no alternative but to value equity directly, a situation we address below.

## 2.1. Use EV when capital structures are different

The critical advantage of using EV is that it allows the valuer to compare the operations of companies with different capital structures. The best example of this is the use of multiples. For now let us assume that multiples are simply a way of comparing value between two companies.

Consider the following example in Table 14.1 of two companies that operate in the same sector, have the same amount of total capital (i.e. same size), generate same revenues, incur same operating expenses, but have different capital structure.

TABLE 14.1 IMPACT OF CAPITAL STRUCTURE ON MULTIPLES

|  | Company A | Company B |
|---|---|---|
| Revenues | 1,000.00 | 1,000.00 |
| Cost of sales | (450.00) | (450.00) |
| **Gross profit** | **550.00** | **550.00** |
| SG&A | (200.00) | (200.00) |
| **EBIT** | **350.00** | **350.00** |
| Interest | - | (100.00) |
| **Profit before tax** | **350.00** | **250.00** |
| Tax | (105.00) | (75.00) |
| **Profit after tax** | **245.00** | **175.00** |
| Enterprise value | 3,200.00 | 3,200.00 |
| Debt | - | (2,000.00) |
| **Equity value** | **3,200.00** | **1,200.00** |
| P/E | 13x | 7x |
| EV/EBIT | 9x | 9x |

What does this example show? It reveals that if we use equity in our valuation multiples, then it is distorted if capital structures vary. In this example, two otherwise identical companies, with only capital structure differences, produce two different P/E calculations. The higher interest expense in Company B reduces the bottom-line profit and so, with an equity multiple approach, the P/E calculation is higher. What is happening here is that the equity multiple is co-mingling operating items and capital structure items. Contrast this with the EV approach. We can see that despite capital structure being different, the enterprise value multiple (EV/EBIT) only reflects the (identical) operations and so is consistent across both. It is worth noting that if we were undertaking some analysis between companies with broadly consistent capital structures then this advantage of EV multiples will clearly diminish in importance.

## 2.2. Use EV when capital intensity is high

If we are valuing a company in an industry with high levels of fixed assets then often we will be concerned about the subjectivity of depreciation numbers. High levels of fixed capital intensity (i.e. the proportion of fixed assets in total assets of the firm) normally result in large depreciation costs. The latitude management has around these material charges means we will often want to use EBITDA as a more robust comparator. This is because that profit measure is before depreciation and amortisation and so is before the impact of any perceived distortion from these items. However, if we want to use EBITDA in valuation multiples we need to use EV, as EBITDA is an enterprise-level profit number, as we explored earlier in the text. Note that we are not suggesting that EBITDA as a measure of profit is not without its own problems. Instead in this context our focus is very much on its utility as a measure for cross-company comparison.

## 2.3. Use EV to separate out financing and operating analysis

Related to the previous point is that EV separates financing and operating decisions within a business. This feature of EV allows a user to consider the quality and value of a company's operations and worry about the capital structure later. This can be important as the two (operating and financing decisions) have very different characteristics. For example, if we consider the example of an airline, financing decisions about the appropriate mix of debt and equity for the business are very different from operating decisions such as which airplane model to construct a fleet around. It is often much easier to refinance and reconfigure an unsuitable capital structure than it is to reconstruct weak operating structures.

## 2.4. Use EV to cope with volatile or negative accounting numbers

If bottom-line earnings (i.e. net income) are negative then we cannot use many of the standard valuation metrics. Given equity multiples, like P/E, use net income as the earnings input, which is post-interest and post-tax, then this is more likely to be negative than if using EBIT or EBITDA in an EV/EBIT or EV/EBITDA multiple.

A similar thought occurs with regard to the volatility of accounting numbers. Such volatility makes analysing trends in multiples very difficult. Again, P/E multiples are more vulnerable to such distortion than EV multiples as net income is post all costs, including interest, which can be particularly volatile. EBIT or EBITDA are less volatile and so this represents another reason for an EV approach.

## 2.5. Use equity for banks and other financial services companies

To use EV requires valuers to distinguish operating items from financing items. For firms operating in non-financial sectors, it is normally straightforward to discriminate between the core operating activities or operating assets (e.g. machines, factories, inventories) and non-core or non-operating assets (which are usually financial assets). However, for a bank this would be much more challenging. The core operating activities of a bank *are* about using financial assets to generate value. In other words, much of the bank's core operating activities and assets are financial in nature (e.g. loans to businesses and individuals, debt securities, derivative financial instruments). That is what banks do. There is no easy separation of assets into operating and financing. If we identify loans on a bank balance sheet, then these cannot be classified as operating or financing – it does not really make sense to think of banks in that way. Hence, for banks, and many other financial institutions, valuers adopt an equity valuation approach rather than EV.

# Stretch yourself

If the decision is made by a valuer to value equity directly, rather than EV, and use the EV bridge to establish the equity value, then there are a number of important challenges that flow from this.

Firstly, relevant measures of cash flow now become 'free cash flow to equity' rather than 'free cash flow to the firm'. This measure of cash flow includes interest and also debt issuances and repayments (see Chapters 26 and 27). Free cash flow to equity can be a much more volatile cash flow measure than the firm-level equivalent.

Secondly, the cost of capital shifts from being a weighted average cost of capital (WACC) figure to a cost of equity figure. This is important as, making some simplifying assumptions, WACC is broadly constant as levels of gearing change. This enables valuers to use the same WACC for each year of a valuation without too much concern that it will be dramatically wrong. However, cost of equity is sensitive to the level of gearing. This is illustrated in Figure 14.1.

## Chapter 14 – When to use enterprise value and when to use equity value

FIGURE 14.1 HOW WACC AND COST OF EQUITY VARY WITH LEVERAGE

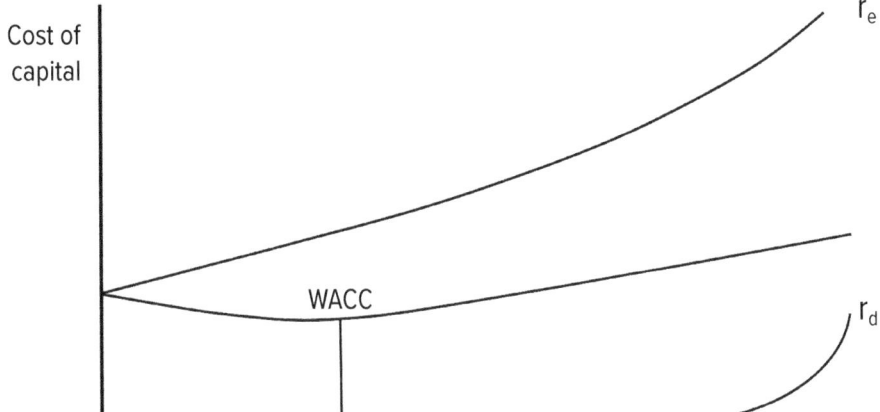

At low to medium levels of debt, WACC gently falls because increasing the use of cheap, tax-deductible debt makes the overall average (WACC) lower. Until we get to very high levels of leverage, the change in WACC is relatively modest. However, you can also observe that the cost of equity is much more sensitive to leverage and increases with higher leverage as shareholders anticipate potential bankruptcy costs. If we are valuing equity directly then it is this volatile cost of equity that we must use. Note that this well-known diagram (Figure 14.1) is very much a simplification but is useful for developing an intuitive understanding of the key point here – if we are valuing equity directly we need to use a volatile cost of equity as it is highly sensitive to leverage; if using EV, and consequently WACC, this is much less of an issue.

# CHAPTER 15
# The different types of valuation models

## Bite size

There is no single universal approach to the valuation of companies. Valuing companies means dealing with uncertainties and with limited information. In such an environment it is best to tackle the valuation problem from different directions, using different models that are based on different assumptions and sources of information. Valuation models can be divided into two broad categories: a) present value-based models, such as Discounted Cash Flow models, Dividend Discount models and Residual Income Valuation models; and b) comparable company-based methods, such as valuation using various equity or enterprise multiples.

## Practitioner focus

Present value-based models are the most straightforward approaches to business valuation as they combine the theoretical ideal with practical applicability. However, such models require high-quality forecasts of company fundamentals, such as earnings, cash flows and future growth rates, as well as an estimation of an appropriate cost of capital (i.e. the discount rate). This is where comparable company-based models (i.e. multiples) come into play. They have lower requirements regarding forecasting of company fundamentals and valuation parameters, relying instead on the degree of comparability and pricing quality of peer group companies.

# Core content

## 1. Why different types of valuation models?

In theory, valuation of companies is simple – at least if we rely on basic theoretical concepts. The value of a company is a function of what an investor can get out of it, in other words the level of future cash flows. These future benefits can be translated into a value number by present value techniques. However, predicting what one can expect to get out of a company in the future is very tricky as there are no crystal balls available and forecasting is always difficult and prone to mistakes. It is not only a problem of building expectations about fundamentals of the company – e.g. the expected revenue for the coming year – but it is also a problem of forecasting the uncertainty related to these fundamental forecasts, i.e. how far the actual outcome for next year's revenue might deviate from the expected value to the upside and the downside.

This gives rise to other valuation approaches that rely less on forecasting fundamentals and dealing with uncertainties, such as the method of multiples. However, for becoming less reliant on forecasting, these alternative models have to pay a price. They are less able to cover all specific characteristics of the target company and have stricter requirements in other dimensions such as data comparability across peer companies and pricing accuracy of peers in capital markets.

As a consequence, investors have to work with different models that have different strengths and weaknesses. To get the best out of these models, it is often necessary to use different ones at the same time and aggregate the results.

This plurality of approaches does not mean that all valuation models are equally relevant or appropriate in all valuation settings. Some models might be deemed more appropriate than others when valuing a company or a business segment operating in a particular sector or circumstance. Hence, aggregation of results generated by different valuation models should not, by default, be based on an equal weighting of single model results. Appropriate weightings should be determined based on careful case-by-case consideration.

## 2. The two core types of valuation models

In generic terms we can distinguish between the following two types of valuation models:
- Present value-based models such as the Discounted Cash Flow (DCF) model, the Dividend Discount Model (DDM) or the Residual Income Valuation (RIV) model require forecasts of future economic benefits, such as future free cash flows, dividends or residual earnings, and appropriate discount rates as an input. For

example, in the case of the DCF model, we should forecast all of the future years' free cash flows, discount them back to today (Year 0) and then sum them, as shown below:

$$Value_0 = \sum_{t=1}^{\infty} \frac{Cash\ flow_t}{(1+r)^t}$$

Where $r$ is the discount rate, and $t$ is the year.

- Comparable company-based valuation models derive the value of a company based on conclusions drawn from peer companies (or peer transactions). Usually in this approach, evidence about the relative pricing of peer companies in capital markets or in M&A transactions is translated into a multiple of a performance reference base such as earnings. Then this multiple is applied to the target company. In simplified terms, the value of the company is here the result of the following valuation model:

$$Value_0 = M_{Peers} \times Reference\ base_{Target}$$

Where $M_{Peers}$ is a multiple that is derived from the capital market pricing (or M&A transaction prices) of peer companies.

It is obvious that the accuracy of comparable company-based valuation crucially depends on the degree of comparability of peers with the target company and the accuracy of peer companies' stock prices (or M&A transaction prices). On the other hand, this model does not explicitly require a detailed period-by-period forecast of future economic benefits such as cash flows, dividends or earnings.

If valuation using multiples is applied based on historical reference bases (and multiples that are derived based on historical reference bases of the peer group as well), then these multiples are called trailing multiples. If it is applied based on one-, two- or three-year forecasted reference bases and respectively derived multiples of the peers, then they are called forward multiples. Later in the book we address multiples in detail.

## 3. Summary of different types and requirements of valuation models

Different valuation models have different strengths and weaknesses. They rely on different assumptions and make use of different information and data. For example, some models are stronger on the degree of comparability with other companies as the data might be widely available and be constructed in a consistent way from company to company. Multiple-based valuations, which make extensive use of audited accounting data might well fit this category of valuation model. On the other hand those models that rely forecasting accuracy (for example, DCF or Dividend Discount models) are naturally exposed to much more uncertain inputs. We can see the following map of different approaches described in this chapter. While multiples are dependent on the availability of comparable companies and the quality of historical accounting data, DCF models are dependent on accuracy of forecast data. As a summary, this two-dimensional decision-making field is depicted in Figure 15.1.

FIGURE 15.1 DIFFERENT VALUATION MODELS AND THEIR NEED FOR FORECASTING ACCURACY AND COMPARABLE DATA

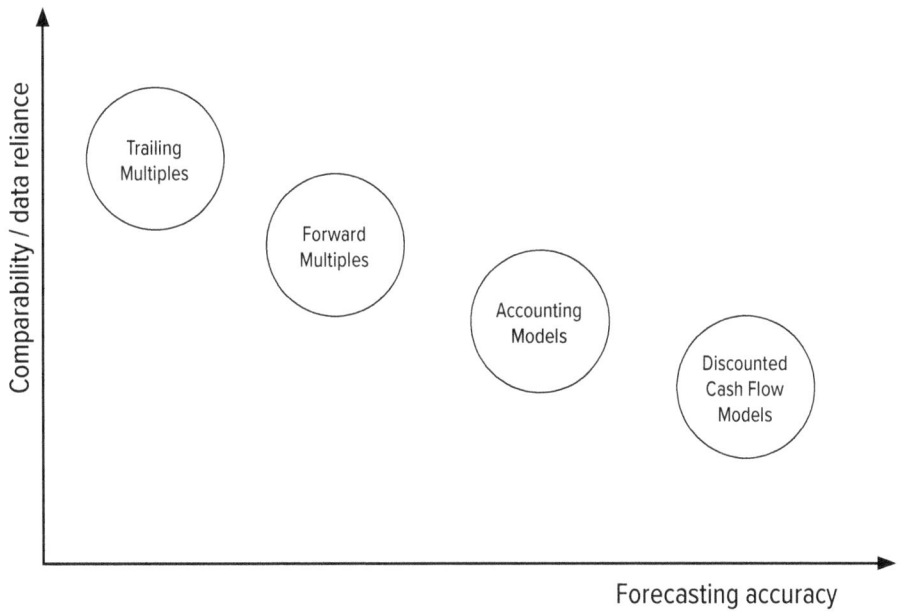

It is important to note that Figure 15.1 does not make a statement about valuation accuracy or performance of the different valuation approaches. It only depicts what is needed in order to perform each of these valuation approaches properly.

# Stretch yourself

The described valuation approaches are not specific models per se but rather are broad umbrella terms for classes of different model variants. For example, the DCF approach comes in many variants, such as an equity value variant (used to estimate the intrinsic value of a company's equity), an entity-value variant (used to estimate the value of the entire enterprise), the adjusted present value approach, etc. The same is true for the comparable company-based valuation approach – there are a number of different variants of multiples (and some are even sector-specific) that can be used to estimate the equity or enterprise value of a company.

Moreover, the described valuation models do not form an exhaustive list of all possible valuation models. In some valuation cases we can see interesting combinations of these generic model types. For example, when valuing young companies (start-ups), or companies where it is difficult to generate long-term projections for cash flows, often so-called venture capital models are applied, which make use of present value-based models for the cash flows of a company in the first years (i.e. up to a forecast horizon that an investor or analyst is comfortable with) and a 'terminal value' or 'continuing value' that is estimated using multiples to capture the value contribution of the years beyond the investor's forecast horizon.

# SECTION E
Multiples-Based Valuation

# CHAPTER 16

# The logic of multiple-based valuations

## Bite size

Multiples express valuation relative to an accounting benchmark. So, we speak of value as 'ten times earnings' or 'two times sales'. This approach to valuation – expressing it in terms of an accounting benchmark – facilitates much clearer and more impactful ways of referring to valuation. In this chapter, our focus is very much on the fundamentals of multiples while the following chapters address equity and enterprise multiples in more detail.

## Practitioner focus

Multiples are used widely in practice. For example, research by Brown et al. (2015)[20] found that multiples, specifically the P/E ratio, were the most frequently used valuation tool. They are simple and intuitive. However, care needs to be taken in their use in practice. Although it is straightforward to establish that a stock trades on (say) ten times earnings (often expressed as '10x' earnings), we need to delve deeper to explore what this means in terms of underlying valuation and potential mispricing.

---

20   Brown, L. D., Call, A. C., Clement, M. B. & Sharp, N. Y. (2015). Inside the "black box" of sell-side financial analysts. *Journal of Accounting Research*, 53(1), 1–47.

# Core content

## 1. Intrinsic versus relative value

We saw in the opening chapter of the book that there are two main approaches to valuation – relative and intrinsic – and that you need to be clear on which approach you are following. The first, which we will term relative valuation, seeks to value an asset based on the valuation in the market of similar assets. For example, if a house on a residential street has sold for $1m, then this might be a good starting point for the valuation of other similar houses on that street or nearby. In the same way, if a UK retailer is valued at 10x earnings then we might value another UK retailer at 10x its earnings. We would need to ensure that the various assets (houses, retail company stocks, etc.) were indeed similar for this approach to work, although we can always make some adjustments. Perhaps we might consider one retailer as riskier than another. In that case we could value it on (say) 9x earnings to reflect this higher risk. As mentioned above, an approach to valuation that is based on the value of other assets in the market is termed relative valuation and is normally done through the use of multiples. It is also commonly referred to as comparable company analysis.

## 2. The basic structure of a multiple

Multiples are a core part of the valuation toolkit for any professional undertaking a valuation or indeed discussing valuation issues. But what is a valuation multiple? The basic structure of a valuation multiple is as follows:

$$Valuation\ multiple = \frac{Market\ value\ measure}{Accounting\ measure}$$

There are two main alternatives for the market value measure – equity value or enterprise value (EV). For the accounting measure, which acts as a benchmark, we have a range of possibilities.

## Chapter 16 – The logic of multiple-based valuations

FIGURE 16.1 WHAT IS A MULTIPLE?

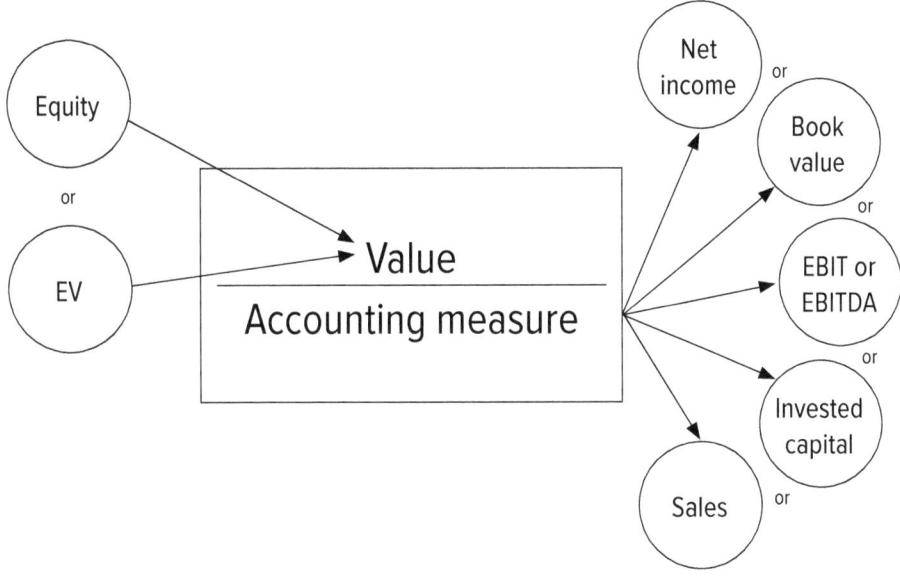

Before discussing these alternatives, illustrated in Figure 16.1, it is important to realise that the accounting measure must be consistent with the valuation measure. For example, net income represents the profit that belongs to the common stockholders. Therefore, it makes sense to relate that to the value of equity investors. Therefore, we get the P/E (price-to-earnings) multiple. This multiple involves an apples-to-apples comparison – an equity profit measure (net income or earnings per share if on a per share basis) divided into the price of an equity share. It would be quite wrong to use, say, earnings before interest and tax (EBIT) as an accounting measure in the denominator if we are using the equity value in the numerator. Why? Because the denominator (EBIT) is not entirely an equity flow, as part of EBIT belongs to debt investors. Consequently, EBIT should be used with EV to ensure we are comparing like with like. We shall revisit this concept in the forthcoming chapters on EV and equity multiples.

Note that equity multiples can be (and typically are) calculated on a per share basis. For example, the P/E multiple can be calculated as a ratio of common shareholder equity to net income, or as a ratio of the price of an equity share (i.e. stock price) to earnings per share (EPS).

## 3. Why do we need multiples?

The easiest way to think of why we need multiples is to consider the difficulty of speaking about the value of a company in absolute terms. Is it meaningful to talk about the market value of a company being, for example, $128.5m? Well not if you have nothing to compare that number to. Is $128.5m, of itself, a high valuation or low valuation? Clearly you would need to be very familiar with the company and its peers to be able to say anything sensible without further information. Comparing the absolute value of two companies is also a pointless exercise. For example, even if we identify that Company X has a higher market value than Company Y it is difficult to say anything further that would be economically literate without more information.

This is where multiples play a key role. If we speak of the valuation of one company's equity as being (say) 10x earnings and another company is trading at 12x earnings, then we have the basis for a useful valuation conversation. Assuming we are happy with these multiple calculations, we can say that the first company is 'cheaper' (relative to the second company), or the second company is more 'expensive' (relative to the first company). In a similar vein, a company's multiples can be compared across time (i.e. using time-series analysis) to compare the company's current valuation relative to its own past valuations. These are simple, useful observations that could not be made without multiples. There are further uses of multiples that we will come to later.

## 4. Types of multiples: equity and EV

There are various ways to classify multiples. The first, which we have introduced already, is to classify multiples into equity and EV multiples. Equity multiples relate a company share price (or total equity) to an accounting equity item (such as book value or EPS). EV multiples, on the other hand, relate the market value of debt and equity (enterprise value) to an appropriate and consistent accounting item such as EBIT, EBITDA or sales that belongs to both the debt and equity holders.

## 5. Types of multiples: stock and flow multiples

The income statement and cash flow on the one hand, and the balance sheet on the other, are very different statements. The former are termed 'flow' statements as they represent flows that occur in specific periods. So, for example, the 2022 income statement shows revenues and costs that relate to 2022. Once the accounting period for 2022 ends, revenues and costs are reset to zero and the accounts begin again. The same process happens with the cash flow statement. Balance sheets are not flow statements as they do not record the 'flow' through one period. Instead, they are cumulative (often referred to as 'stock' statements) and show the cumulative amounts of assets, liabilities and equity at a particular point in time.

Because of its 'cumulative' nature, balance sheet data tend to be much less volatile than flow data. In relation to multiples, we have flow and stock multiples reflecting this difference. An example of a flow multiple would be price-to-earnings (P/E). Earnings come from the income statement, a flow statement, whereas price-to-book (P/B) is a stock multiple as book value of equity comes from the balance sheet (see Figure 16.2 for examples).

One use case for stock multiples is when flow multiples could not be used. For example, if a company has negative EPS, we cannot use P/E, but we may well be able to use P/B.

FIGURE 16.2 DIFFERENT TYPES OF STOCK MULTIPLES

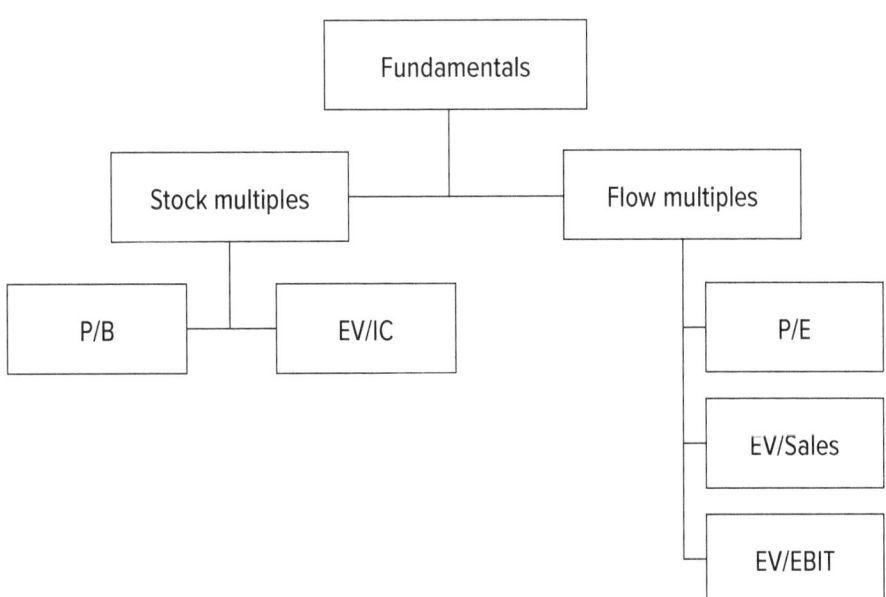

# 6. Types of multiples: forward or trailing multiples

When calculating multiples, we have the option to use historic or forecasted accounting numbers. For example, in calculating a P/E ratio, we could use a historic EPS number. This would be a trailing P/E multiple. On the other hand, we might like to use forecasted EPS, say for next year. This would then become a forward P/E multiple.

# 7. Steps in using multiples

The major steps using multiples are set out in Figure 16.3.

FIGURE 16.3 STEPS IN USING MULTIPLES

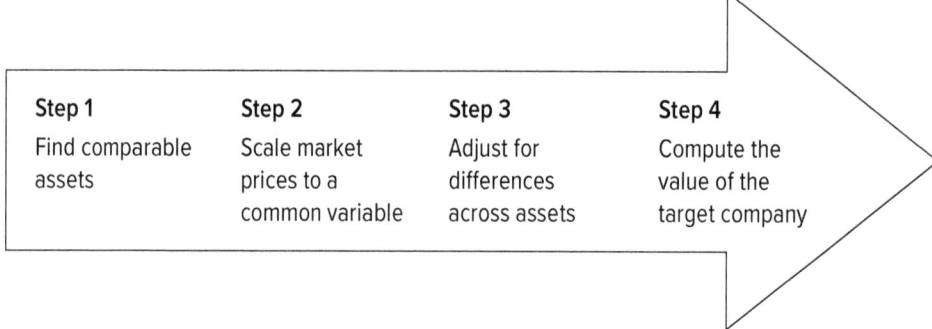

Each step entails making judgements and presents significant challenges for valuers. We shall address each in turn.

## Step 1: Find comparable assets

This is the pool of similar companies that will determine a 'base' or 'benchmark' multiple for our valuation. At a basic level this might appear to be straightforward. The most common initial criteria for identification of comparable companies are sector and size. For example, if we are trying to value a European bank, we might consider the list of European banks presented in Table 16.1 as an initial sample of comparable companies. However, this list may require further refining as large size differences of these banks may hamper their comparability. For example, a larger business can have numerous advantages over smaller ones derived from economies of scale. HSBC Holdings is significantly larger than all other banks in our example and so it could be argued that it faces very different economics from much smaller banks. Therefore, we may want to exclude certain stocks that are dissimilar from the company we are valuing. Additionally, we need to consider if some of these stocks might be excluded from our analysis as they are not sufficiently 'comparable'. For example, the business mix (percentage of business related to investment banking or retail banking) might be different across different banks.

TABLE 16.1 SAMPLE OF MULTIPLES FOR THE EUROPEAN BANKING SECTOR

| Company | Market cap | P/E |
|---|---|---|
| HSBC Holdings PLC | 67,203 | 6.17x |
| BNP Paribas SA | 36,600 | 6.07x |
| UBS Group AG | 36,369 | 8.19x |
| Intesa Sanpaolo SpA | 31,116 | 6.38x |
| Banco Santander SA | 26,380 | 5.8x |
| Nordea Bank Abp | 25,999 | 8.49x |
| ING Groep NV | 23,400 | 6.56x |
| Crédit Agricole SA | 21,347 | 5.46x |
| Credit Suisse Group AG | 20,657 | 7.57x |
| Lloyds Banking Group PLC | 20,309 | 7.25x |
| Barclays PLC | 18,440 | 5.7x |
| DNB ASA | 18,184 | 9.13x |
| KBC Group NV | 17,663 | 8.85x |
| Skandinaviska Enskilda Banken AB | 16,477 | 10.99x |
| UniCredit SpA | 15,719 | 4.78x |
| Banco Bilbao Vizcaya Argentaria SA | 15,683 | 6.19x |
| Swedbank AB | 15,087 | 11.59x |
| Deutsche Bank AG | 14,645 | 2.75x |
| Banca Mediolanum SpA | 4,559 | 18.77x |
| Mean | | 7.72x |
| Median | | 6.56x |

# Step 2: Scale market prices to a common variable

This means choosing an appropriate multiple. As set out in the chapter, the choice will be between EV and equity multiples and stock and flow multiples. We will address the pros and cons of individual multiples in the next two chapters.

# Step 3: Adjust for differences across assets

In Step 1 we discussed the basic approach to identifying comparable companies. However, even if we do include companies that are comparable, we may still want to make adjustments to the relevant multiple. For example, if I am valuing a bank, I might simply get the average multiples for other banks and use this as a benchmark multiple. But even if all of these banks are similar, establishing the average might be difficult. The example in Table 16.1 illustrates one of the challenges of establishing a base for a multiple-based valuation. The calculated mean P/E value might be distorted by a number of outliers such as Banca Mediolanum SpA (18.77x), Skandinaviska Enskilda Banken AB (10.99x) on the high side, and Deutsche Bank AG (2.75x) on the low side.

Hence, to reduce the impact of outliers, it might be better to use the median instead of a simple average. We may also consider other dimensions of peers' comparability. For example, if we decided that Barclays had higher risk than the average risk of the companies in the comparable universe then we might wish to adjust our median multiple of 6.56x to a lower figure to reflect this. These adjustments tend to be highly judgemental and subjective.

### Step 4: Compute the value of the target company

At a simplistic level this merely entails applying the computed average multiple (emerging from steps 1–3 above) to the target company's relevant accounting number (e.g. EPS). Of course, if we are using equity multiples this will directly provide the valuer with an estimate of the equity value. If using an EV multiple, we will (obviously) derive the EV from applying the multiple to the chosen accounting item. Therefore, if we require the equity value then we will need to use the EV bridge to derive equity.

# Stretch yourself

### Multiples – pricing or valuation?

In this introductory chapter we have described multiples as a (relative) valuation methodology. However, we need to be careful here as there are strong arguments that multiples are more about *pricing* than valuation.

The cornerstone of this argument is that if we use the market to drive a valuation measure then we are accepting, to some degree at least, that the market is right. For instance, an analyst using valuation multiples of Delta Airlines to value another airline is assuming the starting point (the market's valuation of Delta) is meaningful. But the market's valuation of Delta Airlines reflects its price on the market driven by sentiment, momentum as well as fundamentals and myriad other factors.

Penman (2011), in his text *Accounting for Value*, puts it succinctly – *"when calculating value to challenge price, beware of using price in the calculation"*. This quote illustrates the inherent circularity in using multiples. If we use multiples to value a company, then price is clearly in that multiple (for example the 'P' in P/E). Imagine we establish that the P/E for Singapore Airlines is 12x and use this to value another airline, Japanese Airlines, which has a profit of $100m. Our valuation of Japanese Airlines would be:

*Value (of Japanese Airlines) = Singapore Airlines' P/E × Earnings of Japanese Airlines*

$$Value = 12 \times \$100 = \$1{,}200m$$

We now check the market value of Japanese Airlines, and it is $1,100m; we conclude that this company is mispriced (i.e. 'overvalued') by the market by $100m. The potential flaw in this approach is that we started the valuation process by assuming that the market is efficient and 'correct' for Singapore Airlines (at a P/E of 12x) to argue that the market is not correct for Japanese Airlines (i.e. that it is mispriced by $100m). So, when using multiples, we must always be aware of this inherent circularity. The solution is to ensure multiples are used alongside other valuation methods rather than as a valuation methodology of itself.

# CHAPTER 17

# Equity multiples

## Bite size

In common with many aspects of valuation there are equity and enterprise value (EV) versions of multiples. In this chapter we explore the two most important equity multiples: price to earnings (P/E) and price to book (P/B).

## Practitioner focus

The P/E ratio is probably the most popular and widely used multiple in practice. However, it does have some important weaknesses that are vital for practitioners to be familiar with. Furthermore, we need to think about different ways of calculating the multiple to ensure we understand the choices of how to use it in practice.

## Core content

Equity multiples have a number of advantages. Firstly, the valuation will often be of the equity portion of the business, and this relates directly to share prices. Although we can use the EV bridge to achieve a similar outcome (see Chapter 13), equity multiples enable the valuer to dispense with this extra step. Also, there can be judgements involved with market values in the EV bridge, which are not required if we start with equity multiples in the first place. Secondly, equity multiples are very familiar to investors and other users in comparison with EV multiples.

In terms of disadvantages, the most important one is probably that equity multiples co-mingle operating items and capital structure (financial) items. This means that if we use an equity multiple, we cannot easily unpick the underlying drivers from those related to the operations of the business and those related to the capital structure (mix of debt and equity finance). This makes comparisons between companies with different capital structures tricky. Furthermore, equity multiples use accounting numbers that are vulnerable to accounting distortion. For example, net income, or earnings per share (EPS), is the profit number at the very end of the income statement and so is exposed to all accounting judgements made to income statement items above it. In addition, such numbers are often more volatile.

# 1. Price to earnings multiple (P/E)

**Overview:** The P/E multiple is one of the most commonplace valuation metrics, if not the most popular. It is simple to calculate and has been widely used for many decades, meaning lots of historical data are available from a wide range of sources.

The ratio relates the price paid for a share to the EPS that the firm produces:

$$\frac{P}{E} = \frac{Share\ price}{EPS}$$

Usage points:

- **Per share or total basis:** The P/E is normally calculated on a per share basis but can also be calculated in total:

$$\frac{P}{E} = \frac{Market\ capitalisation\ of\ the\ company}{Net\ income}$$

- **Capital structure:** Should be used with caution if comparing companies with different capital structures.

- **Trailing or forward:** The P/E calculation that relates today's price (or market capitalisation) to the most recently reported EPS (or net income) figure is called the trailing P/E multiple, as it uses a historic earnings number. This can be designated as '$P_0/E_0$', with $P_0$ meaning today's share price and $E_0$ the last reported earnings. We can also calculate a forward P/E using a forecast earnings number and this would be designated as $P_0/E_1$, i.e. today's share price divided by next year's forecast earnings.

- **Loss making:** If earnings are negative then the multiple cannot be used as the result is not meaningful.

- **Earnings normalisation:** If earnings are distorted, for example due to non-recurring items, then adjustments would normally be made to eliminate these distortive items.

- **Accounting policy:** Like most accounting numbers, diversity in accounting policy might distort the multiple. EPS is especially vulnerable as it is a profit number after all items have been deducted or added in the calculation of income.

- **Apples-to-apples comparison:** The numerator and denominator in all multiples must be consistent. In this case the price of an equity share should be compared with the earnings that flow to equity investors. Let us consider the income statement of The Coca-Cola Company presented in Table 17.1.

TABLE 17.1 CONSOLIDATED STATEMENT OF INCOME (THE COCA-COLA COMPANY) (IN MILLIONS EXCEPT PER SHARE DATA)

| Year Ended December 31 | 2020 |
|---|---|
| Net Operating Revenues | $ 33,014 |
| Cost of goods sold | 13,433 |
| Gross Profit | 19,581 |
| Selling, general and administrative expenses | 9,731 |
| Other operating charges | 853 |
| Operating Income | 8,997 |
| Interest income | 370 |
| Interest expense | 1,437 |
| Equity income (loss) – net | 978 |
| Other income (loss) – net | 841 |
| Income Before Income Taxes | 9,749 |
| Income taxes | 1,981 |
| Consolidated Net Income | 7,768 |
| Less: Net income (loss) attributable to noncontrolling interests | 21 |
| Net Income Attributable to Shareowners of The Coca-Cola Company | $ 7,747 |

Which profit number would we use for our P/E calculation? We want the profit after all other sources of finance and tax have been deducted. We can see this figure appears to be 'consolidated net income' in the income statement above. However, there is a further item related to non-controlling interests ('Net income (loss) attributable to non-controlling interests'). These are outsiders who own part of same entities within the Coca-Cola group. For example, Coca-Cola might own 80% of its Brazilian subsidiary and third parties own the remaining 20%. Therefore, we need to deduct the 20% as it is not owned by the shareholders of The Coca-Cola Company, and we call this deduction 'non-controlling interests'. When calculating the P/E multiple we exclude non-controlling interests and so in this case the correct net income number is $7,747.

FIGURE 17.1 COMPOSITION OF CONSOLIDATED NET INCOME

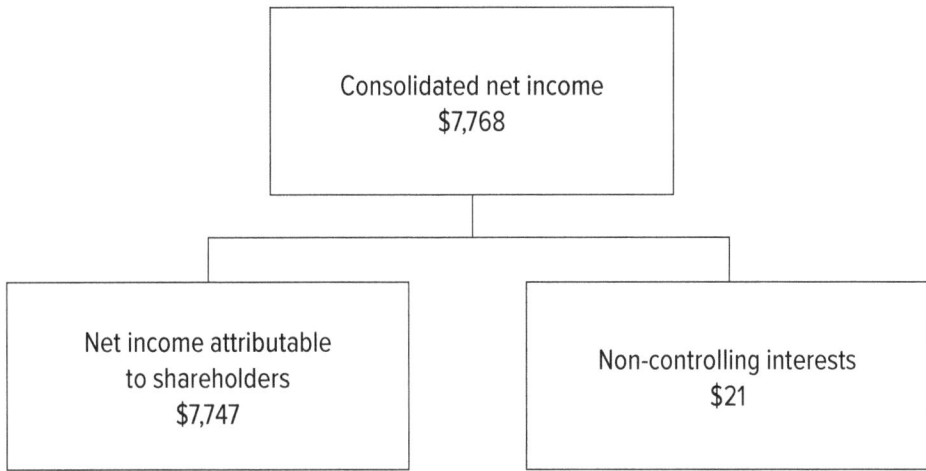

## 2. Price to book value multiple (P/B)

**Overview:** The P/B multiple is also a relatively popular metric, particularly for firms in the financial sector (see Chapter 19). In a similar way to the P/E multiple, the wide availability of historic data means that it can be calculated and analysed over long periods of time, as needed.

The multiple relates the price of a share to the book value per share (BVPS) from the balance sheet:

$$\frac{P}{B} = \frac{Share\ price}{BVPS}$$

**Usage points:**

- **Per share or total basis:** The P/B multiple is normally calculated on a per share basis but can also be calculated in total:

$$\frac{P}{B} = \frac{Market\ capitalisation\ of\ the\ company}{Book\ value\ of\ equity}$$

- **Capital structure:** In a similar way to the P/E multiple, it is less useful for comparisons between companies with large differences in capital structures.
- **P/B is a stock multiple:** As the accounting measure in P/B multiple (i.e. the denominator) is a balance sheet number, this is a 'stock' multiple. These multiples are often very useful where a flow multiple (such as P/E) is negative, such as when a company makes a loss. Negative multiples are meaningless, but book value of equity is unlikely to be negative for most companies and so P/B may be an alternative.
- **Use book value from 'today':** Whereas we can have trailing or forward P/E multiples we generally do not have the same for stock multiples such as P/B. The book value will always be today's (i.e. current) book value.
- **Accounting policy:** Like most accounting numbers, diversity in accounting policy might distort the multiple. Book value is especially vulnerable as it will be impacted by accounting policy choices over many years.

# Stretch yourself

In the text above we calculated the P/E multiple as:

$$\frac{P}{E} = \frac{\text{Share price}}{\text{EPS}}$$

We can relate this to a Dividend Discount Model (DDM) covered in Chapters 21–22. In a basic variant of DDM that assumes a constant growth rate of future dividends, we have:

$$P_0 = \frac{D_1}{r_e - g}$$

Where $P_0$ is today's equity value, $D_1$ is dividend forecast for the next period, $r_e$ is the cost of equity capital, and $g$ is the constant long-term growth rate.

If we divide both sides of this formula by earnings from the next period ($E_1$), we get:

$$\frac{P_0}{E_1} = \frac{D_1/E_1}{r_e - g}$$

We can see here that on the left-hand side we now have a forward P/E multiple (i.e. $\frac{P_0}{E_1}$), and the numerator on the right-hand side of the formula is the ratio of dividends to earnings (i.e. $D_1/E_1$). This ratio is normally referred to as the dividend payout ratio and shows the percentage of profits paid out as a dividend. The right-hand side now provides the theoretical drivers of the forward P/E multiple. These are dividend growth rate ($g$), cost of equity ($r_e$) and the future/expected payout ratio ($D_1/E_1$). This depiction of the P/E ratio is often referred to as the target or fair multiple. In other words, it represents a theoretically correct multiple.

How might we use this? It is unlikely that if we estimate growth, cost of equity and payout we would get a result that ties in perfectly with a P/E multiple observed in the market. This is because there will be many divergent views on growth prospects, cost of equity inputs and the balance between payouts and retentions of future earnings. However, we might input our estimates into this formula to see how far the theoretical multiple is from the observed multiple. For example, if we saw that, based on our forecast inputs, the theoretical model gave us a P/E of 12x, while the firm was trading on a P/E of 9x, then we might conclude that this would be an undervalued firm. The other way of using this approach is to exploit the market as an information source. In other words, we can work backwards from the P/E observed in the market to establish what inputs the market is using (this technique is also referred to as reverse engineering). For example, imagine we are confident that our estimates of $r_e$ and dividend payout ratio are accurate. We could input these into the formula above and using the observed market P/E work backwards to solve for the implied growth rate ($g$) that the market is using:

$$g = r_e - \frac{D_1/E_1}{P_0/E_1}$$

# CHAPTER 18
# Enterprise value multiples

## Bite size

As we have seen in previous chapters, when making comparisons, enterprise value (EV) offers significant advantages over valuing equity directly. In particular it enables comparisons between companies with different capital structures. This advantage extends to comparisons using multiples – whereas equity multiples (such as P/E) reflect both operations and capital structure, EV multiples only reflect the value of operations.

## Practitioner focus

EV multiples are used extensively in practice. Despite most investment professionals and valuers ultimately wanting to value an equity stake in a firm, using EV multiples provides a much stronger basis for analysis as they are not distorted by capital structure issues. Importantly, in financial services-related sectors, such as banks and insurance companies, the difficulty of distinguishing operating items from financing items means that EV does not really work. In these sectors, equity multiples dominate.

## Core content

### 1. Advantages of EV multiples

EV multiples have a number of advantages over using equity multiples.

- **Allow the user to focus on measures that minimise accounting distortion**: As EV multiples use accounting numbers such as earnings before interest and taxes (EBIT) and earnings before interest, taxes, depreciation, and amortisation (EBITDA), they are less vulnerable to accounting policy choices and certain volatile items.

- **Avoid the influence of capital structure:** This advantage has been well signalled in the text – EV multiples, unlike equity multiples, are consistent irrespective of capital structure.

- **EV multiples value the entire firm:** Unlike equity multiples, EV multiples do not just reflect the value of one part of the overall funding. They address the value of all of the operations.

## 2. Who owns the profit?

An important point to revisit as we think about EV multiples is regarding who owns the profit number we are embedding in our multiple. For equity multiples we use net income (in total or per share in the form of earnings per share (EPS)) whereas for EV multiples we use EBIT or EBITDA in most cases. Figure 18.1 links the profit and ownership. Net income is an equity flow and so, as we saw in the previous chapter, the relevant multiple only reflects the value of equity (i.e. P/E). As EBIT and EBITDA are owned by both the debt and equity holders we need to include the market value of both of these items in any multiple that uses EBIT or EBITDA. This ensures an 'apples-to-apples' comparison.

FIGURE 18.1 WHO OWNS THE PROFIT?

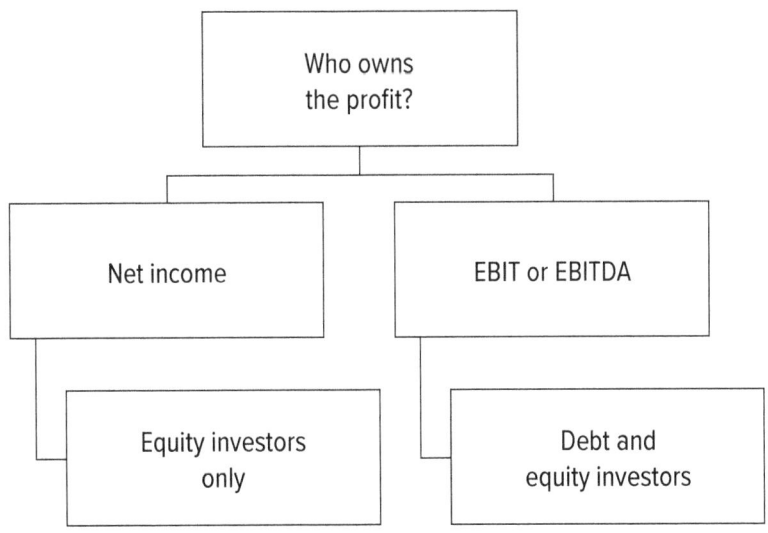

# 3. Specific EV multiples

## EV/EBIT and EV/EBITDA

**Overview:** These are the most widely used EV metrics and have wide applicability for a broad suite of industries. They express the value of the operations relative to an operating earnings number, either before or after depreciation and amortisation. The multiple is expressed as:

$$\frac{EV}{EBIT \; or \; EBITDA}$$

Usage points:

- **Critical difference is 'DA':** The critical difference between both multiples is that the EV/EBITDA multiple removes the impact of 'DA' (depreciation and amortisation) from the calculation. This can be useful as both these items require significant judgement and so by reversing them out comparisons can be more straightforward to understand. However, DA represent the capex costs of the company, which must be covered and so care must be taken not to ignore these. Using EBITDA, as against EBIT, might cause valuers to omit important information about the efficiency of capex from their analysis.

- **Pre-tax:** In both EBIT- and EBITDA-form this ratio is a pre-tax multiple, which is fine if we are comparing companies that are facing similar tax rate environments. But if instead we are looking at international comparisons, then we may need to use 'Net operating profit after tax' (NOPAT) instead, to capture these tax differentials. To calculate NOPAT we multiply EBIT by (1 − Tax rate).

## EV/IC

**Overview:** This is the stock EV multiple. It relates the value of the operations of the firms to the capital that has been invested, be it debt or equity. This multiple essentially relates the market value of debt and equity (EV) to the book value of debt and equity (i.e. invested capital, IC), and is a useful metric for tangible asset-intensive industries (see Chapter 19).

$$\frac{EV}{Invested \; capital}$$

Usage points:

- **Use when EBIT or EBITDA is negative:** In common with other stock multiples one use case is where the equivalent flow multiple, in this case EV/EBIT or EBITDA, has a negative earnings number. A multiple does not work if any of the inputs are negative. It would be unlikely that invested capital could ever be negative. So, the EV/IC multiple should almost always be available for use.
- **Compares book and market values:** As mentioned earlier the essence of this multiple is in the comparison between book values and market values. The P/B ratio is only concerned with the comparison of the equity portion, whereas in the case of EV/IC we are comparing both the debt and equity market values against debt and equity book values. If a company is expected to achieve a return on invested capital (RoIC) higher than its cost of capital (WACC) then theoretically we would expect this multiple to be higher than 1x.

# Stretch yourself

### Using a trading comparables table

We have covered a wide range of topics on multiples in the various preceding chapters. In practice, work on multiples is often brought together in a comparables (often referred to as 'comps') table, an example of which is provided in Table 18.1 for the retail sector in the UK and US. The table contains a mixture of useful information for valuers and investors and allows quick comparisons. We have deliberately included a table with some questionable areas to draw out some of the learning points.

Looking at Table 18.1 we can see that the first column defines those companies that the analyst views as belonging to the same sector. This is important, as being classified into a particular sector brings with it important benchmarks for multiples given that different sectors trade on different multiples. Often it would be well established within the market which constituents make up the 'sector', but even in a relatively straightforward sector like retail we can question those companies included in the comps table in Table 18.1. For example, is it appropriate to compare Boohoo, an online-only provider of clothing, with JD Sports, which has a large number of stores selling sportswear? Additionally, the business mix of Marks & Spencer and Sainsbury's contains a significant amount of food sales – are these appropriate companies to compare against non-food retailers? Many analysts would suggest food retailers such as Sainsbury's and Marks & Spencer should be excluded from this group.

## TABLE 18.1 RETAIL SAMPLE TRADING COMPARABLES TABLE

| Company Name | Market Data | | | Financial Data | | Valuation | |
|---|---|---|---|---|---|---|---|
| | Price per Share | Market Cap (in millions) | TEV (in millions) | Earnings (in millions) | EBITDA (in millions) | P/E | EV/EBITDA |
| JD Sports | £1.52 | £7,240.00 | £8,400.00 | £618.80 | £1,229.87 | 11.7x | 6.8x |
| Foot Locker | $30.54 | $3,010.00 | $5,600.00 | $427.56 | $1,450.78 | 7.0x | 3.9x |
| ASOS | £15.93 | £1,790.00 | £1,920.00 | £82.34 | £326.53 | 21.7x | 5.9x |
| Boohoo | £0.87 | £1,140.00 | £1,080.00 | £71.47 | £125.44 | 16.0x | 8.6x |
| Marks and Spencer | £1.56 | £3,140.00 | £6,170.00 | £368.98 | £855.76 | 8.5x | 7.2x |
| Sainsbury | £2.60 | £5,930.00 | £11,500.00 | £933.86 | £1,962.46 | 6.4x | 5.9x |
| Dick's Sporting Goods | $106.97 | $9,310.00 | $11,180.00 | $849.45 | $1,940.97 | 11.0x | 5.8x |
| DFS Furniture | £2.07 | £490.00 | £960.00 | £62.82 | £248.06 | 7.8x | 3.9x |
| Halfords Group | £2.57 | £550.00 | £770.00 | £60.64 | £161.43 | 9.1x | 4.8x |
| Average | | | | | | 11.01x | 5.85x |
| Median | | | | | | 9.07x | 5.86x |

The first three columns of numerical information provide market data that would be drawn from one of the many well-established data vendors such as Bloomberg, FactSet or CapIQ, for example. We can see from the market cap column that DFS and Halfords are much smaller than the other companies, in particular JD Sports and Dick's Sporting Goods. This is important as smaller companies are, in general, higher risk and also face less favourable economies of scale. Rather than 'Operating Enterprise Value' (OEV), the table shows 'Total Enterprise Value' (TEV). TEV represents the value of the core operations of the business plus the market value of any non-core investments these firms may have (please refer to Chapter 11 for further discussion of OEV and TEV).

The next section of the table shows some financial data for earnings (net income) and EBITDA. It is commonplace to include some accounting-based data. However, we would want to see the period for which this is provided more clearly. Is this historical data? Last 12 months (LTM) or a one-year forecast? We have no idea based on the information provided. A better approach would be to clearly identify the period in question. This also applies to the two multiples provided. We welcome the inclusion of both EV and equity multiples, but we need to know the period for the accounting number. Also, as we have included a US company in the comparables table (Dick's Sporting Goods), we would need to be careful drawing conclusions from any comparison of EBITDA. These are pre-tax multiples, and Dick's Sporting Goods may face a very different tax regime from the other companies in the table.

Finally, we can see the distortive impact of outlier multiples. ASOS has a P/E of 21.7x, far ahead of the other companies. Including this in our arithmetic average lifts the mean to 11.01x. In cases like this the median ('middle') value becomes more meaningful and, arguably, a better measure of central tendency for the overall sector.

# CHAPTER 19

# Sector-specific multiples

## Bite size

We have now looked at the most widely used multiples across both enterprise value (EV) and equity. These remain the most important multiples for you to master. However, these multiples, and other derivations, tend to be used in specific sectors rather than in every sector. In this chapter we examine which multiples might be used in specific sectors and explore the rationale for this.

## Practitioner focus

The vast majority of valuations are carried out on specific companies in specific sectors. The economic drivers, underlying economics and key metrics can differ widely across industries. This is particularly the case of banks, insurance, real estate and extractive industries. Therefore, to use the material on multiples covered in earlier chapters we need to be able to adapt it to particular sectors.

## Core content

Table 19.1 provides a comprehensive list of multiples with comments on their usage in specific industries. It is important to realise that the core multiples still dominate. The multiples we have already looked at in some detail – P/E, P/B, EV EBITDA and EV/IC – remain some of the most common forms of multiples seen in practice. However, as mentioned already, in some industries these multiples may be more or less common. Additionally, specialist multiples have been developed over the years, especially where core multiples do not capture the drivers of a business.

## TABLE 19.1. MULTIPLES AND SECTOR USAGE

| Multiple | Sectors, types of companies | Explanation and commentary |
|---|---|---|
| EV/Revenue (sometimes adapted to EV/Operational metric) | • Early-stage companies<br>• Loss-making companies | • An alternative to earnings if they are negative<br>• Must be used with caution as ultimately profits need to be generated<br>• Revenue recognition policy becomes key as it drives the entire valuation<br>• If a company is 'pre-revenue' then a relevant operating metric might be more useful. For example, a more relevant calculation in such a case might be: $$\frac{EV}{Order\ Book}$$ |
| EV/EBIT | Broad range of sectors in industries where capital structure varies (almost every industry) | • A very widely used metric where leverage diversity is most important (e.g. beverages)<br>• Vulnerable to divergent capital intensity in that depreciation policy can distort EBIT<br>• EBIT would normally be 'cleaned' of non-recurring and non-operating items<br>• NOT used for financial services companies<br>• Often used for a sum-of-the-parts (SOTP) valuation |
| EV/EBITDA | Wide ranging use including Aerospace, Autos, Chemicals, Mining, Pharma, Telcos and Utilities | • Most relevant in high asset intensity (or divergent asset intensity) situations, as depreciation policy becomes an important (and subjective) issue<br>• EBITDA warning – even if excluded from our multiple, the cost of assets needs to get reflected in valuations in other ways |
| EV/EBITDAR (no longer used widely but included for information) | Used instead of EV/EBIT where extensive use is made of operating leases. Mainly Retail, Leisure, Luxury and Transport | • R = operating lease rentals, all pre-tax so no adjustment<br>• New standard IFRS 16 *Leases* makes this ratio less important going forward as lease rentals have been excluded from earnings |
| EV/EBITA | Used when amortisation is potentially distortive (as some companies grow by M&A whereas others do not) but depreciation less significant (and so can be left unadjusted). Applies to various media sub-sectors (e.g. gaming) and technology-related sectors | • Often calculated in addition to other EV metrics<br>• Remember goodwill, often the most significant intangible, is not amortised under IFRS or US GAAP. Therefore, we are referring to the amortisation of brands, customer lists and software development costs where they are amortised |

## Chapter 19 – Sector-specific multiples

| Multiple | Sectors, types of companies | Explanation and commentary |
|---|---|---|
| EV/IC | Chemicals, utilities and certain other asset-intensive industries | • Rarely mentioned but no good reasons for it not to be used |
| EV/Barrel of reserves | Oil & Gas | • This can be usefully compared to the cash flows per barrel to see what the market is pricing into the shares |
| P/NAV | Real Estate, Oil & Gas and Mining | • NAV = Net asset value<br>• NPV = Net present value<br>• Stocks may trade at a premium or discount to NAV and this is captured by this multiple<br>• Mining use P/NPV which is a very similar ratio |
| P/E | In particular for financial institutions, but widely used | • Even in sectors where this might not be a useful metric (e.g. divergent capital structures) it remains in use given its widespread and historic popularity<br>• Often using normalised 'cash' earnings, excluding both non-recurring items and amortisation<br>• Also useful for comparing between sectors as it is calculated by almost every analyst |
| P/B | Financial institutions (e.g. banks, insurance) | • Many financial assets on bank balance sheets are at fair value so book value moves from being an outdated historic measure to a more meaningful one dominated by fair values<br>• Cannot use EV multiples for these sectors, so this is the only stock multiple for financial institutions |
| P/Tangible book | Banks | • This is the same as P/B except that goodwill is removed<br>• Here the idea is that goodwill is an inherently subjective accounting number and reversing it out leaves us with a more conservative and meaningful measure |
| PEG ratio | Technology and other high-growth sectors or companies | • Scales P/E by the expected earnings growth rate<br>• Challenge is to agree on a single growth rate for companies that are often growing quickly and in a volatile manner |

# Stretch yourself

Even though this has been mentioned elsewhere, it is worth repeating here. When choosing between EV and equity multiples it is important to consider the industry in question. To use EV, and its associated multiples, requires valuers to distinguish operating items from financing items. For a manufacturing sector it is normally straightforward to discriminate between the operations (machines, factories, inventories, for example) and the supporting financing (debt and equity). However, for a financial institution, such as a bank, this would be much more challenging. The operations of a bank *are* financing in nature. That is what banks do. There is no easy separation of assets into operating and financing. If we identify loans on a bank balance sheet, then these cannot be classified as operating or financing – it does not really make sense to think of banks in that way. Hence for banks, and many other financial institutions, valuers adopt an equity valuation approach, and use equity value multiples, rather than EV multiples.

# SECTION F
# Present Value Models: the Dividend Discount and Free Cash Flow Models

# CHAPTER 20
# Stages in present value-based models

## Bite size

While the theoretical ideal of a present value-based valuation model (e.g. Dividend Discount Model, Discounted Cash Flow model or Residual Income Valuation model) is quite straightforward, its practical application is rather complex. One of the key reasons for this complexity is the fact that valuers have to build expectations about the future of the company, but this future is by its very nature uncertain. A way of dealing with this challenge is to make forecasts of cash flows, earnings or dividends in different stages, such as: a visible period for which detailed forecasts can be made for the short-term horizon; a transitional period for the mid-term horizon; and a terminal value period for the long-term horizon.

## Practitioner focus

The quality of each present value-based valuation depends ultimately on the valuer's ability to breathe life into the forecasts model, i.e. to set proper assumptions about the future expected cash flows, earnings or other relevant value drivers of the company. To better deal with the inevitable uncertainty surrounding every forecasting of cash flows or other value drivers, it is advisable to perform these tasks in stages. For example, a phase of detailed forecasts for the time horizon where the degree of certainty of the forecast is still relatively high (referred to as 'visible period') and a phase of simplified assumption-setting for the time horizon where the degree of certainty is rather low (referred to as 'terminal value period'). Between these two phases we may insert a transitional phase ('transitional period') to bridge the former with the latter.

# Core content

## 1. The key practical problems of every present value-based valuation model

While valuation models are straightforward in theory, in practice they are quite a challenge. The two main challenges for real-world application are:

- Several valuation parameters are not observable or can only be estimated with a margin of error; for example, certain components of our discount rates – such as the equity risk premium or the beta (the risk parameter in the capital asset pricing model). These have to be derived indirectly or based on an imperfect set of data.
- Present value-based valuation models require valuers to build expectations about the future realisation of cash flows or other value drivers. By the very nature of making forecasts in a world of uncertainty, even experienced valuation experts are prone to make errors.

While the observability problem can often be managed (more or less well) within a certain range of assumptions, the forecasting problem can corrupt whole valuations very quickly. Over and above the challenge of forecasting there is also a question of how to map different forecasts with different degrees of certainty from a technical point of view in our models.

## 2. The two approaches for producing forecasts for valuation models

From a technical viewpoint, there are two extremes in how to make forecasts of cash flow (or other value drivers) for a present value-based valuation model. The first one is very detailed, while the second one is more simplistic.

- On the one hand, forecasts of a value driver (e.g. cash flow) can be constructed by generating itemised forecasts of all individual components of the cash flow. In this approach, the valuer will generate forecasts of all individual drivers of individual revenue streams, expenses, balance sheet items, tax effects, and so on. This approach requires detailed fundamental analysis of the company's business and financials.
- On the other hand, forecasts can be made in a very simplistic way by just linking the cash flow (the resulting total) of a particular period to the cash flow of an earlier period with a rate of development (i.e. a growth rate). This is obviously the minimum effort approach to forecasting.

While the first approach is more sophisticated and accurate, and looks preferable to the second one, there are two important practical limitations to consider. First, there might be time restrictions that prevent valuers to go deeper into fundamental analysis of the company and hence to forecast each component of the cash flow separately. And second, there might simply be information restrictions – whether because of a lack of information availability in general or because of a low visibility due to an uncertain future – that would not allow valuers to make a detailed component-by-component cash flow forecast with the necessary degree of accuracy.

Under these two limitations, a simplistic forecast of 'growing' cash flows might prove a more practical approach; in addition, it offers clear time advantages. However, as a matter of course, combinations of both approaches are also possible.

## 3. The standard two-stage and three-stage approaches to valuation

The choice between a two-stage and a three-stage forecasting approach usually depends on:

- the forecasting time horizon: the longer away from the valuation date the particular forecasting period is, the lower the visibility and the more a simplistic approach makes sense, all other things being equal; and
- the complexity of the business model: the more dynamic and more complex the business is, the earlier the forecasting visibility decreases.

If the forecasting horizon can be reasonably split into two stages, then the preferred model is described as a 'two-stage model'. The first stage is a short-term (say three to five years) detailed forecast horizon – we refer to it as a 'visible' forecast period – and the second is referred to as a 'terminal' value period. A terminal value captures the value that arises from the end of the visible forecast period to infinity.

FIGURE 20.1 TWO-STAGE MODEL

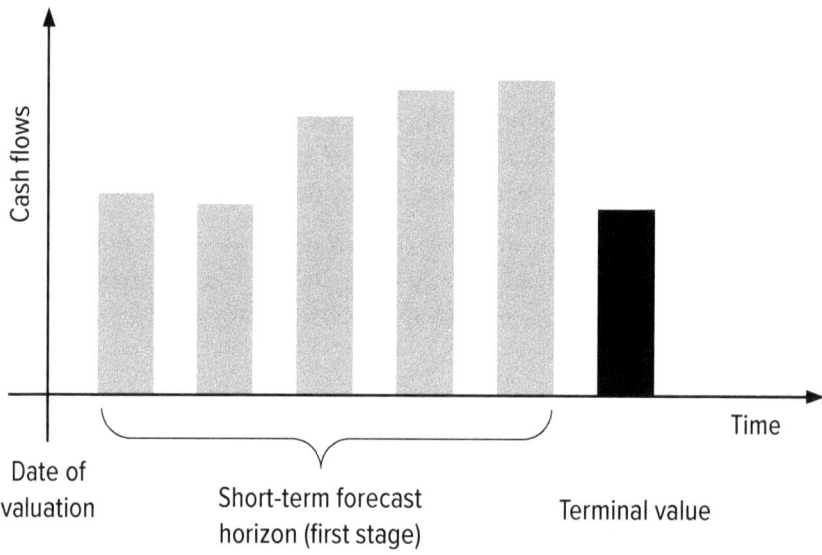

As a hard cut between these two stages is not always realistic, a bridge stage is often (but not always) included to smooth the transition. This stage – referred to as the 'transitional period' – often gradually adjusts key valuation parameters such as revenue growth rates, cost ratios, margins, capital expenditures per revenue ratios, etc., to the terminal value steady state.

FIGURE 20.2 THREE-STAGE MODEL

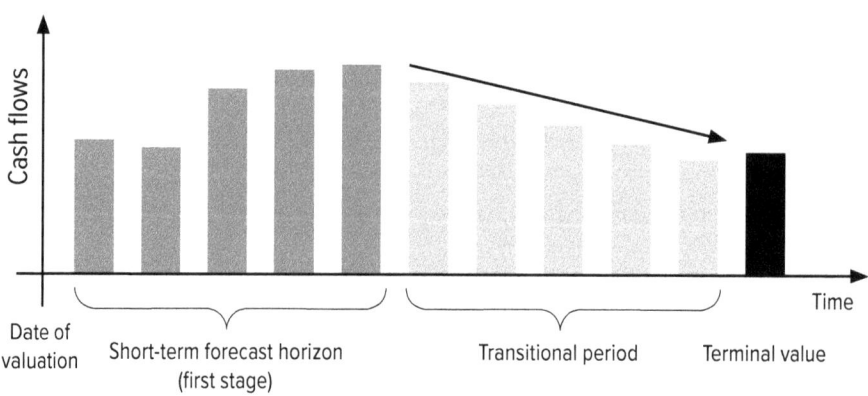

The length of a stage can vary materially – except for the terminal value stage, which runs on to infinity. The higher the visibility and information quality the longer is the first stage – i.e. the 'visibility period' where explicit forecasts can be generated for each year of the period. And the longer the adjustment processes take, the longer should the second stage (i.e. the 'transitional period') be, and vice versa.

# Stretch yourself

Building a present value-based valuation model with two or three stages is standard in practical business valuation. However, nothing prevents the valuer from applying more stages – usually by adding different transitional phases. This is a reasonable approach when there are: a) different value drivers with different impact times (e.g. fast margin normalisation but longer revenue growth normalisation); or b) single-projects with a finite but long-term useful life (e.g. a power plant that runs another 20 years and will not be replaced) while the rest of the business is a going concern business.

There is also the case of a single-stage valuation model. Such a model is applied for pure-play finite-life projects (i.e. that only require a finite-horizon forecasting until the end of the project) or in case of quick-and-dirty value indications (a terminal value stage starting in the very first period). A single-stage model can also be applied to value mature, steady-state companies that can be reasonably expected to grow at a constant, sustainable growth rate forever.

# CHAPTER 21
# The logic of the Dividend Discount Model

## Bite size

The most general model to value a company is the Dividend Discount Model (DDM). As the name suggests, the future dividends of a company are discounted using the present value technique in order to determine the value of the equity of the company. It is important to understand the basic logic of the DDM in order to be ready for analytically more sophisticated models such as the Discounted Cash Flow or the Residual Income Valuation models, which are discussed in later chapters. The DDM works well in theory, but in practice it has limitations if companies are rather young, are in a distressed situation or in a non-steady-state.

## FIGURE 21.1 HOW DIVIDENDS TURN INTO VALUE

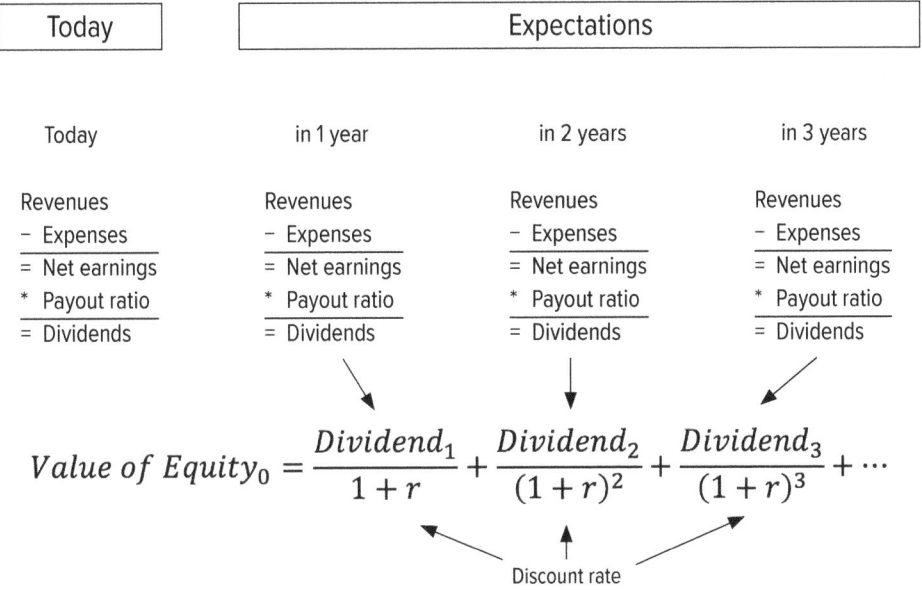

# Practitioner focus

The value of a company is determined by what an investor can get out of the company in the future. Neglecting any non-financial benefits such as prestige or similar, it is the cash that will flow to investors in the future that matters here for valuation (monetary perspective). The simplest concept of cash flowing to investors is the periodical dividend payments. If an investor can build a proper expectation of future dividends, he can use these dividend expectations as an input to its present value model, and discount them in order to get the value of the company – *voilà* the DDM. As dividends only flow to shareholders (i.e. equity investors), it is the equity value that is the result of the DDM.

# Core content

## 1. What matters for investors when determining values

For setting up a sound present value model it requires both a proper derivation of discount rates (the denominator of the present value formula) and an apt determination of the expected benefits from the company to be valued (the numerator of the present value formula). In this chapter we focus on the numerator. In general, an investor can expect different benefits from investing in a company.

Of course, expected benefits are not always purely financial in nature. A founding investor of a company may take the prestige of being a successful entrepreneur as a benefit from holding stakes in the company (and believe it or not, in many small and mid-sized companies it is exactly this that matters most to the founder-shareholders). But prestige is not a good concept to bring into present value models. It is also rarely paid for in transactions. Hence, in business valuation we restrict ourselves to expected financial benefits.

When focusing on financial benefits there are still different ways how an equity investor can receive them. The easiest way is to receive periodical dividends from the company, i.e. payouts of the company to its shareholders. But investors can also benefit from share price appreciations and monetise these capital gains by selling the shares. Hence, the total financial benefit that the investor would receive in a given year can be expressed as follows:

$$\begin{aligned}Total\ financial\ benefit_1 \\ = Dividend_1 \\ + \big(Market\ value\ of\ equity_{End\ of\ Period\ 1} \\ - Market\ value\ of\ equity_{Beginning\ of\ Period\ 1}\big)\end{aligned}$$

In this chapter we focus on the dividend component, and we will show that this focus is enough for determining today's proper (i.e. intrinsic) value of the equity of the company – at least in a theoretical framework, and also in practice if investors are able to make sound forecasts of the dividend stream.

## 2. Where dividends come from

In order to better understand the concept of the DDM it is necessary to understand where dividends come from. For this, imagine a company that produces certain goods. This company will generate revenues by selling the goods to its customers. This is where cash flows into the company. However, for producing the goods and bringing it to the customers the company is also facing several costs, i.e. cash outflows – buying supplier goods, paying employees in the production departments, paying employees in the supporting departments (Human Resources, Finance & Tax, etc.), paying the rent for the factories and the offices, etc. If it is partly financed with debt, it has to pay interest on this debt and repay it at some point in the future. And it has to pay taxes.

## FIGURE 21.2 CASH FLOWING THROUGH THE COMPANY

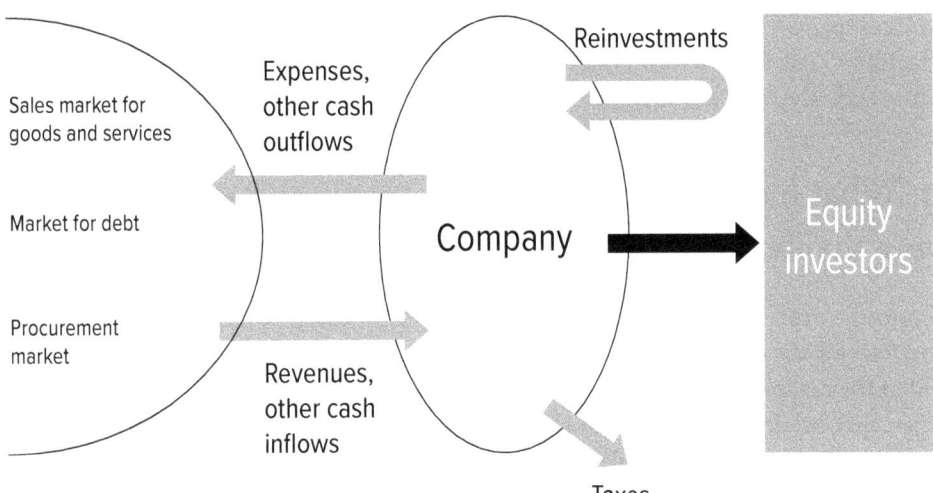

What is left on a net-basis after all these transactions is the net income of the company (in accounting terms). As long as revenues are higher than the sum of all expenses, net earnings is a positive number.

Of course, the accounting view is not the same as the cash perspective (investments in machines are real cash outflows that only show up as expenses in the form of annual depreciation charges, etc.). But for the basic understanding of what happens inside a company this explanation should suffice.

## FIGURE 21.3 FROM REVENUE GENERATION TO DIVIDEND PAYMENTS

    Revenues
- Expenses
= Operating earnings
- Interest payments
= Earnings before tax
- Taxes
= Net earnings
× Payout ratio
= **Dividends**

With this remaining amount of money (i.e. net income) the company can now do two things: it can give the money back to equity investors; or it can keep the money within the company. Of course, any combination of both is also a possibility. If the company decides to pay out (at least parts) of net income to investors, then investors receive a dividend. This is where it comes from.

## 3. What happens to money (net income) not paid out as a dividend?

From the explanations above it seems that it is a bit discretionary how much of the net income the company pays out. If the management decides to pay out a lot or even all of the net income as dividends, then investors will receive a higher dividend. If the management decides to pay out only a little part or even nothing of the net income as a dividend, then investors will receive only a small dividend or even nothing. How can this concept which obviously depends on management discretion be a sound concept for the valuation of a company?

The key for understanding this lies in the analysis of what happens with the part of the net income that is not paid out as a dividend, the part that is ploughed back (or 'retained') by management. In fact, this part is not lost for investors. Even if in this particular period it will not show up as a dividend it serves as a promise for future dividends.

Imagine two companies. Company A pays out all of its net income as dividends while Company B decides to keep 20% of the net income inside the firm to reinvest it, e.g. for buying new machines or building a new plant, or similar. The dividend in this particular period will be higher for Company A than for Company B. But by reinvesting parts of the net income, Company B paves the way for higher future dividends because with new machines or a new plant the company can produce and sell more goods and generate higher net income in future periods. Figure 21.4 provides an illustration of how dividend payout affects future dividends. Here, Company A pays out from its net income as dividends, while Company B pays out 80% as dividends and reinvests the remaining 20% of net income into an increasing capacity each and every period. In this example we also assume that the reinvestments of Company B are value neutral, i.e. the present value of all future benefits from these capacity additions equals the amount of investment necessary to set up these capacity additions (such investment projects are also often referred to as zero net present value (NPV) investment).

## FIGURE 21.4 HOW PAYOUT RATIOS AFFECT FUTURE DIVIDENDS

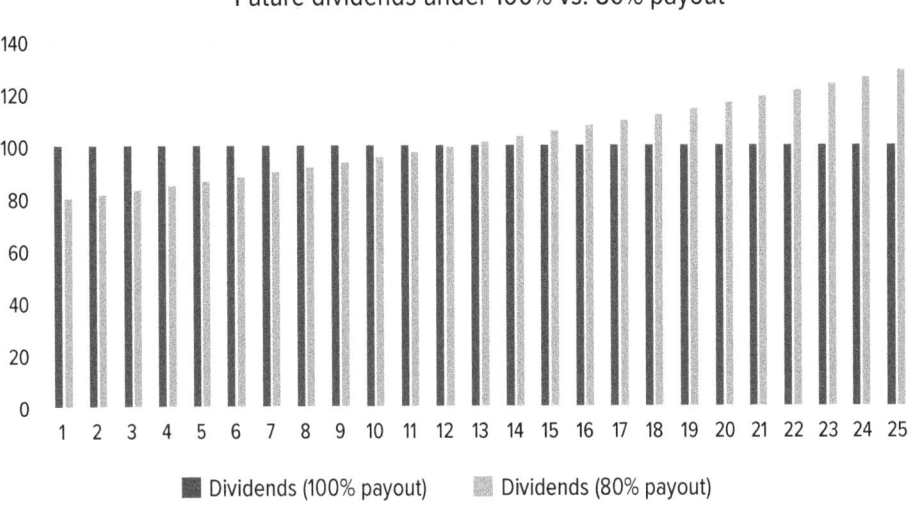

As we can see, the future capacity additions give rise to higher net income in the future and hence to higher future dividends (in every period, 80% of the net income of this period). As long as these capacity additions are value neutral (i.e. represent zero NPV investments) we get the same present value for both cases.

In this context it can be shown mathematically that under constant dividend assumption the classical DDM that was shown earlier in Figure 21.1 takes the following form:

$$Value\ of\ equity_0 = \frac{Dividend_1}{r}$$

In a similar vein, it can be shown that, under an assumption that dividends grow at a constant growth rate ($g$) forever, the classical DDM obtains the following form:

$$Value\ of\ equity_0 = \frac{Dividend_1}{r - g}$$

This expression is also commonly referred to as the Gordon Growth model.

Dividends are a function of earnings and the payout ratio $q$ (i.e. the percentage of earnings that is paid out to shareholders). The long-term (or 'sustainable') growth rate $g$ itself can be expressed as a function of the 'plough-back' (or 'earnings retention') ratio $1-q$, (i.e. is the percentage of earnings that is kept within the company) and the return on equity (ROE) on these reinvested funds. This leads to the following expression of the DDM:

$$Value\ of\ equity_A = \frac{Net\ income_1 \times q}{r - ROE \times (1 - q)}$$

In our example we assume a constant ROE for all future years, and throughout subsequent examples use this formula to compute the growth rate. For a net income of $100 and 100% payout (i.e. $q=100$) and assuming that the discount rate is 10%, the following equation applies:

$$Value\ of\ equity_A = \frac{100}{0.1} = \$1{,}000$$

If 20% of this net income is ploughed back and assumed to earn an ROE equalling the cost of equity of 10% we get:

$$Value\ of\ equity_B = \frac{100 \times 0.8}{0.1 - 0.1 \times (1 - 0.8)} = \frac{80}{0.1 - 0.02} = \$1{,}000$$

This highlights how important it is to not only look at one particular periodical dividend but rather to look at all future expected dividends when determining values.

## 4. So does it even matter how much of net income a company pays out?

In a famous paper published in 1961, two Nobel Prize laureates, Franco Modigliani and Merton Miller, proposed and proved a theorem that it does not matter (for the valuation of a company) how much of the net income is paid out as dividends. Admittedly, they proved it in a much more sophisticated way than we have shown it above.[21] However, they also relied on the assumption that all plough-backs of net

---

21 See: Miller, M. & Modigliani, F. (1961). Dividend policy, growth, and the valuation of shares. *The Journal of Business*, 34, 411–433.

income are value neutral (and some more restrictive assumptions such as perfect capital markets, no taxes, etc.). If one does not know better, it is certainly a fair assumption to assume value-neutrality in a particular valuation case.

But what if analysis shows that the management is able to invest in value increasing (i.e. positive NPV) projects? In fact, it should be the job of the management to find profitable projects. Certainly, such projects are not easy to find but this is exactly why managers are employed. If there are profitable projects things are different. In this case, keeping part of the net income inside the company and not paying them out would increase the value of the company. We illustrate this below for our above-mentioned companies A and B, but now with higher ROE of 12% from the reinvestments of Company B.

$$Value\ of\ equity_A = \frac{100}{0.1} = \$1{,}000$$

$$Value\ of\ equity_B = \frac{100 \times 0.8}{0.1 - 0.12 \times (1 - 0.8)} = \$1{,}052.6$$

Of course, it should not be forgotten that there are several real-world situations where management reinvests in only low-profitability (i.e. zero or negative NPV) projects (e.g. because management wrongly assess the projects). In this case reinvestment is value-destructive, as illustrated below for Company B that has an ROE of 8%.

$$Value\ of\ equity_A = \frac{100}{0.1} = \$1{,}000$$

$$Value\ of\ equity_B = \frac{80}{0.1 - 0.016} = \$952$$

You can see how important it is to understand the basic economics of what happens inside the company in order to set up a proper valuation model.

# Stretch yourself

There is always a relationship between the rate of return on reinvestments (ROE) and the payout ratio. Usually, a firm has access to only a limited number of 'good' (positive NPV) projects and the marginal rate of return of every next best project decreases. This means one usually cannot play around with payout ratios and return assumptions independently from each other in practice.

FIGURE 21.5 INVESTMENT OPPORTUNITY SET OF A COMPANY

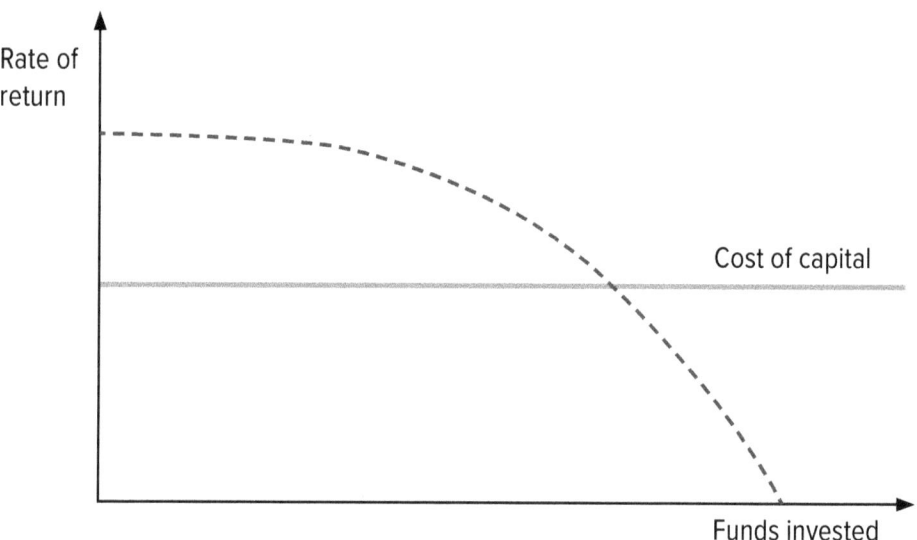
– – – – – Marginal rate of return on the last $ reinvested

# CHAPTER 22

# How (and when) does the Dividend Discount Model work?

## Bite size

The Dividend Discount Model (DDM) is quite easy to apply in theory. However, the proper calibration of the model in practice is often a problem. The main challenge is to forecast the dividends, a number that is not always only driven by the economic situation of the company but often also by company management's less predictable discretionary dividend policy.

## Practitioner focus

If you want to run a DDM it is first necessary to derive the dividends from the corporate accounts, then to make a sound forecast of the dividend path in the future. However, this is not always easy in practice. Depending on the company and its economic conditions, in particular when dividend streams are unstable over time, it is not advisable to apply the DDM.

## Core content

### 1. Deriving dividends from corporate accounts

The starting point of the application of the DDM is to understand how to derive the dividends from corporate accounts. Usually, dividends are a function of net income and the payout ratio (accounting view). However, if you want to know what a fair payout ratio is – or at least what maximum payout ratio is possible – you also need to have a clear view on the cash situation of the company or, more specifically, the amount of free cash flow that the company generates in each period.

The notion of free cash flow differs from net income (which is an accounting notion). This is because free cash flow takes into account some cash outflows (e.g. investments into fixed assets [capital expenditures] and working capital) and some cash inflows (e.g. increase in debt) that are not part of the company's profit and loss statement. In other words, these inflows and outflows of cash affect the company's free cash flow but do not affect the reported net income. Furthermore, the company's profit and loss statement includes certain non-cash expenses (often referred as accruals), such as depreciation and amortisation expense. These non-cash expenses affect the company's reported net income but do not affect its free cash flow. See below for a simplified version of this two-sided view – accounting and cash – to derive dividend potentials.

FIGURE 22.1 DETERMINING DIVIDEND POTENTIAL FROM CORPORATE ACCOUNTS

| Accounting View | Cash View |
|---|---|
| Revenues<br>− Expenses<br>= Operating Earnings<br>− Interest Payments<br>= Earnings before Tax<br>− Taxes<br>= Net Earnings<br>× Payout Ratio<br>= **Dividends** | Operating Earnings<br>+ Depreciation/Amortisation<br>− Increase in Working Capital<br>− Tax Rate × Operating Earnings<br>= Operating Cash Flow<br>− Investments in Fixed Assets<br>= Free Cash Flow<br>− Interest Payments<br>+ Tax Rate × Interest Payments<br>+ Increase in Financial Liabilities<br>= **Free Cash Flow attributable to equity holders**<br>(= Dividend Potential) |

# 2. Understanding the future path of dividends

Once you have determined the dividend potential of a company, you are ready to make a forecast of future dividends. This can be done based on a fundamental analysis assuming that a company follows a so-called residual dividend policy. Residual dividend policy means that as long as the firm has profitable investment opportunities it will invest at least a part of net income and reduce the dividend potential in this particular period (but increase the dividend potential of future periods). If no such opportunities exist, the firm will pay out all net income as dividends.

The best way of performing such a forecast is a three-step approach. Step one: analyse the fundamental situation of the company and the investment opportunity set. Step two: forecast the profit and loss statement, the balance sheet and the cash flow statement for each period. Step three: determine the dividends for each future period.

## 3. Running the model

Imagine Company A sells goods to end-consumers. It is operating in a mature market and does not have a lot of attractive (i.e. positive net present value) new investment opportunities. However, it must incur maintenance capital expenditures in order to keep its production facilities in a proper state. It is assumed that the company invests an amount equal to its annual depreciation charge each year for this maintenance and replacement.

After preparing a profit and loss, balance sheet and cash flow statement forecast you can see that following a residual dividend policy the company can pay out 100% of their earnings as dividends on a sustainable basis. Moreover, earnings are assumed to be stable over time as the company does not grow by investments. The DDM here looks as follows:

$$Value\ of\ equity_A = \frac{Dividend_{stable}}{1+r} + \frac{Dividend_{stable}}{(1+r)^2} + \cdots = \frac{Dividend_{stable}}{r}$$

Company B is more dynamic than Company A. It is operating in a high-growth environment and makes a lot for investments in new facilities. According to your analysis the company is not able to pay dividends at all during the first two years (i.e. $Dividend_1$ and $Dividend_2$ are equal to zero). After this time, however, it is assumed that it will grow strongly over two years just to turn into a moderate stable growth phase thereafter. Here the DDM looks as follows (dividend payments for Years 3 till 5 are explicitly forecasted).

$$Value\ of\ equity_B = \frac{Dividend_3}{(1+r)^3} + \frac{Dividend_4}{(1+r)^4} + \frac{\frac{Dividend_5}{(r - g_{long-term})}}{(1+r)^4}$$

## 4. What about stock price appreciation?

So far, we have only talked about the dividend component of financial benefits. But is this really sufficient for setting up a proper valuation model? In the previous chapter we commented that there are different ways of realising financial benefits for investors: while holding the shares investors would be receiving cash dividends, but at some future point in time investors would sell the shares for cash. Where is this latter component in our valuation model?

The good news is – it is not forgotten! It is inherent in our DDM. For understanding this, let us have a look at the Gordon Growth model presented in Chapter 21 as a starting point. Recall that the Gordon Growth model assumes that the company pays dividends forever that increase at a constant rate. Let us assume that the company is paying $80 in dividends, the constant growth rate of dividends is 2% and the cost of equity is 10%. In this case, the value of equity is:

$$Value\ of\ equity_0 = \frac{Dividend_1}{r-g} = \frac{80}{0.1-0.02} = \$1{,}000$$

Let us now assume that the investor plans to sell the shares in one year. In this case she would receive two components: the dividend for Year 1 and the share price at the end of Year 1 (immediately after dividend payments). The dividend for Year 1 is of course $80. The share price at the end of Year 1 is equal to the present value (of all future dividends) at the end of Year 1, because in a rational and efficient market investors will pay the present value of future dividends to get the shares. Because dividends are assumed to grow at a constant growth rate ($g$ = 2%), the share price at the end of Year 1 can be computed using the Gordon Growth model:

$$Value\ of\ equity_1 = \frac{Dividend_2}{r-g} = \frac{Dividend_1 \times (1+g)}{r-g} = \frac{80 \times (1+0.02)}{0.1-0.02} = \$1{,}020$$

Note that $Dividend_2$ serves as a starting dividend for this present value model, and $Dividend_2 = Dividend_1 \times (1 + g)$ because dividends are assumed to grow at a constant growth rate $g$. To compute today's share price we need to add together the present value of all future financial benefits that the investor expects to receive; that is, the present value of $Dividend_1$ and the value of shares at the end of Year 1 ($Value\ of\ equity_1$). Expressed formulaically:

$$Value\ of\ equity_0 = \frac{Dividend_1}{1+r} + \frac{Value\ of\ equity_1}{1+r}$$

By substituting the above numbers, we get:

$$Value\ of\ equity_0 = \frac{80}{1+0.1} + \frac{1020}{1+0.1} = \$1{,}000$$

As the fair price of a stock is nothing other than the value of future dividends, a valuation model based on forecasted dividends covers all necessary value effects.

## 5. When does the DDM work in practice (and when not)?

The DDM can be used in practice to value dividend-paying companies. The model can work well as long as it is possible to generate reliable and realistic dividend forecasts. And it is exactly this forecasting problem that sets limits to the DDM. Companies are not always following a smooth dividend path and a residual dividend policy that make a forecast of dividends simple. The application of the DDM is particularly problematic if:

- companies are not in a steady state, i.e. young and growing companies or distressed companies
- companies do not follow a residual dividend policy but rather other policies that are not linked to the company's underlying economic performance, such as a dividend stability-oriented policy, which leads to a certain amount of payouts or a clientele-based policy where management focuses on the needs of investors (income generation, retirement needs, tax effects, etc.).

# Stretch yourself

While not discussed in this chapter, the discount rate itself is also not always independent of the path of dividends. Companies with strong growth of dividends often show a higher uncertainty profile than companies that are in a mature and stable-dividend state. Moreover, paying out dividends can also affect the financing situation of the company (as available funds can also be used for paying out debt instead of paying dividends), which then impacts the capital structure risk of the company. This again highlights how important it is to have a holistic view on the company when setting up a valuation model.

# CHAPTER 23

# Free cash flow to the firm (FCFF) – talk-through

## Bite size

If we want to move beyond dividends (see Chapters 21 and 22), then we enter the world of free cash flow (FCF). There are different versions of FCF available for valuation purposes. In this chapter, we discuss the concept of FCF to the firm (FCFF) and the valuation process that is based on FCFF.

## Practitioner focus

As FCFF keeps operating and non-operating elements separate, it is the standard approach to discounted cash flow (DCF) valuation in practice. We deal with the alternative, and less commonly used, free cash flow to equity (FCFE) approach in Chapter 26.

## Core content

### 1. Free cash flow to the firm (FCFF)

FCFF is the cash flow **available** to pay interest to lenders and dividends to shareholders. In practice, we derive FCFF in two steps. In the first step we work with the operating elements of the income statement (Table 23.1).

## TABLE 23.1 CALCULATION OF NET OPERATING PROFIT AFTER TAXES (NOPAT)

| | |
|---|---|
| 1. Sales | X |
| 2. 'Cash' operating expense (i.e. CoGS and SG&A) | (X) |
| **EBITDA** | **X** |
| 3. D&A expenses | (X) |
| **EBIT** | **X** |
| 4. Tax on operations | (X) |
| **NOPAT** | **X** |

*CoGS: cost of goods sold; D&A: depreciation and amortisation; EBIT: earnings before interest and taxes; EBITDA: earnings before interest, taxes, depreciation and amortisation; NOPAT: net operating profit after taxes; SG&A: selling, general and administrative.*

The second step is driven by the operating elements of the cash flow statement (see Table 23.2).

## TABLE 23.2 CALCULATION OF NET REINVESTMENT OF NOPAT

| | |
|---|---|
| 5a. (Increase)/decrease in inventory | (X) / X |
| 5b. (Increase)/decrease in receivables | (X) / X |
| 5c. Increase/(decrease) in payables | X / (X) |
| **(Investment in)/release of NOWC (A)** | **(X) / X** |
| 6. Capex | (X) |
| D&A expenses | X |
| **Net investment in non-current assets (B)** | **(X)** |
| **Net reinvestment of NOPAT (A+B)** | **(X)** |

*NOWC: net operating working capital; capex: capital expenditures; D&A: depreciation and amortisation; NOPAT: net operating profit after taxes.*

The calculation is completed as shown in Table 23.3.

## TABLE 23.3 COMPLETION OF FCFF CALCULATION

| | |
|---|---|
| **NOPAT** | **X** |
| Net reinvestment of NOPAT (to grow net operating asset base) | (X) |
| **FCFF** | **X** |

Now that we have laid out the elements of our FCFF calculation clearly, we can see the key assumptions that drive our forecasts.

In Chapter 5 we briefly touched on the main drivers of sales and operating, D&A and tax expenses. Let us consider some of these in more detail (see Table 23.4).

## TABLE 23.4 KEY DRIVERS OF NOPAT

| Forecast | Forecast driver |
|---|---|
| 1. Sales | Sales growth rates |
| 2. 'Cash' operating expenses | Operating expense margins |
| 3. D&A expenses* | D&A margins |
| 4. Tax on operations** | Effective tax rates (ETRs) |

\* It may seem wrong to see the non-cash D&A expenses included in a cash-flow calculation. However, we need to tax the operations (EBIT) of the business and in the real world the cost of purchasing non-current assets is tax deductible. The tax deduction will often be different from the accounting depreciation numbers but these will usually act as a reasonable proxy. However, we must remember that D&A expenses are not actual cash outflows, so we must add them back before completing our calculation, as we do in the second part.

\*\* We must be careful not to pick up the tax expenses that we forecast in our income statements as these are based on EBT. They are 'levered', i.e. after accounting for interest expenses. This is because in the real world, interest expenses are tax deductible. However, FCFF must remain purely operational and so we need to calculate 'unlevered' taxes free from the impact of interest expenses. Therefore, we have to calculate new tax expenses based on EBIT, i.e. profits before accounting for interest expenses. If the tax rate $t$ is known, the tax on operations can be calculated by $EBIT \times t$.

Thus, we arrive at net operating profit after tax (NOPAT). This term may seem tautologous, but the net refers to the D&A expenses rather than the taxes.

In Chapters 6 and 7 we touched upon drivers of net operating working capital and capex (see Table 23.5).

## TABLE 23.5 KEY DRIVERS OF NET REINVESTMENT

| Forecast | Forecast driver |
|---|---|
| 5a/b/c. Increases/decreases in inventories, receivables and payables* | Inventory, receivable and payable days |
| 6. Capex** | Capex-to-D&A multiples |

\* These drive the net investment in (or release of) NOWC, i.e. how much NOPAT is reinvested into growing the shorter-term net operating asset (NOA) base of the business.

\*\* In effect, having already captured the maintenance (or replacement) element (D&A expenses) within NOPAT, we now only deduct the incremental growth (or expansionary) element of capex (the net of total capex and D&A), i.e. how much NOPAT is reinvested into growing the longer-term NOA base.

Thus, we arrive at FCFF available to make financial payments to lenders and shareholders, i.e. interest, debt repayments and dividends.

## 2. Cost of capital

As FCFF belongs to debt and equity providers, risk is captured using the weighted average cost of capital (WACC), which reflects the risks perceived and returns required by these lenders and shareholders. The WACC is calculated as the cost of debt and the cost of equity blended according to the proportions of debt and equity in the company's capital structure (see Chapter 9).

## 3. Growth rate

We forecast out FCFF for a certain number of years – the 'visible' period. In theory, this should last as long as the company has a competitive advantage and until it settles into a more long-term steady state. In practice, analysts will often use a round number, such as five or ten years. The company will continue to generate FCFF and create value beyond this visible period and we usually assume that this will continue into perpetuity. We call this the terminal period and the value of all the FCFF generated during this period, as at the beginning of the period, is the terminal value (TV). As the terminal period continues into perpetuity, even modest levels of growth will have a significant impact. This is why the TV is where growth is fundamentally captured in this model.

There are two main ways to approach the calculation of the TV. The first is multiples-based, using for example an EBITDA multiple:

$$TV = Final\ EBITDA\ forecast \times Terminal\ \frac{EV}{EBITDA}\ multiple$$

This has the advantage of being relatively quick and easy. However, it involves switching from a DCF to a multiples-based approach part way through the valuation, which is an odd thing to do. It also has the disadvantage that the key driver of the TV, i.e. growth, is implicit (it is baked into the terminal EV/EBITDA multiple – higher means more growth and vice versa) rather than being explicit. It is far better for our key assumptions to be transparent. If this method is used, then the terminal multiple should usually be lower than the equivalent current multiple, as it will reflect the lower-growth assumption of the terminal period.

It is better, and more common in practice, to keep to a DCF approach using a version of the Gordon Growth model:

$$TV = \frac{Next\ FCFF\ forecast}{WACC - Terminal\ growth\ rate}$$

Where:

*Next FCFF forecast = Final visible FCFF forecast × (1 + Terminal growth rate)*

This also has the advantage that the terminal growth assumption is explicit. This is extremely important as this is one of our – if not our single – most important assumptions and the valuation will be highly sensitive to changes to it. This is problematic as we do not know what the terminal growth rate of the business will be. In practice, we often use a long-term GDP growth rate, as anything higher would imply that the company will eventually achieve world domination.

Once we have captured the three key elements of cash, risk/time value of money, and growth, we can pull these together to arrive at our implied EV. We are performing a classic two-stage DCF valuation (see Chapter 20 for models with more than two stages). So, we must discount the FCFF forecasts for the visible period (Stage 1) back to their present values using the WACC. We must also discount the TV back from the beginning of the terminal period (Stage 2) to its present value, also using the WACC (Figure 23.1).

FIGURE 23.1 THE THREE ELEMENTS OF THE FCFF MODEL

| Stage 1<br>Visible period<br>Free cash flow to firm (FCFF) forecasts<br>**CASH** | Stage 2<br>Terminal period<br>Terminal value (TV)<br>**GROWTH** |
|---|---|

| Weighted average cost of capital (WACC)<br>**RISK/time value of money** |
|---|

We thus arrive at the EV, capturing the operational value of the business:

$$EV = PV\ of\ FCFF\ forecasts + PV\ of\ TV$$

## 4. The bridge

Equity investors are going to want to go further and build the bridge from enterprise to equity value and then on to a share price.[22]

As the EV only captures the value of operations, we need to add on the value of any financial (or other non-operating) assets that the company owns. From this total pool of value, we then have to deduct all claims that precede those of the shareholders (for example, those of the debtholders), i.e. all financial (or other non-operating) liabilities. The shareholders only own the residual value after these prior claims have been met (Figure 23.2, Table 23.6).

FIGURE 23.2 THE EV BRIDGE

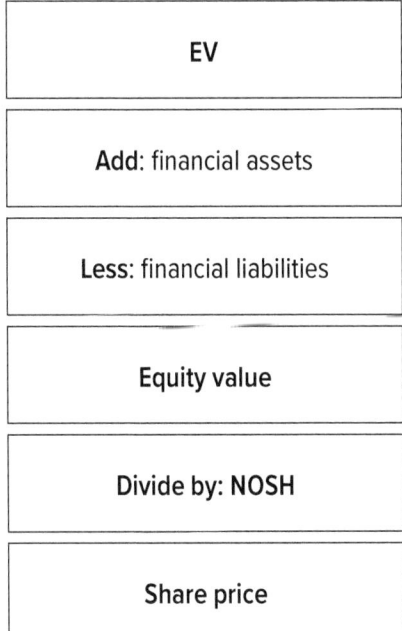

---

22  The EV bridge was already covered in an early chapter of the text. We have repeated the concepts here to make this chapter a complete FCFF walk-through without having to check the previous chapter.

TABLE 23.6 THE DETAILED ELEMENTS OF THE EV BRIDGE

| EV | X |
|---|---|
| *Add: financial/non-operating assets* | |
| 1. Cash and cash equivalents | X |
| 2. Other non-operating assets | X |
| *Less: financial/non-operating liabilities* | |
| 3. Debt | (X) |
| 4. Non-controlling interests | (X) |
| **Equity value** | X |
| 5. **Divide by**: Number of outstanding shares | X |
| **Implied share price** | X |

We normally use the most up-to-date balance sheet at the time of our valuation to create the list of assets and liabilities that we need to capture in the bridge, although we might need to be wary of using accounting values:

1. **Cash and cash equivalents** – cash is cash, so we will probably just take the number from the balance sheet, assuming it is not too out of date.

2. **Other non-operating assets** – we must make sure that we capture the value of any other non-operating assets, e.g. equity method investments (EMIs), which do not form part of the core operations of the business.

Thus, we arrive at the total pool of value available to **all** claimants.

3. **Debt** – the book value of debt will often be close to its fair or market value but not the same. Normally, we will look in the notes to the financial statements where the company may disclose the fair value of its debt.

4. **Non-controlling interests (NCIs)** – these are minority shareholders in subsidiaries of the parent, so they are **not** common stockholders in the parent. The value of their claim must be deducted. (In effect, the EV captures 100% of the value of all subsidiaries, even if they are not 100% owned, so we have to manually deduct the value of the NCI's share.)

Thus, we arrive at the equity value which belongs to, and must be divided among, the common stockholders.

5. **Number of outstanding shares ('NOSH')** – we need to be careful. Ideally, we want an up-to-date number as at our valuation date. This may involve taking the most recent financial report and rolling that number forward using regulatory filings. We also need to make sure that we use the outstanding shares:

*Outstanding shares = Issued shares − Treasury shares*

The company may have issued 100m shares and then subsequently bought back 10m of those. If they cancel those 10m shares, then they are no longer in issue and naturally fall out of the stock count. If they do not cancel those 10m shares and hold them as treasury stock then, technically, they are still in issue, but the company holds shares in itself, which is a nonsense, and these must still be taken out of the stock count. So, either way the correct 'NOSH' would be 90m (Table 23.7).

TABLE 23.7 NOSH CALCULATION

|  | Bought back stock cancelled | Bought back stock held |
|---|---|---|
| Issued | 90m | 100m |
| Treasury | – | (10m) |
| Outstanding | 90m | 90m |

Finally, we divide the equity value by the NOSH to arrive at our implied share price:

$$Implied\ share\ price = \frac{Equity\ value}{Nosh}$$

# Stretch yourself

In some valuations, you might want to consider the dilutive impact on the number of shares (NOSH) of stock options (and other similar instruments, e.g. warrants, restricted stock units). These will usually only have a significant impact on the valuation if a large number of such instruments have been issued, relative to the 'NOSH', as a form of remuneration. This can be seen, for example, in tech companies.

## CHAPTER 24

# Free cash flow to the firm (FCFF) – walk-through

## Bite size

In this chapter, we walk through a numerical example of FCFF valuation, as set out in the previous chapter. So, we tackle the cash, risk and growth elements to arrive at an enterprise value (EV). We then build the bridge from EV to equity value and on to an implied share price.

## Practitioner focus

In practice, analysts build their valuation models in Microsoft Excel. This is our weapon of choice because it has several tools that allow for flexibility in our valuation, which is very useful when we are dealing with an uncertain future. We discuss some of these tools in the next chapter.

## Core content

### 1. How to forecast FCFF

Let us use an example of a hypothetical mature company to illustrate how our expectations and assumptions can be used for generating the forecasts of the components of FCFF. The historical and forecast data for the company are shown in Table 24.1.

## TABLE 24.1 FCFF FORECASTS

| Example Corp in USDm (unless stated) | Year 0 Historical | Year 1 Forecast | Year 2 Forecast | Year 3 Forecast | Year 4 Forecast | Year 5 Forecast | Year 6 Forecast | Year 7 Forecast | Year 8 Forecast | Year 9 Forecast | Year 10 Forecast |
|---|---|---|---|---|---|---|---|---|---|---|---|
| Sales | 100.0 | 104.7 | 109.3 | 113.8 | 118.1 | 122.2 | 126.2 | 129.8 | 133.2 | 136.3 | 139.0 |
| *Sales growth rates* | 5.0% | 4.7% | 4.4% | 4.1% | 3.8% | 3.5% | 3.2% | 2.9% | 2.6% | 2.3% | 2.0% |
| Cash operating expenses (CoGS and SG&A) | (72.0) | (75.2) | (78.3) | (81.2) | (84.1) | (86.8) | (89.3) | (91.7) | (93.8) | (95.7) | (97.3) |
| *Cash operating expense margins* | 72.0% | 71.8% | 71.6% | 71.4% | 71.2% | 71.0% | 70.8% | 70.6% | 70.4% | 70.2% | 70.0% |
| **EBITDA** | **28.0** | **29.5** | **31.0** | **32.5** | **34.0** | **35.5** | **36.8** | **38.2** | **39.4** | **40.6** | **41.7** |
| Depreciation and amortisation expenses | (2.0) | (2.1) | (2.2) | (2.3) | (2.4) | (2.4) | (2.5) | (2.6) | (2.7) | (2.7) | (2.8) |
| *D&A as a % of Sales* | 2.0% | 2.0% | 2.0% | 2.0% | 2.0% | 2.0% | 2.0% | 2.0% | 2.0% | 2.0% | 2.0% |
| **EBIT** | **26.0** | **27.4** | **28.9** | **30.3** | **31.7** | **33.0** | **34.3** | **35.6** | **36.8** | **37.9** | **38.9** |
| Tax on operations | (6.2) | (6.6) | (7.0) | (7.4) | (7.7) | (8.1) | (8.4) | (8.8) | (9.1) | (9.4) | (9.7) |
| *Effective tax rates (ETRs) on EBIT* | 24.0% | 24.1% | 24.2% | 24.3% | 24.4% | 24.5% | 24.6% | 24.7% | 24.8% | 24.9% | 25.0% |
| **NOPAT** | **19.8** | **20.8** | **21.9** | **22.9** | **23.9** | **24.9** | **25.9** | **26.8** | **27.6** | **28.4** | **29.2** |
| (Incr) / decr in inventories | (1.6) | (1.4) | (1.4) | (1.4) | (1.3) | (1.3) | (1.2) | (1.2) | (1.1) | (1.0) | (0.9) |
| *Inventories* | 27.6 | 29.0 | 30.4 | 31.8 | 33.2 | 34.5 | 35.7 | 36.9 | 38.0 | 39.0 | 40.0 |
| *Inventory days* | 140 days | 141 days | 142 days | 143 days | 144 days | 145 days | 146 days | 147 days | 148 days | 149 days | 150 days |
| (Incr) / decr in receivables | (1.9) | (1.8) | (1.8) | (1.8) | (1.8) | (1.7) | (1.7) | (1.6) | (1.5) | (1.4) | (1.3) |
| *Receivables* | 32.9 | 34.7 | 36.5 | 38.3 | 40.1 | 41.9 | 43.6 | 45.2 | 46.7 | 48.2 | 49.5 |
| *Receivables days* | 120 days | 121 days | 122 days | 123 days | 124 days | 125 days | 126 days | 127 days | 128 days | 129 days | 130 days |
| Incr / (decr) in payables | 0.7 | 0.7 | 0.6 | 0.6 | 0.5 | 0.5 | 0.4 | 0.3 | 0.3 | 0.2 | 0.1 |
| *Payables* | 19.7 | 20.4 | 21.0 | 21.6 | 22.1 | 22.6 | 23.0 | 23.4 | 23.6 | 23.8 | 24.0 |
| *Payables days* | 100 days | 99 days | 98 days | 97 days | 96 days | 95 days | 94 days | 93 days | 92 days | 91 days | 90 days |
| **Net investment in NOWC** | **(2.8)** | **(2.6)** | **(2.6)** | **(2.6)** | **(2.6)** | **(2.6)** | **(2.5)** | **(2.5)** | **(2.4)** | **(2.3)** | **(2.1)** |
| Capex | (5.1) | (5.1) | (5.1) | (5.2) | (5.2) | (5.2) | (5.2) | (5.1) | (5.1) | (5.0) | (4.9) |
| *Capex-to-D&A multiples* | 2.50x | 2.43x | 2.35x | 2.28x | 2.20x | 2.13x | 2.05x | 1.98x | 1.90x | 1.83x | 1.75x |
| Depreciation and amortisation expenses | 2.0 | 2.1 | 2.2 | 2.3 | 2.4 | 2.4 | 2.5 | 2.6 | 2.7 | 2.7 | 2.8 |
| **Net investment in non-current assets** | **(3.1)** | **(3.0)** | **(3.0)** | **(2.9)** | **(2.8)** | **(2.8)** | **(2.6)** | **(2.5)** | **(2.4)** | **(2.2)** | **(2.1)** |
| **Net reinvestment of NOPAT** | **(5.9)** | **(5.6)** | **(5.6)** | **(5.5)** | **(5.4)** | **(5.3)** | **(5.2)** | **(5.0)** | **(4.8)** | **(4.5)** | **(4.2)** |
| **Free cash flow to firm** | **13.9** | **15.2** | **16.3** | **17.4** | **18.5** | **19.6** | **20.7** | **21.8** | **22.9** | **23.9** | **25.0** |

**Sales growth rates**. The company has historical sales of $100m, which have grown 5.0% from the previous year. This is already a relatively mature company, and we believe that they will not be able to maintain this growth rate. So, we have assumed that the sales growth rate will gradually decline to a more sustainable terminal rate of 2.0% over the visible period. In the absence of a more sophisticated approach, we have assumed a simple linear decline over time.

**Cash operating expense margins**. The company has historical cash operating expenses of $72.0m (for the purposes of simplicity we have aggregated cost of goods sold (CoGS) and selling, general and administrative (SG&A)), giving a cash operating expense margin of 72.0%. As the company grows, it might achieve some economies of scale, for example buying in materials in greater volumes and achieving better unit purchase prices. We have also assumed that as sales growth declines, the company might spend a relatively smaller proportion of its income on expenses like advertising and marketing. So, we have assumed that the cost base will decline slightly relative to sales over the visible period to 70.0%. Again, we have assumed a simple linear improvement over time.

**Depreciation and amortisation (D&A) as a % of sales**. Our historical and sector analysis has shown that D&A expenses consume a reasonably stable 2.0% of sales income over time. We have no reason to believe that this will change significantly in the future and so we have maintained this level throughout our visible period.

**Effective tax rates (ETRs) on EBIT**. Our analysis of mature companies in the same sector and tax jurisdiction shows that they incur a fairly stable ETR of 25.0%. Our analysis of the case company also shows that its ETR has been slightly lower than this as it has been growing faster and investing in new assets to fuel this growth. As such, it has been receiving more generous tax deductions than the sector peers. As its growth and investment gradually decline toward the industry average, we would expect its ETR to gradually return to the more normal level of 25.0%.

**Inventory days**. The company's management guidance suggests they are concerned they have been holding too little inventory. The company therefore expects its inventory levels and holding periods to increase slightly over time, and we have followed this guidance. We have used the inventory days (and CoGS) forecasts to project the year-end inventory. We have then compared this to the previous year-end's inventory to calculate the increase or decrease over the year and its cash flow impact. In this case, the relative increase in inventories is cash-flow negative.

**Receivables days**. Our historical and cross-sector analysis shows that the company has traditionally been slightly less generous with its customer collection periods than its competitors. As its sales growth declines the company plans to defend its position by allowing customers longer credit periods. So, we are assuming that receivables days will increase slightly over the forecast period. As before, we have used the receivables days (and sales) forecasts to project the year-end receivables. We have then compared this to the previous year-end's receivables to calculate the increase or decrease over the year and the cash flow impact. The increasing credit periods will be cash-flow negative for the company.

**Payables days.** Again, historical and cross-sector analysis shows that the company has traditionally demanded slightly more generous credit periods from suppliers than its competitors. Management is slightly concerned that this may damage some of their supplier relationships and reduce their access to key supplies. To reduce this risk, they plan to gradually reduce their supplier payment periods over time. As before, we have used the payables days (and CoGS) forecasts to project year-end payables. We have then compared this to the previous year-end's payables to calculate the increase or decrease over the year and the cash flow impact. The decreasing credit periods will be cash-flow negative for the company.

The net of the changes in inventory, receivables and payables shows us overall how much net operating profit after taxes (NOPAT) the company will have to reinvest to grow its shorter-term net operating working capital (NOWC) base.

**Capex-to-D&A multiples.** Historically, to take advantage of growth opportunities and achieve higher growth rates, the company has had capex-to-D&A multiples far greater than 1.00x, reflecting a need for maintenance and significant expansionary capex. As the company's expected rate of growth declines over the visible period, we can expect the need for expansionary capex, and the capex-to-D&A multiples, to decline. However, they should remain above 1.00x, as we are still forecasting growth in Year 10 and beyond and so we still need growth capex. We multiply the forecast capex-to-D&A multiple with D&A forecast to project the level of gross capex, and the difference between gross capex and D&A shows the net investment in the company's non-current asset base.

The sum of net investment NOWC and net investment in non-current assets shows the total amount of net reinvestment of NOPAT in the company's net operating assets. This then gets us to FCFF forecasts, as shown in Table 24.1.

# 2. Cost of capital

## 2.1 Cost of debt

TABLE 24.2 COST OF DEBT CALCULATION

| Risk-free rate | 4.0% |
|---|---|
| Credit risk premium | 2.0% |
| **Cost of debt (pre-tax)** | **6.0%** |
| Marginal tax rate | 25.0% |
| **Cost of debt (post-tax)** | **4.5%** |

One of the most common methods of determining the cost of debt is to add a credit risk premium (which is specific to our case company) to a risk-free rate in a given jurisdiction. As the FCFF forecasts are in US dollars, we have used a US-dollar risk-free rate. At the time of writing, the yield on benchmark ten-year US Treasuries is approximately 4%. To determine the credit risk premium, we would analyse the company's historical financial statements. Investigation of the notes to the company's financial statements shows that on average, historically, the company's effective interest rate (EIR) on their bank loans and bonds is about 2% above the risk-free rate for the given period. So, in our cost of debt projections we have settled on a pre-tax cost of debt of 6% (0.04 + 0.02 = 0.06).

In order to be consistent with our FCFF assumptions above, we have used a terminal marginal tax rate of 25%. This rate should ideally be the same as the rate we have trended to over our visible period. If the government is subsidising the cost of the company's debt finance to the tune of 25%, then after the beneficial impact of this interest tax shield the company only really incurs the remaining 75% (1 − 0.25 = 0.75). So, we arrive at a post-tax cost of debt of 4.5% (0.06 × [1 − 0.25] = 0.045).

## 2.2 Cost of equity

TABLE 24.3 COST OF EQUITY CALCULATION

| Risk-free rate | 4.0% |
|---|---|
| Equity risk premium | 6.0% |
| Adjusted beta | 0.80 |
| **Cost of equity** | **8.8%** |

We estimate cost of equity using the Capital Asset Pricing Model (CAPM), which was introduced in Chapter 9. We start with the same risk-free rate as we used above (4%). After consulting a variety of sources using both historical analysis and implied market studies, we arrive at a sensible equity risk premium for US markets of approximately 6%. In conjunction with the risk-free rate, this implies a compound annual return on US equities of about 10% (0.04 + 0.06 = 0.1) on average. This acts as a good sanity check on our calculation. If this total seems reasonable, we can proceed. If not, we may need to adjust our assumptions.

Example Corp. is not involved in a particularly high-risk activity and so we would expect a beta of less than 1. Again, after consulting a variety of sources using two-year/weekly and five-year/monthly regressions of narrower and broader market indices on the company's stock returns, we have settled on an adjusted beta of 0.80.

Using CAPM, we arrive at an overall cost of equity of 8.8% (0.04 + 0.06 × 0.8 = 0.088).

## 2.3 Weighted average cost of capital (WACC) calculation

After analysis of the company's balance sheets, looking up the value of its debt and the market value of its equity, listening to management guidance on their financing strategy and studying other similar companies, we have assumed that on average, over the longer term, debt will represent (or own) about 20% of EV. Therefore, equity will represent (or own) the other 80% (1 − 0.2).

TABLE 24.4 WACC CALCULATION

| | |
|---|---|
| Risk-free rate | 4.0% |
| Credit risk premium | 2.0% |
| **Cost of debt (pre-tax)** | **6.0%** |
| Marginal tax rate | 25.0% |
| **Cost of debt (post-tax)** | **4.5%** |
| Risk-free rate | 4.0% |
| Equity risk premium | 6.0% |
| Adjusted beta | 0.80 |
| **Cost of equity** | **8.8%** |
| Debt/Enterprise value | 20.0% |
| Equity/Enterprise value | 80.0% |
| **Weighted average cost of capital** | **7.94%** |

Using data in Table 24.4, we can then pull these separate elements together to arrive at our WACC:

$$WACC = (0.045 \times 0.2) + (0.088 \times 0.8) = 0.0794 \; (or \; 7.94\%)$$

We shall use this WACC figure as the discount rate to compute the present value of future FCFF in our discounted cash flow (DCF) valuation model.

## 3. Growth and terminal value

We have already forecast FCFF for Year 10 ($25.0m). In line with our top-line sales growth rates trending down to 2.0% by the end of the visible period, we have assumed that the business will continue at this growth rate ($g$) on average throughout the terminal period. This is certainly no greater than a sensible long-term GDP growth rate assumption and so the company will not achieve world domination. We can therefore estimate FCFF for Year 11 to be $25.5m ($25.0$m \times [1 + 0.02]$).

TABLE 24.5 TERMINAL VALUE CALCULATION

| | |
|---|---|
| Free cash flow to firm – Year 10 | 25.0 |
| Terminal growth rate | 2.0% |
| **Free cash flow to firm – Year 11** | **25.5** |
| Weighted average cost of capital | 7.94% |
| Terminal growth rate | 2.0% |
| **Terminal value as at Time 10** | **429.3** |

We can now estimate the terminal value (TV) of our company, i.e. its EV as at the end of Year 10. Conceptually, what is TV? It is as though we are planning to buy the business at the end of Year 0, own it for the next ten years, pocketing the FCFF it generates during that period, and then sell it at the end of Year 10. The TV is our best guess as to what value we will be able to sell the business for at the end of Year 10. TV is the present value (as at the end of Year 10) of an infinite series of FCFF generated after Year 10. Because we assume that these free cash flows will grow at the same terminal growth rate ($g$) forever, we can compute TV by using the Gordon Growth model:

$$TV_{Year\ 10} = \frac{FCFF_{Year\ 11}}{(WACC - g)}$$

Using data from Tables 24.4 and 24.5, we obtain:

$$TV_{Year\ 10} = \frac{\$25.5m}{(0.0794 - 0.02)} = \$429.3m$$

## 4. Pulling it all together to arrive at EV

As we already have the cash element in the form of the FCFF forecasts for Years 1 to 10, the TV and WACC, we can now compute our estimate of EV using the following formula:

$$EV_0 = \sum_{t=1}^{10} FCFF_t \times \frac{1}{(1+WACC)^t} + TV_{Year\ 10} \times \frac{1}{(1+WACC)^{10}}$$

## Chapter 24 – Free cash flow to the firm (FCFF) – walk-through

For the sake of simplicity, and as is often done in practice, we have assumed that the cash flows arise at the end of each year and our valuation date is the end of Year 0. We refer to term $\frac{1}{(1+WACC)^t}$ as a discount factor. If we multiply each of the future FCFFs by its corresponding discount factor and sum all ten products, we arrive at the present value of FCFF of the visible period (Stage 1). Using data from Table 24.6, we arrive at the present value of Stage 1 FCFF of $130.9m. We then compute the present value of TV (Stage 2) by multiplying $TV_{Time\ 10}$ by the discount factor for Year 10 ($429.3m × 0.47 = $201.8m). We then simply add the present values of Stage 1 and Stage 2 to arrive at the EV ($130.9 + $201.8m = $332.7m), the value of the operations of the business.

### TABLE 24.6 CALCULATION OF EV

| Example Corp in USDm (unless stated) | Year 0 | Year 1 | Year 2 | Year 3 | Year 4 | Year 5 | Year 6 | Year 7 | Year 8 | Year 9 | Year 10 |
|---|---|---|---|---|---|---|---|---|---|---|---|
| | Historical | Forecast | Forecast | Forecast | Forecast | Forecast | Forecast | Forecast | Forecast | Forecast | Forecast |
| Free cash flow to firm | | 15.2 | 16.3 | 17.4 | 18.5 | 19.6 | 20.7 | 21.8 | 22.9 | 23.9 | 25.0 |
| Terminal value using a TGR of 2.0% | | | | | | | | | | | 429.3 |
| Discount factors using a WACC of 7.94% | | 0.93 | 0.86 | 0.80 | 0.74 | 0.68 | 0.63 | 0.59 | 0.54 | 0.50 | 0.47 |
| Present value of visible period | 130.9 | 40% | | | | | | | | | |
| Present value of terminal period | 201.8 | 60% | | | | | | | | | |
| Enterprise value | 332.7 | | | | | | | | | | |

At this point it is a good idea to calculate the proportions of the EV coming from each stage. In this case we have a 40/60 split. This weighting towards the terminal period is not uncommon as eternity is a long time. The problem would have been exacerbated if we had chosen a shorter visible period (e.g. five years) and could be improved if we chose a longer visible period (e.g. 15 or 20 years or more). We are also more likely to get this kind of split if the business is already fairly mature and there is not a significant growth differential between the visible and terminal periods.

## 5. The EV bridge

TABLE 24.7 THE EV BRIDGE

| Enterprise value | 332.7 | |
|---|---|---|
| Add: financial / non-operating assets | | |
| Cash & cash equivalents | 7.2 | |
| Non-operating assets | 32.6 | |
| Less: financial / non-operating liabilities | | |
| Debt | (70.7) | |
| Non-controlling interests | (50.5) | |
| Equity value | 251.3 | |
| Number of outstanding shares (m) | 9.9 | |
| Implied share price (USD) | 25.38 | |

**Add: financial/non-operating assets**

**Cash and cash equivalents.** This is simply taken from the balance sheet as at the end of Year 0.

**Non-operating assets.** This is the value of equity method investments (EMIs), also taken from the balance sheet as at the end of Year 0.

This gives a total pool of available value of $372.5m ($332.7*m* + $7.2m + $32.6*m*).

**Less: financial/non-operating liabilities**

**Debt.** This is the fair value of the debt taken from the notes to the financial statements, which is slightly higher than the balance sheet figure of $68.2m.

**Non-controlling interests.** The company owns 60% of a Canadian subsidiary. In effect, 100% of the value of the subsidiary has been captured in the EV. So, we have deducted the value of the 40% owned by the minority (or non-controlling shareholders), which has again been taken from the balance sheet as at the end of Year 0.

This makes a total value of pre-equity claims of $121.2m ($70.7m + $50.5m). If we deduct this from the total pool of value available, we arrive at the equity value of $251.3m ($372.5m − $121.2m).

**Number of outstanding shares** – the company has 10.0m shares in issue but has bought back and holds 0.1m as treasury stock, giving an outstanding share count of 9.9m (10.0m − 0.1m).

Thus, we finally arrive at an implied share price of $25.38 ($251.3m / 9.9m).

# Stretch yourself

We have now walked through an entire FCFF DCF valuation. However, how do we know if our valuation is sensible and internally consistent? In order to satisfy ourselves (and others) of this, we will have to perform some sense checks, in the form of returns and DuPont analysis. Also, our valuation is based on many assumptions about the future. These are uncertain and so we will need to be able to flex our valuation to deal with this. We can do this using scenario analysis for our key FCFF drivers (upside/base/downside scenarios) and sensitivity analysis for our time value of money (WACC) and terminal growth (TV) assumptions. We cover these more sophisticated tools and topics in the next chapter.

# Appendix

TABLE 24.8 THE ENTIRE FCFF DCF VALUATION

| Example Corp in USDm (unless stated) | Year 0 Historical | Year 1 Forecast | Year 2 Forecast | Year 3 Forecast | Year 4 Forecast | Year 5 Forecast | Year 6 Forecast | Year 7 Forecast | Year 8 Forecast | Year 9 Forecast | Year 10 Forecast |
|---|---|---|---|---|---|---|---|---|---|---|---|
| **Free cash flow to firm forecasts** | | | | | | | | | | | |
| Sales | 100.0 | 104.7 | 109.3 | 113.8 | 118.1 | 122.2 | 126.2 | 129.8 | 133.2 | 136.3 | 139.0 |
| Sales growth rates | 5.0% | 4.7% | 4.4% | 4.1% | 3.8% | 3.5% | 3.2% | 2.9% | 2.6% | 2.3% | 2.0% |
| Cash operating expenses (CoGS and SG&A) | (72.0) | (75.2) | (78.3) | (81.2) | (84.1) | (86.8) | (89.3) | (91.7) | (93.8) | (95.7) | (97.3) |
| Cash operating expense margins | 72.0% | 71.8% | 71.6% | 71.4% | 71.2% | 71.0% | 70.8% | 70.6% | 70.4% | 70.2% | 70.0% |
| **EBITDA** | **28.0** | **29.5** | **31.0** | **32.5** | **34.0** | **35.5** | **36.8** | **38.2** | **39.4** | **40.6** | **41.7** |
| Depreciation and amortisation expenses | (2.0) | (2.1) | (2.2) | (2.3) | (2.4) | (2.4) | (2.5) | (2.6) | (2.7) | (2.7) | (2.8) |
| D&A as a % of Sales | 2.0% | 2.0% | 2.0% | 2.0% | 2.0% | 2.0% | 2.0% | 2.0% | 2.0% | 2.0% | 2.0% |
| **EBIT** | **26.0** | **27.4** | **28.9** | **30.3** | **31.7** | **33.0** | **34.3** | **35.6** | **36.8** | **37.9** | **38.9** |
| Tax on operations | (6.2) | (6.6) | (7.0) | (7.4) | (7.7) | (8.1) | (8.4) | (8.8) | (9.1) | (9.4) | (9.7) |
| Effective tax rates (ETRs) on EBIT | 24.0% | 24.1% | 24.2% | 24.3% | 24.4% | 24.5% | 24.6% | 24.7% | 24.8% | 24.9% | 25.0% |
| **NOPAT** | **19.8** | **20.8** | **21.9** | **22.9** | **23.9** | **24.9** | **25.9** | **26.8** | **27.6** | **28.4** | **29.2** |
| (Incr) / decr in inventories | (1.6) | (1.4) | (1.4) | (1.4) | (1.3) | (1.3) | (1.2) | (1.2) | (1.1) | (1.0) | (0.9) |
| Inventories | 27.6 | 29.0 | 30.4 | 31.8 | 33.2 | 34.5 | 35.7 | 36.9 | 38.0 | 39.0 | 40.0 |
| Inventory days | 140 days | 141 days | 142 days | 143 days | 144 days | 145 days | 146 days | 147 days | 148 days | 149 days | 150 days |
| (Incr) / decr in receivables | (1.9) | (1.8) | (1.8) | (1.8) | (1.8) | (1.7) | (1.7) | (1.6) | (1.5) | (1.4) | (1.3) |
| Receivables | 32.9 | 34.7 | 36.5 | 38.3 | 40.1 | 41.9 | 43.6 | 45.2 | 46.7 | 48.2 | 49.5 |
| Receivables days | 120 days | 121 days | 122 days | 123 days | 124 days | 125 days | 126 days | 127 days | 128 days | 129 days | 130 days |
| Incr / (decr) in payables | 0.7 | 0.7 | 0.6 | 0.6 | 0.5 | 0.5 | 0.4 | 0.3 | 0.3 | 0.2 | 0.1 |
| Payables | 19.7 | 20.4 | 21.0 | 21.6 | 22.1 | 22.6 | 23.0 | 23.4 | 23.6 | 23.8 | 24.0 |
| Payables days | 100 days | 99 days | 98 days | 97 days | 96 days | 95 days | 94 days | 93 days | 92 days | 91 days | 90 days |
| **Net investment in NOWC** | **(2.8)** | **(2.6)** | **(2.6)** | **(2.6)** | **(2.6)** | **(2.6)** | **(2.5)** | **(2.5)** | **(2.4)** | **(2.3)** | **(2.1)** |
| Capex | (5.1) | (5.1) | (5.1) | (5.2) | (5.2) | (5.2) | (5.2) | (5.1) | (5.1) | (5.0) | (4.9) |
| Capex-to-D&A multiples | 2.50x | 2.43x | 2.35x | 2.28x | 2.20x | 2.13x | 2.05x | 1.98x | 1.90x | 1.83x | 1.75x |
| Depreciation and amortisation expenses | 2.0 | 2.1 | 2.2 | 2.3 | 2.4 | 2.4 | 2.5 | 2.6 | 2.7 | 2.7 | 2.8 |
| **Net investment in non-current assets** | **(3.1)** | **(3.0)** | **(3.0)** | **(2.9)** | **(2.8)** | **(2.8)** | **(2.6)** | **(2.5)** | **(2.4)** | **(2.2)** | **(2.1)** |
| **Net reinvestment of NOPAT** | **(5.9)** | **(5.6)** | **(5.6)** | **(5.5)** | **(5.4)** | **(5.3)** | **(5.2)** | **(5.0)** | **(4.8)** | **(4.5)** | **(4.2)** |
| **Free cash flow to firm** | **13.9** | **15.2** | **16.3** | **17.4** | **18.5** | **19.6** | **20.7** | **21.8** | **22.9** | **23.9** | **25.0** |

## Chapter 24 – Free cash flow to the firm (FCFF) – walk-through

| | | |
|---|---|---|
| Add: financial / non-operating assets | | |
| Cash & cash equivalents | 7.2 | |
| Non-operating assets | 32.6 | |
| Less: financial / non-operating liabilities | | |
| Debt | (70.7) | |
| Non-controlling interests | (50.5) | |
| **Equity value** | **249.2** | |
| Number of outstanding shares (m) | 9.9 | |
| **Implied share price (USD)** | **25.17** | |
| **Weighted average cost of capital calculation** | | |
| Risk-free rate | 4.0% | |
| Credit risk premium | 2.0% | |
| **Cost of debt (pre-tax)** | **6.0%** | |
| Marginal tax rate | 25.0% | |
| **Cost of debt (post-tax)** | **4.5%** | |
| Risk-free rate | 4.0% | |
| Equity risk premium | 6.0% | |
| Adjusted beta | 0.80 | |
| **Cost of equity** | **8.8%** | |
| Debt / Enterprise value | 20.0% | |
| Equity / Enterprise value | 80.0% | |
| **Weighted average cost of capital** | **7.94%** | |
| **Terminal value calculation** | | |
| Free cash flow to firm – Year 10 | 25.0 | |
| Terminal growth rate | 2.0% | |
| **Free cash flow to firm – Year 11** | **25.5** | |
| Weighted average cost of capital | 7.94% | |
| Terminal growth rate | 2.0% | |
| **Terminal value as at Time 10** | **428.7** | |

| | | | | | | | | | | |
|---|---|---|---|---|---|---|---|---|---|---|
| Terminal value using a TGR of 2.0% | | | | | | | | | | 428.7 |
| Discount factors using a WACC of 7.94% | 0.93 | 0.86 | 0.80 | 0.74 | 0.68 | 0.63 | 0.59 | 0.54 | 0.50 | 0.47 |
| Present value of visible period | 130.9 | 40% | | | | | | | | |
| Present value of terminal period | 199.7 | 60% | | | | | | | | |
| Enterprise value | 330.6 | | | | | | | | | |

# CHAPTER 25

# Free cash flow to the firm (FCFF) – food for thought

## Bite size

In this chapter, we revisit the key elements of cash, risk and growth, as well as the bridge and our overall valuation, and address a number of more complex issues.

## Practitioner focus

In practice, producing forecasts that are reasonable and consistent is difficult. Therefore, good analysts will build sense checks into their models to ensure they are achieving these aims. Also, valuation is based on the future, which is highly uncertain. So, we do not want models that are carved in stone but ones that are highly flexible and allow us to ask and answer questions, such as what happens to my valuation if the future looks different from what we are most expecting.

## Core content

### 1. Cash, risk and growth

#### 1.1 Sense checks

We have previously mentioned the idea of using asset turnover as a sense check on the consistency of our growth and investment assumptions. We can now demonstrate this using our example from the previous chapter.

## TABLE 25.1. ASSET TURNOVER CALCULATIONS

| Example Corp in USDm (unless stated) | Year 0 | Year 1 | Year 2 | Year 3 | Year 4 | Year 5 | Year 6 | Year 7 | Year 8 | Year 9 | Year 10 |
|---|---|---|---|---|---|---|---|---|---|---|---|
| | Historical | Forecast | Forecast | Forecast | Forecast | Forecast | Forecast | Forecast | Forecast | Forecast | Forecast |
| Sales | 100.0 | 104.7 | 109.3 | 113.8 | 118.1 | 122.2 | 126.2 | 129.8 | 133.2 | 136.3 | 139.0 |
| Opening non-current assets | | 60.0 | 63.0 | 65.9 | 68.8 | 71.7 | 74.4 | 77.1 | 79.6 | 82.0 | 84.2 |
| Add: capex | | 5.1 | 5.1 | 5.2 | 5.2 | 5.2 | 5.2 | 5.1 | 5.1 | 5.0 | 4.9 |
| Less: D&A expenses | | (2.1) | (2.2) | (2.3) | (2.4) | (2.4) | (2.5) | (2.6) | (2.7) | (2.7) | (2.8) |
| Closing non-current assets | 60.0 | 63.0 | 65.9 | 68.8 | 71.7 | 74.4 | 77.1 | 79.6 | 82.0 | 84.2 | 86.3 |
| Inventories | 27.6 | 29.0 | 30.4 | 31.8 | 33.2 | 34.5 | 35.7 | 36.9 | 38.0 | 39.0 | 40.0 |
| Receivables | 32.9 | 34.7 | 36.5 | 38.3 | 40.1 | 41.9 | 43.6 | 45.2 | 46.7 | 48.2 | 49.5 |
| Payables | (19.7) | (20.4) | (21.0) | (21.6) | (22.1) | (22.6) | (23.0) | (23.4) | (23.6) | (23.8) | (24.0) |
| NOWC | 40.8 | 43.4 | 46.0 | 48.6 | 51.2 | 53.8 | 56.3 | 58.7 | 61.1 | 63.4 | 65.5 |
| Net Operating Assets (or Invested Capital) | 100.8 | 106.3 | 111.9 | 117.4 | 122.9 | 128.2 | 133.3 | 138.3 | 143.1 | 147.6 | 151.8 |
| Asset (or capital) turnover | 0.99x | 0.98x | 0.98x | 0.97x | 0.96x | 0.95x | 0.95x | 0.94x | 0.93x | 0.92x | 0.92x |

If non-current assets were $60m at the end of the historical year, we can keep track of the running total by adding capex and deducting depreciation and amortisation (D&A) expenses each year. If we add this to our net operating working capital (NOWC), we have the net operating asset base (or invested capital). If we compare sales to this asset or capital base, we arrive at asset (or capital) turnover, i.e. how many dollars of sales does the company make for each dollar of capital invested in its net operating asset base.

In our example, this is declining slightly over the forecast period. What we want to avoid is the classic 'hockey-stick' profile, where asset turnover grows significantly over time. This would be unrealistically optimistic and would suggest an inconsistency between our sales growth and investment assumptions. This provides a feedback loop – if necessary, we can go back and dial down our sales growth assumptions and/or dial up our investment assumptions until we are satisfied that the resulting asset turnover profile is reasonable.

We can extend this idea of sense checks into returns analysis (Table 25.2).

TABLE 25.2 ROIC CALCULATIONS

| Example Corp in USDm (unless stated) | Year 0 | Year 1 | Year 2 | Year 3 | Year 4 | Year 5 | Year 6 | Year 7 | Year 8 | Year 9 | Year 10 |
|---|---|---|---|---|---|---|---|---|---|---|---|
| | Historical | Forecast | Forecast | Forecast | Forecast | Forecast | Forecast | Forecast | Forecast | Forecast | Forecast |
| NOPAT | 19.8 | 20.8 | 21.9 | 22.9 | 23.9 | 24.9 | 25.9 | 26.8 | 27.6 | 28.4 | 29.2 |
| Net Operating Assets (or Invested Capital) | 100.8 | 106.3 | 111.9 | 117.4 | 122.9 | 128.2 | 133.3 | 138.3 | 143.1 | 147.6 | 151.8 |
| Return on Invested Capital (RoIC) | 19.6% | 19.6% | 19.5% | 19.5% | 19.5% | 19.4% | 19.4% | 19.4% | 19.3% | 19.3% | 19.2% |

If we compare NOPAT with the capital base (i.e. net operating assets), we arrive at RoIC (return on invested capital) or RoNOAs (return on net operating assets), i.e. how many dollars of NOPAT does the company make for each dollar of capital invested in its net operating asset base. In our visible period, this is declining slightly, suggesting a gradual diminishing of returns over time. Again, we want to avoid the 'hockey-stick' profile, where returns grow significantly over time. This provides a broader feedback loop – if necessary, we can go back and dial down any/all of our NOPAT assumptions and/or dial up our investment assumptions until we are satisfied that the resulting returns profile is reasonable.

Before doing this, we might want to interrogate the numbers further by disaggregating (or decomposing) the returns into their component parts (i.e. the classic 'DuPont' analysis):

$$RoIC = \frac{NOPAT}{Net\ operating\ assets} = \frac{EBIT}{Sales} \times (1 - ETR) \times \frac{Sales}{Net\ operating\ assets}$$

## TABLE 25.3 DUPONT ANALYSIS OF ROIC

| Example Corp in USDm (unless stated) | Year 0 | Year 1 | Year 2 | Year 3 | Year 4 | Year 5 | Year 6 | Year 7 | Year 8 | Year 9 | Year 10 |
|---|---|---|---|---|---|---|---|---|---|---|---|
| | Historical | Forecast | Forecast | Forecast | Forecast | Forecast | Forecast | Forecast | Forecast | Forecast | Forecast |
| EBIT | 26.0 | 27.4 | 28.9 | 30.3 | 31.7 | 33.0 | 34.3 | 35.6 | 36.8 | 37.9 | 38.9 |
| Sales | 100.0 | 104.7 | 109.3 | 113.8 | 118.1 | 122.2 | 126.2 | 129.8 | 133.2 | 136.3 | 139.0 |
| EBIT margins | 26.0% | 26.2% | 26.4% | 26.6% | 26.8% | 27.0% | 27.2% | 27.4% | 27.6% | 27.8% | 28.0% |
| Effective tax rates (ETRs) on EBIT | 24.0% | 24.1% | 24.2% | 24.3% | 24.4% | 24.5% | 24.6% | 24.7% | 24.8% | 24.9% | 25.0% |
| Sales | 100.0 | 104.7 | 109.3 | 113.8 | 118.1 | 122.2 | 126.2 | 129.8 | 133.2 | 136.3 | 139.0 |
| Net Operating Assets (or Invested Capital) | 100.8 | 106.3 | 111.9 | 117.4 | 122.9 | 128.2 | 133.3 | 138.3 | 143.1 | 147.6 | 151.8 |
| Asset (or capital) turnover | 0.99x | 0.98x | 0.98x | 0.97x | 0.96x | 0.95x | 0.95x | 0.94x | 0.93x | 0.92x | 0.92x |
| Return on Invested Capital (RoIC) | 19.6% | 19.6% | 19.5% | 19.5% | 19.5% | 19.4% | 19.4% | 19.4% | 19.3% | 19.3% | 19.2% |

In our forecasts, the operating profit margins ($\frac{EBIT}{Sales}$) are increasing over time, as we have assumed that the cash operating expense margins will decline – partly due to economies of scale and partly due to relatively reduced spending on advertising and marketing (see Chapter 24). In isolation, this would drive returns up. This effect will be tempered somewhat by Example Corp's effective tax rates (ETRs) increasing back towards an industry-average level (see Chapter 24), which, in and of itself, would reduce returns.

In this example, the upward impact of earnings before interest and tax (EBIT) margins is also tempered by the slight decrease in asset turnover ratio ($\frac{Sales}{Net\ operating\ assets}$), shaded in Table 25.3. If our forecast returns were getting out of control, the DuPont breakdown would help us to identify why and enable us to correct any errors and inconsistencies in our forecast drivers.

For the sake of good modelling habits, we can then check that these DuPont analysis-based RoIC numbers agree back to the original calculations (in Table 25.2 above), i.e. that they net to zero. This gives us confidence that our breakdown of returns is correct.

## 1.2 Uncertainty and flexibility

Our valuation is based on forecasts, but we do not know what the future sales growth rates and the other cash flow drivers will be. In order to manage these uncertainties, it is useful to build flexibility into our valuations. One way to do this is using scenarios. For example, we can build our best guess as to what we think future sales growth rates will be, our 'base case', and we can then create more optimistic 'upside cases' and more pessimistic 'downside cases'. Even if we do not use formal statistical analysis, it is useful to think of this like a probability distribution, with the most likely outcome in the centre and then less likely outcomes deviating from that central point:

TABLE 25.4 SALES GROWTH SCENARIO ANALYSIS

| Example Corp in USDm (unless stated) | Year 0 | Year 1 | Year 2 | Year 3 | Year 4 | Year 5 | Year 6 | Year 7 | Year 8 | Year 9 | Year 10 |
|---|---|---|---|---|---|---|---|---|---|---|---|
| | *Historical* | *Forecast* | *Forecast* | *Forecast* | *Forecast* | *Forecast* | *Forecast* | *Forecast* | *Forecast* | *Forecast* | *Forecast* |
| *Sales growth rates – upside case* | 5.0% | 4.8% | 4.6% | 4.4% | 4.2% | 4.0% | 3.8% | 3.6% | 3.4% | 3.2% | 3.0% |
| *Sales growth rates – base case* | 5.0% | 4.7% | 4.4% | 4.1% | 3.8% | 3.5% | 3.2% | 2.9% | 2.6% | 2.3% | 2.0% |
| *Sales growth rates – downside case* | 5.0% | 4.6% | 4.2% | 3.8% | 3.4% | 3.0% | 2.6% | 2.2% | 1.8% | 1.4% | 1.0% |
| Sales – upside case | 100.0 | 104.8 | 109.6 | 114.4 | 119.3 | 124.0 | 128.7 | 133.4 | 137.9 | 142.3 | 146.6 |
| Sales – base case | 100.0 | 104.7 | 109.3 | 113.8 | 118.1 | 122.2 | 126.2 | 129.8 | 133.2 | 136.3 | 139.0 |
| Sales – downside case | 100.0 | 104.6 | 109.0 | 113.1 | 117.0 | 120.5 | 123.6 | 126.3 | 128.6 | 130.4 | 131.7 |

So, above we have our original sales growth rate assumptions, as well as higher and lower ones, which then drive different sets of sales forecasts.

All other things being equal, this would also lead to higher and lower implied share prices (Table 25.5).

## TABLE 25.5 IMPLIED SHARE PRICES

| Scenario | $ |
|---|---|
| Upside case | 25.84 |
| **Base case** | **25.38** |
| Downside case | 24.50 |

The same logic could also be applied to all of the other cash flow drivers. It could even be applied to the risk drivers in the weighted average cost of capital (WACC) calculation and the growth drivers in the terminal value calculation, although, in practice, analysts often use a different approach to flex these elements.

The WACC and the terminal growth rate are usually the two inputs to which our valuation is most sensitive. This is problematic, as they are also two of the most uncertain. Analysts often manage this uncertainty by performing sensitivity analysis – what if the WACC and the terminal growth rate are higher or lower than our estimates? Again, even if we do not perform a formal statistical analysis, it is still useful to think of these variations like a probability distribution.

We can analyse these variations one at a time (one-dimensional), as illustrated in Table 25.6.

## TABLE 25.6 SENSITIVITY ANALYSIS – VARYING WACC

| | Implied share price ($) under varying WACC | | | | |
|---|---|---|---|---|---|
| WACC | 8.44% | 8.19% | 7.94% | 7.69% | 7.44% |
| Implied share price | 22.44 | 23.75 | 25.38 | 26.71 | 28.40 |

As the WACC decreases (increases), the implied share price increases (decreases). So, all other things being equal, we can test a range of possible WACCs around our best estimate and see a range of different implied share prices.

## TABLE 25.7 SENSITIVITY ANALYSIS – VARYING TERMINAL GROWTH RATE

| | Implied share price ($) under varying terminal growth rate | | | | |
|---|---|---|---|---|---|
| WACC | 1.0% | 1.5% | 2.0% | 2.5% | 3.0% |
| Implied share price | 22.09 | 23.51 | 25.38 | 27.13 | 29.49 |

Similarly, in Table 25.7 we see that, all other things being equal, as the terminal growth assumption increases (decreases), the implied share price increases (decreases). Once more we are able to test a range of terminal growth rates and see a range of implied share prices.

We can also analyse these variations at the same time (two-dimensional):

TABLE 25.8 SENSITIVITY ANALYSIS – VARYING WACC AND TERMINAL GROWTH RATE

| Implied share price (USD) sensitivity | | | | | |
|---|---|---|---|---|---|
| Terminal growth rate | | | Weighted average cost of capital | | |
| 25.17 | 8.44% | 8.19% | 7.94% | 7.69% | 7.44% |
| 1.0% | 19.90 | 20.96 | 22.09 | 23.31 | 24.63 |
| 1.5% | 21.08 | 22.25 | 23.51 | 24.88 | 26.36 |
| 2.0% | 22.44 | 23.75 | 25.38 | 26.71 | 28.40 |
| 2.5% | 24.03 | 25.51 | 27.13 | 28.90 | 30.86 |
| 3.0% | 25.91 | 27.61 | 29.49 | 31.56 | 33.87 |

As the WACC decreases and the terminal growth rate increases, the implied share price increases. When the sensitivity analysis uses the 'base case' WACC (7.94%) and terminal growth rate (2.0%), we can check that it arrives at our original implied share price ($25.38). So, we can test a range of different WACCs and terminal growth rates at the same time.

This is a quick and easy way of flexing our valuation with regard to these two key but highly uncertain drivers.

## 2. Terminal growth rate

In Chapter 23, we stated that there are two methods for calculating the terminal value – the multiples-based approach and the Gordon Growth model, and we preferred the latter, i.e.:

$$TV = \frac{Next\ FCFF\ forecast}{WACC - Terminal\ growth\ rate}$$

We also noted that in practice valuers often use a long-term GDP growth rate as a proxy for terminal growth rate. However, there is a second approach for calculating the terminal value, which is anchored on a company's own expected fundamentals rather than the expected growth rate of the economy:

*Fundamental growth rate (g) = Reinvestment rate (b) × Incremental RoIC (r)*

This quantifies the growth rate as being the product of the proportion of NOPAT reinvested (i.e. incremental invested capital) and the return generated on that incremental invested capital. So, if our prediction is that in the long term a company will be reinvesting 20% (0.2) of its NOPAT and generating an incremental return of 10% (0.1) on that reinvested NOPAT,[23] then its NOPAT will be growing at 2% (0.02) per year:

$$0.02(2\%) \, (g) = 0.2(20\%) \, (b) \times 0.1(10\%) \, (r)$$

Under a constant reinvestment rate, the company's net reinvestment of NOPAT (which is the sum of investment in net operating working capital and net investment in non-current assets) will also grow at 2%. This translates into 2% growth rate in FCFF, as FCFF is the difference between NOPAT and net reinvestment of NOPAT (see Chapter 23).

TABLE 25.9 ADJUSTED TERMINAL VALUE CALCULATION

| NOPAT – Year 10 | 29.2 | |
| --- | --- | --- |
| Terminal growth rate | 2.0% | g |
| **NOPAT – Year 11** | **29.8** | |
| Terminal RoIC | 10.0% | r |
| Terminal reinvestment rate | 20.0% | b = g/r |
| Terminal payout ratio | 80.0% | |
| **Free cash flow to firm – Year 11** | **23.8** | |
| Weighted average cost of capital | 7.94% | |
| Terminal growth rate | 2.0% | |
| **Terminal value as at Time 10** | **400.9** | |

To predict FCFF for Year 11 instead of starting with FCFF for Year 10 (as we did in Chapter 24), we start with NOPAT for Year 10. We first forecast NOPAT for Year 11 by applying the terminal growth rate ($29.2m × [1 + 0.02] = $29.8m). We can then convert this NOPAT figure into FCFF for Year 11 ($29.8m × 0.8 = $23.8m). Our assumption that in the long term the company will be reinvesting 20% (0.2) of its NOPAT implies that the other 80% (1 - 0.2) will be available to pay out to their lenders and shareholders (i.e. FCFF). We can see that this is lower than the Year 11 FCFF forecast we calculated in Chapter 24 ($25.5m). When we use the Gordon Growth formula to convert this into a terminal value as at Year 10 ($23.8m / [0.0794 - 0.02] = $400.9m), we can see that this is a fair amount lower than

---

23  The law of diminishing returns suggests that return on capital will trend towards cost of capital over the long term. Example Corp has a WACC of 8% and we have assumed the returns in our analysis above continue their gradual decline to a terminal return of 10%. We are assuming they will maintain a differential of 2% – what Warren Buffett would call an 'economic moat'.

the Chapter 24 figure ($429.3m). These differences are driven by different implied/assumed reinvestment rates of NOPAT. In Chapter 24 (Table 24.1) the terminal period's implied reinvestment rate of NOPAT was 14.4% ($4.2m / $29.2*m*), whereas in our above example we assumed a 20% reinvestment rate of NOPAT.

# 3. Bridge

## 3.1 The 3 Cs

We have stated previously that the enterprise value (EV) captures the operational value of the business. More than this, EV is the **continuing**, **core** and **controlled** value of operations (Figure 25.1).

FIGURE 25.1 THE 3 CS

| Continuing | Core | Controlled |
|---|---|---|
| • We only forecast **continuing** activities.<br>• So, we only capture continuing value in the EV.<br>• Therefore, if Example Corp had any non-continuing ('one-off', abnormal, exceptional or non-recurring) assets (liabilities), they would have to have been added (subtracted) separately in the bridge. For the sake of simplicity, we have assumed that Example Corp does not have any but a good example would be a one-off legal claim. | • We only forecast **core** activities.<br>• So, we do not capture any non-core value in the EV. Equity method investments (EMIs) are usually considered non-core.<br>• This is why we added the value of Example Corp's EMIs as a separate item in the bridge ('non-operating assets'). | • We forecast all **controlled** activities.<br>• So, we capture the value of everything that is controlled, whether or not it is owned, in the EV.<br>• This is why we deducted the portion of the value of subsidiaries not owned by Example Corp (i.e. owned by minority shareholders – NCIs) in the bridge.<br>• So, by the time we arrive at equity value it only reflects the value of the subsidiaries actually owned by the parent. |

## 3.2 Bridge waterfall chart

As we saw in Chapter 13, we often display the EV bridge using a waterfall chart, so that we can clearly see the transition from enterprise to equity value (Figure 25.2). The version in Chapter 13 differs a little in terminology and it is useful to be aware of both. So, for example, we can present debt as net debt (debt less surplus cash) or deduct debt and add back cash as we have done in Figure 25.2. Either way we end up with an identical result.

FIGURE 25.2 EV TO EQUITY VALUE BRIDGE – WATERFALL CHART

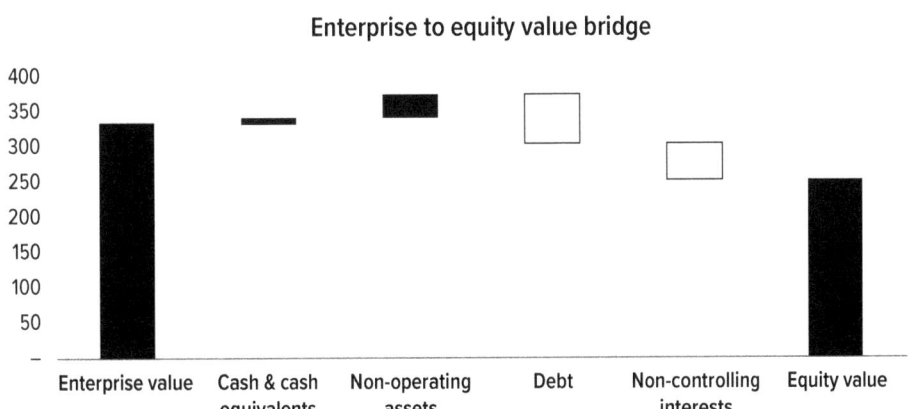

It is easy to see that the key adjustments are the non-operating assets (EMIs), the debt and the NCIs.

## 4. Value versus price

Once we have built the mechanics to compute fundamental share value, it can be a useful exercise to adjust the drivers in our model so that it arrives at the current market price (we can also place this within the context of the 52-week high and low, or even longer). This will help us to understand what the market is currently pricing in, and we can decide whether we agree with these market assumptions or not.

We may, for example, conclude that the market is underestimating the company's future growth potential, so there is a difference between the market price and our fundamental valuation – as Warren Buffett is often quoted as saying, *"Price is what you pay. Value is what you get."* We also have to be careful to understand whether, and if so how (i.e. via what 'catalyst'), the market might come round to our way of thinking – as John Maynard Keynes is quoted as having said, *"The market can stay wrong longer than you can stay liquid."*

So, having arrived at a fundamental share value (and equity value and EV), we can use this to help us decide whether we want to buy, hold or sell this stock, given our fundamental valuation versus the market price.

# Stretch yourself

### Three-stage discounted cash flow (DCF)

Further to our discussion above about alternative approaches to calculating TVs, there is another option for dealing with valuations with large, sensitive and somewhat opaque terminal values. Instead of building a two-stage DCF valuation (with just a visible and a terminal period), it is possible to build a three-stage DCF valuation – with a visible period, a transitional period and then a terminal period (Figure 25.3).

FIGURE 25.3 THREE-STAGE DCF

| Stage 1<br>Visible period | Stage 2<br>Transitional period | Stage 3<br>Terminal period |
|---|---|---|
| • This is the higher growth/higher return period.<br>• During this initial period, the company will usually have a significant competitive advantage. | • During this transitional period, growth and returns will decline, or 'fade'.<br>• In particular, the return on capital will fade towards (possibly even to) the cost of capital.<br>• This might be due to competitors entering the market and eroding the company's growth and returns.<br>• In practice, this can take a very long time (possibly decades), which can be somewhat impractical to model.<br>• This also raises the question of the profile of the fading growth and returns – will it be linear, concave, convex, sinusoidal? | • During this final period, growth and returns will be steady.<br>• (Technically, if return on capital equals cost of capital, growth becomes irrelevant.)<br>• This leaves the terminal period and the terminal value as a much smaller and less significant portion of the overall valuation and makes the valuation more transparent. |

However, three-stage valuation is far less commonly used in practice.

# CHAPTER 26
# Free cash flow to equity (FCFE) – talk-through

## Bite size

In this chapter, we discuss the background to free cash flow to equity (FCFE) and talk through the entire process from start to finish.

## Practitioner focus

If we are equity analysts or investors, not unreasonably, we might occasionally want a complete equity focus. Therefore, even though FCFE breaks the normal rule of keeping operating and non-operating (or financing) elements separate, we might be pragmatic and use it anyway. Additionally, in the case of valuation of financial institutions, the lines between the operating and the financing elements are often blurred and hence FCFE approaches are more common for these business models. Moreover, in some countries (such as Germany) variants of this approach (the so-called *Ertragswertverfahren* in German) are the core technique in certain legal or tax-related valuation settings.

# Core content

## 1. Free cash flow to equity

If we want to go a step beyond dividends **actually** paid to shareholders (see Chapters 21 and 22), we could forecast FCFE. This is the cash flow **available** to pay dividends to shareholders (and to fund share buybacks), as opposed to the dividends actually paid.

In practice, we divide the FCFE calculation into two parts. The first is driven by the elements of the income statement (Table 26.1).

TABLE 26.1 CALCULATION OF NET INCOME

| | |
|---|---|
| 1. Sales | X |
| 2. 'Cash' operating expense (i.e. CoGS and SG&A) | (X) |
| **EBITDA** | **X** |
| 3. D&A expenses | (X) |
| **EBIT** | **X** |
| 4. Interest expenses | (X) |
| **EBT** | **X** |
| 5. Tax expense | (X) |
| **Net income** | **X** |

The second is driven by the elements of the cash flow statement (Table 26.2).

TABLE 26.2 CALCULATION OF NET REINVESTMENT OF NET INCOME

| | |
|---|---|
| 6a. (Increase)/decrease in inventory | (X) / X |
| 6b. (Increase)/decrease in receivables | (X) / X |
| 6c. Increase/(decrease) in payables | X / (X) |
| **(Investment in)/release of net operating working capital (NOWC) (A)** | **(X) / X** |
| 7. Capex | (X) |
| D&A expenses | X |
| **Net investment in non-current assets (B)** | **(X)** |
| **Net reinvestment (A + B)** | **(X)** |

The calculation is completed as shown in Table 26.3.

## Chapter 26 – Free cash flow to equity (FCFE) – talk-through

TABLE 26.3 COMPLETION OF FCFE CALCULATION

| Net income | X |
|---|---|
| Net reinvestment of net income (to grow net operating asset base) | (X) |
| 8. Debt raised/(repaid) | X / (X) |
| FCFE | X |

Thus, we convert the profits that belong to shareholders (net income) into the cash flows that belong to shareholders (FCFE).

Now that we have laid out the elements of our FCFE calculation clearly, we can see the key assumptions that drive our forecasts.

In Chapter 5 we explored some of the key drivers of net income (see Table 26.4).

TABLE 26.4 KEY DRIVERS OF NET INCOME

| Forecast | Forecast driver |
|---|---|
| 1. Sales | Sales growth rates |
| 2. 'Cash' operating expense | Operating expense margins |
| 3. D&A expenses* | D&A margins |
| 4. Interest expenses | Effective interest rates (EIRs) |
| 5. Tax expenses** | Effective tax rates (ETRs) |

\* It may seem wrong to see the non-cash D&A expenses included in a cash-flow calculation. However, we need to tax the profits (EBT) of the business and in the real world the cost of purchasing non-current assets is tax deductible. The tax deduction might be different from the accounting depreciation numbers but these will usually act as a reasonable proxy. However, we must remember that D&A expenses are not actual cash outflows, so we must add them back before completing our calculation as we do in the second part (see Table 26.2).

\*\* Free cash flow to the firm (FCFF) had to remain purely operational and so we had to calculate 'unlevered' taxes, free from the impact of interest expenses. So, we had to calculate new tax expenses based on EBIT, i.e. profits before deducting interest expenses (see Chapter 24). By definition FCFE mixes operating and non-operating (or financing) elements, such as interest expenses. So, we can use the normal 'levered' tax expenses based on EBT, i.e. profits after accounting for interest expenses. If the tax rate $t$ is known, the tax on operations can be calculated by $EBT \times t$.

Thus, we arrive at net income.

Table 26.5 shows what we saw in Chapters 6 and 7.

TABLE 26.5 KEY DRIVERS OF NET REINVESTMENT

| Forecast | Forecast driver |
|---|---|
| **6a/b/c**. Increases/decreases in inventories, receivables and payables* | Inventory, receivable and payable days |
| **7**. Capex** | Capex-to-D&A multiples |
| **8**. Debt raised/(repaid)*** | Debt-to-EBITDA multiples |

\* These drive the net investment in (or release of) NOWC, i.e. how much net income is reinvested into growing the shorter-term NOA base of the business.

\*\* In effect, having already captured the maintenance (or replacement) element (D&A expenses) within net income, we now just deduct the incremental growth (or expansionary) element of capex (the net of total capex and D&A), i.e. how much net income is reinvested into growing the longer-term NOA base.

\*\*\* Debt raised can be used to help fund NOA growth investments, as well as dividends and buybacks. Debt repaid will be a further drain on net income and FCFE.

Thus, we arrive at FCFE available to make payments to shareholders, i.e. dividends and share buybacks.

## 2. Cost of capital

As FCFE only belongs to equity providers, risk is captured using just the cost of equity, which reflects the risks perceived and returns required by these shareholders. The **cost of equity** can be estimated using the Capital Asset Pricing Model (CAPM), as explained in Chapters 9 and 10.

## 3. Growth rate

We forecast out FCFE for a certain number of years, the 'visible' period. In theory, this should last as long as the company has a competitive advantage and until it settles into a more long-term 'steady state'. In practice, analysts will often use a round number, such as five or ten years. The company will continue to generate FCFE and create equity value beyond this visible period and we usually assume that this will continue into perpetuity. We call this the terminal period and the value of all the FCFE generated during this period, as at the beginning of the period, is the terminal value (TV). As the terminal period continues into perpetuity, even modest levels of growth will have a significant impact. This is why the TV is where growth is fundamentally captured in this model.

There are two main ways to approach the calculation of the TV. The first is multiples-based using an earnings multiple, for example:

$$TV = Final\ net\ income\ forecast \times Terminal\ P/E\ multiple$$

This has the advantage of being relatively quick and easy. However, it involves switching from a discounted cash flow (DCF) to a multiples-based approach part way through the valuation, which is an odd thing to do. It also has the disadvantage that the key driver of the TV, i.e. growth, is implicit (it is baked into the terminal P/E multiple – higher means more growth and vice versa) rather than being explicit. It is far better for our key assumptions to be transparent. If this method is used, then the terminal multiple should usually be lower than the equivalent current multiple, as it will reflect the lower-growth assumption of the steady state.

The second approach is to keep to a DCF methodology using a version of the Gordon Growth model:

$$TV = \frac{Next\ FCFE\ forecast}{Cost\ of\ equity - Terminal\ growth\ rate}$$

Where:

$$Next\ FCFE\ forecast = Final\ visible\ FCFE\ forecast \times (1 + Terminal\ growth\ rate)$$

This approach has the advantage that the terminal growth assumption is explicit. This is extremely important as this is one of our, if not our single, most important assumptions and the valuation will be highly sensitive to changes to it. This is problematic as we do not know what the long-term growth rate of the business will be. In practice, we often use a long-term GDP growth rate, as anything higher would imply that the company will eventually achieve world domination.

Once we have captured the three key elements – FCFE, cost of equity capital and growth rate – we can pull these together to arrive at our implied equity value. We are performing a classic two-stage DCF valuation (see Chapter 20 for models with more than two stages). So, we must discount the FCFE forecasts for the visible period (Stage 1) back to their present values using the cost of equity. We must also discount the TV back from the beginning of the terminal period (Stage 2) to its present value, also using the cost of equity (see Figure 26.1).

FIGURE 26.1 THE THREE ELEMENTS OF THE FCFE MODEL

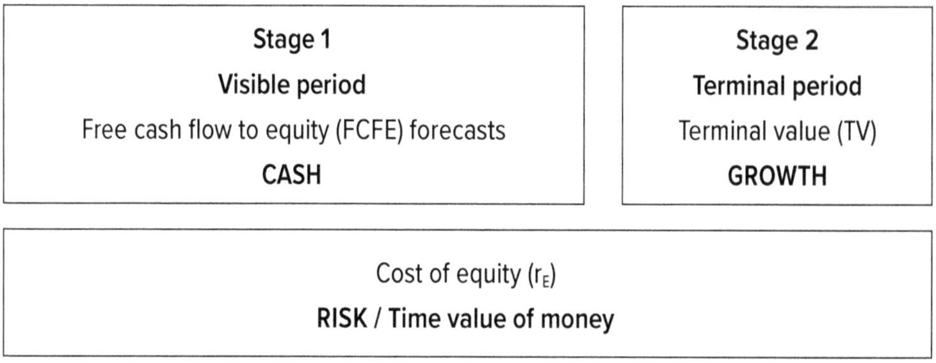

| Stage 1 | Stage 2 |
|---|---|
| Visible period | Terminal period |
| Free cash flow to equity (FCFE) forecasts | Terminal value (TV) |
| CASH | GROWTH |

Cost of equity ($r_E$)

RISK / Time value of money

We thus arrive at the equity value:

$$Equity\ value = PV\ of\ FCFE\ forecasts + PV\ of\ TV$$

Having arrived directly at the equity value, unlike with FCFF we do not need to construct a bridge. However, we must still divide the equity value by the number of outstanding shares. Please see Chapter 23 for further details on how to work out the appropriate measure of the number of shares.

# Stretch yourself

We must maintain consistency between the currency of our FCFE and the currency of our cost of equity (see Chapter 30) in order to ensure that the assumptions 'baked' into both, e.g. inflation expectations, are consistent. So, the risk-free rate will be the yield on government debt of the currency of our FCFE, i.e. if the FCFE is in US dollars, the risk-free rate will be a US Treasury yield. Normally, we will use ten-year government bonds as this is not dissimilar to the average period over which companies raise and refinance their medium-to-long-term debt. Also, ten-year government debt markets are often the most liquid and therefore give the best proxy for the risk-free rate.

## CHAPTER 27

# Free cash flow to equity (FCFE) – walk-through and food for thought

## Bite size

In this chapter, we walk through a numerical example of free cash flow to equity (FCFE) valuation, as set out in the previous chapter. We tackle the cash, risk and growth elements to arrive at an equity value and an implied share price.

## Practitioner focus

Building internally consistent, sensible and defensible valuations is hard. Therefore, it is important that we perform sense checks on our valuations. We discuss this further in the 'Stretch yourself' section at the end of this chapter.

## Core content

### 1. Cash

Below we begin our example of a hypothetical, reasonably mature company to illustrate how our drivers are used to generate forecasts for the components of our FCFE calculations. Historical and forecast data for the company are shown in Table 27.1.

## TABLE 27.1 NET INCOME FORECASTS

| Example AG in EURm (unless stated) | Year 0 | Year 1 | Year 2 | Year 3 | Year 4 | Year 5 | Year 6 | Year 7 | Year 8 | Year 9 | Year 10 |
|---|---|---|---|---|---|---|---|---|---|---|---|
| | *Historical* | *Forecast* | *Forecast* | *Forecast* | *Forecast* | *Forecast* | *Forecast* | *Forecast* | *Forecast* | *Forecast* | *Forecast* |
| **Free cash flow to equity forecasts** | | | | | | | | | | | |
| Sales | 1,000.0 | 1,037.5 | 1,073.8 | 1,108.7 | 1,142.0 | 1,173.4 | 1,202.7 | 1,229.8 | 1,254.4 | 1,276.3 | 1,295.5 |
| Sales growth rates | 4.00% | 3.75% | 3.50% | 3.25% | 3.00% | 2.75% | 2.50% | 2.25% | 2.00% | 1.75% | 1.50% |
| Cash operating expenses (CoGS and SG&A) | (780.0) | (811.3) | (841.9) | (871.4) | (899.9) | (927.0) | (952.5) | (976.4) | (998.5) | (1,018.5) | (1,036.4) |
| Cash operating expense margins | 78.0% | 78.2% | 78.4% | 78.6% | 78.8% | 79.0% | 79.2% | 79.4% | 79.6% | 79.8% | 80.0% |
| **EBITDA** | **220.0** | **226.2** | **231.9** | **237.3** | **242.1** | **246.4** | **250.2** | **253.3** | **255.9** | **257.8** | **259.1** |
| Depreciation and amortisation expenses | (30.0) | (31.1) | (32.2) | (33.3) | (34.3) | (35.2) | (36.1) | (36.9) | (37.6) | (38.3) | (38.9) |
| D&A as a % of Sales | 3.0% | 3.0% | 3.0% | 3.0% | 3.0% | 3.0% | 3.0% | 3.0% | 3.0% | 3.0% | 3.0% |
| **EBIT** | **190.0** | **195.1** | **199.7** | **204.0** | **207.8** | **211.2** | **214.1** | **216.4** | **218.3** | **219.5** | **220.2** |
| Interest expenses | (30.3) | (30.7) | (31.1) | (31.4) | (31.6) | (31.7) | (31.7) | (31.7) | (31.6) | (31.4) | (31.1) |
| Effective interest rates (EIRs) on Debt | 5.50% | 5.45% | 5.40% | 5.35% | 5.30% | 5.25% | 5.20% | 5.15% | 5.10% | 5.05% | 5.00% |
| **EBT** | **159.8** | **164.4** | **168.7** | **172.6** | **176.3** | **179.5** | **182.3** | **184.7** | **186.7** | **188.1** | **189.1** |
| Tax expenses | (46.4) | (47.9) | (49.3) | (50.6) | (51.9) | (53.0) | (54.0) | (54.9) | (55.6) | (56.3) | (56.7) |
| Effective tax rates (ETRs) on EBT | 29.0% | 29.1% | 29.2% | 29.3% | 29.4% | 29.5% | 29.6% | 29.7% | 29.8% | 29.9% | 30.0% |
| **Net income** | **273.2** | **280.9** | **288.1** | **294.7** | **300.7** | **306.1** | **310.7** | **314.6** | **317.8** | **320.1** | **321.6** |

**Sales growth rates**. The company has historical sales of €1,000m, which have grown 4% from the previous year. This is already a relatively mature company and we believe that they will not be able to maintain this growth rate. So, we have assumed that the sales growth rate will gradually decline to a more sustainable long-term rate of 1.5% over the visible period. In the absence of a more sophisticated approach, we have assumed a simple linear decline over time.

**Cash operating expense margins**. The company has historical cash opex of €780m (for the purposes of simplicity we have aggregated cost of goods sold (CoGS) and selling, general and administrative (SG&A) expenses), giving a cash opex margin of 78%. We have assumed that as sales growth declines, the company might spend a relatively higher proportion of its income on expenses like advertising and marketing to defend its market share. So, we have assumed that the cost base will increase slightly relative to sales over the visible period to 80%. Again, we have assumed a simple linear increase over time.

**Depreciation and amortisation (D&A) as a % of sales**. Our historical and sector analysis has shown that D&A expenses consume a reasonably stable 3% of sales income over time. We have no reason to believe that this will change significantly in the future and so we have maintained this level throughout our visible period.

**Effective interest rates (EIRs) on debt**. Analysis of Example AG's historical financial statements (including notes) suggests that the company suffers an interest rate of approximately 5.5% on its bank loans. We have assumed that the company will slightly de-lever over time (see below) and so will suffer a slightly lower credit spread and overall interest rate. We have assumed that this will reduce to 5% over the visible period.

**Effective tax rates (ETRs) on EBT**. Our analysis of mature companies in the same sector and tax jurisdiction shows that they suffer a fairly stable ETR of 30%. Example AG's ETR has been slightly lower than this as it has engaged in some complicated tax structuring. Over time, we expect the benefit of this to diminish and so we expect their ETR to gradually return to the more normal level of 30%.

So, we can see the net income we expect the company to generate.

## TABLE 27.2 NET INVESTMENT IN NET OPERATING WORKING CAPITAL (NOWC) FORECASTS

| Example AG in EURm (unless stated) | Year 0 | Year 0 | Year 1 | Year 2 | Year 3 | Year 4 | Year 5 | Year 6 | Year 7 | Year 8 | Year 9 | Year 10 |
|---|---|---|---|---|---|---|---|---|---|---|---|---|
| | Historical | Historical | Forecast | Forecast | Forecast | Forecast | Forecast | Forecast | Forecast | Forecast | Forecast | Forecast |
| (Incr) / decr in inventories | | | (13.9) | (13.6) | (13.3) | (13.0) | (12.6) | (12.2) | (11.6) | (11.0) | (10.3) | (9.6) | (8.7) |
| Inventories | 296.0 | 309.9 | 323.4 | 336.7 | 349.8 | 362.4 | 374.6 | 386.2 | 397.3 | 407.6 | 417.2 | 425.9 |
| Inventory days | | 145.0 days | 145.5 days | 146.0 days | 146.5 days | 147.0 days | 147.5 days | 148.0 days | 148.5 days | 149.0 days | 149.5 days | 150.0 days |
| (Incr) / decr in receivables | | | (10.4) | (10.2) | (10.0) | (9.7) | (9.4) | (9.1) | (8.7) | (8.2) | (7.7) | (7.1) | (6.5) |
| Receivables | 222.5 | 232.9 | 243.0 | 253.0 | 262.7 | 272.2 | 281.3 | 290.0 | 298.2 | 305.9 | 313.0 | 319.4 |
| Receivables days | | 85.0 days | 85.5 days | 86.0 days | 86.5 days | 87.0 days | 87.5 days | 88.0 days | 88.5 days | 89.0 days | 89.5 days | 90.0 days |
| Incr / (decr) in payables | | | 8.6 | 8.3 | 8.0 | 7.6 | 7.2 | 6.7 | 6.2 | 5.7 | 5.1 | 4.4 | 3.7 |
| Payables | 226.5 | 235.1 | 243.4 | 251.4 | 259.0 | 266.3 | 273.0 | 279.2 | 284.9 | 290.0 | 294.4 | 298.1 |
| Payables days | | 110.0 days | 109.5 days | 109.0 days | 108.5 days | 108.0 days | 107.5 days | 107.0 days | 106.5 days | 106.0 days | 105.5 days | 105.0 days |
| Net investment in NOWC | | | (15.7) | (15.4) | (15.3) | (15.1) | (14.9) | (14.5) | (14.1) | (13.6) | (13.0) | (12.3) | (11.5) |

**Inventory days**. Example AG's management guidance suggests they have been holding slightly too little inventory. The company expects its inventory levels and holding periods to increase slightly over time, and we have followed this guidance. We have used the inventory days (and CoGS) forecasts to project year-end inventory. We have then compared this with the previous year-end's inventory to calculate the increase or decrease over the year and its cash flow impact. In this case, the relative increase in inventories is cash-flow negative.

**Receivables days**. Our historical and cross-sector analysis shows that the company has traditionally been slightly less generous with its customer collection periods than its competitors. As its sales growth declines, the company plans to defend its position by addressing this issue. So, we are assuming that receivables days will increase slightly over the visible period. As before, we have used the receivables days (and sales) forecasts to project year-end receivables. We have then compared this with the previous year-end's receivables to calculate the increase or decrease over the year and the cash flow impact. The increasing credit periods will be cash-flow negative for the company.

**Payables days.** Again, historical and cross-sector analysis shows that the company has traditionally demanded slightly more generous credit periods from suppliers than its competitors. Management is slightly concerned that this may damage some of their supplier relationships and reduce their access to key supplies. To reduce this risk, they plan to gradually reduce their supplier payment periods over time. As before, we have used the payables days (and CoGS) forecasts to project year-end payables. We have then compared this with the previous year-end's payables to calculate the increase or decrease over the year and the cash flow impact. All other things being equal, the decreasing credit periods would be cash-flow negative. However, in this case, the growth of CoGS overpowers this and the overall cash flow impact is actually positive.

The net of the changes in inventory, receivables and payables shows us overall how much net income the company will have to reinvest to grow its shorter-term NOWC base.

## TABLE 27.3 COMPLETION OF FCFE FORECASTS

| Example AG in EURm (unless stated) | Year 0 | Year 0 | Year 1 | Year 2 | Year 3 | Year 4 | Year 5 | Year 6 | Year 7 | Year 8 | Year 9 | Year 10 |
|---|---|---|---|---|---|---|---|---|---|---|---|---|
|  | Historical | Historical | Forecast | Forecast | Forecast | Forecast | Forecast | Forecast | Forecast | Forecast | Forecast | Forecast |
| Capex |  | (60.0) | (59.4) | (58.6) | (57.5) | (56.2) | (54.6) | (52.7) | (50.5) | (48.2) | (45.6) | (42.8) |
| *Capex-to-D&A mutliples* |  | *2.00x* | *1.91x* | *1.82x* | *1.73x* | *1.64x* | *1.55x* | *1.46x* | *1.37x* | *1.28x* | *1.19x* | *1.10x* |
| Depreciation and amortisation expenses |  | 30.0 | 31.1 | 32.2 | 33.3 | 34.3 | 35.2 | 36.1 | 36.9 | 37.6 | 38.3 | 38.9 |
| Net investment in non-current assets |  | (30.0) | (28.3) | (26.4) | (24.3) | (21.9) | (19.4) | (16.6) | (13.7) | (10.5) | (7.3) | (3.9) |
| Net reinvestment of net income |  | (45.7) | (43.7) | (41.7) | (39.4) | (36.8) | (33.9) | (30.7) | (27.2) | (23.5) | (19.5) | (15.3) |
| Debt raised / (repaid) |  |  | 11.0 | 13.2 | 12.0 | 10.8 | 9.5 | 8.1 | 6.7 | 5.2 | 3.7 | 2.1 | 0.5 |
| Debt | 539.0 |  | 550.0 | 563.2 | 575.2 | 586.0 | 595.6 | 603.7 | 610.4 | 615.6 | 619.3 | 621.3 | 621.8 |
| *Debt-to-EBITDA mutliples* |  |  | *2.50x* | *2.49x* | *2.48x* | *2.47x* | *2.46x* | *2.45x* | *2.44x* | *2.43x* | *2.42x* | *2.41x* | *2.40x* |
| Free cash flow to equity |  |  | 238.5 | 250.3 | 258.4 | 266.1 | 273.5 | 280.3 | 286.7 | 292.6 | 297.9 | 302.6 | 306.7 |

**Capex-to-D&A multiples**. Historically, to take some advantage of growth opportunities and achieve relatively higher growth rates, the company has had capex-to-D&A multiples greater than 1.0x, reflecting a need for maintenance and some expansionary capex. As the company's expected rate of growth declines over the visible period, we expect the need for expansionary capex to decline and so the capex-to-D&A multiples can reduce. However, they should remain a little above 1.0x, as we are still forecasting some growth in Year 10 and beyond and so we still need some growth capex.

So, we can see the level of gross capex and net investment in the company's non-current asset base and the net reinvestment of net income in net operating assets overall.

**Debt-to-EBITDA multiples**. Example AG has a debt-to-EBITDA (earnings before interest, taxes, depreciation and amortisation) multiple of 2.5x. Management guidance with regards to their financing strategy is that as they continue to mature, they plan to de-lever slightly, relatively speaking. They are aiming for a debt-to-EBITDA multiple of 2.4x, which we have accepted as reasonable and achievable. As with NOWC, we have used the debt-to-EBITDA forecasts to project year-end debt levels and have then backed out the increase/decrease and the cash flow impact. All other things being equal, the decreasing debt-to-EBITDA multiples would be cash-flow negative for the company. However, in this case, the growth of EBITDA overpowers this, and the overall cash flow impact is actually positive. Although this declines to a negligible level over the visible period.

This then brings us to our FCFE forecasts.

# 2. Risk

TABLE 27.4 COST OF EQUITY CALCULATION

| Risk-free rate | 3.0% |
|---|---|
| Equity risk premium | 5.5% |
| Adjusted beta | 0.90 |
| **Cost of equity** | **7.95%** |

As the FCFE forecasts are in euros, we have used a euro risk-free rate. As at time of writing, the yield on benchmark ten-year German government bunds is about 3% (0.03).

After consulting a variety of sources using both historical analysis and implied market studies, we arrive at a sensible equity risk premium for developed European markets of about 5.5% (0.055). In conjunction with the risk-free rate, this implies a compound annual return on developed European equities of about 8.5% (0.03 + 0.055 = 0.085) on average. This acts as a good sanity check on our calculation. If this total seems reasonable, we can proceed. If not, we may need to adjust our assumptions.

Example AG is not involved in a particularly high-risk activity and so we would expect a beta of less than 1. Again, after consulting a variety of sources using two-year/weekly and five-year/monthly regressions and using narrower and broader market indices, we have settled on an adjusted beta of 0.90. Using the Capital Asset Pricing Model (CAPM), we arrive at a risk premium of 4.95% (0.055 × 0.90 = 0.0495), and an overall cost of equity of 7.95% (0.03 + 0.0495 = 0.0795).

# 3. Growth

TABLE 27.5 FCFE YEAR 11 CALCULATION

| Free cash flow to equity – Year 10 | 306.7 |
|---|---|
| Terminal growth rate | 1.5% |
| **Free cash flow to equity – Year 11** | **311.3** |

We have already forecast FCFE for Year 10 (€306.7m). In line with our top-line sales growth rates trending down to 1.5% by the end of the visible period, we have assumed that the business will continue at this growth rate on average throughout the terminal period. This is definitely no greater than a sensible long-term GDP growth rate assumption and so this company is certainly not going to achieve world domination. We can therefore estimate FCFE for Year 11 to be €311.3m (€306.7m × [1 + 0.015]).

TABLE 27.6 TERMINAL VALUE CALCULATION

| Free cash flow to equity – Year 10 | 306.7 |
|---|---|
| Terminal growth rate | 1.5% |
| **Free cash flow to equity – Year 11** | **311.3** |
| Cost of equity | 7.95% |
| Terminal growth rate | 1.5% |
| **Terminal value as at Year 10** | **4,826.7** |

We can then feed this information into the Gordon Growth model, to arrive at:

$$TV_{Year\ 10} = \frac{€311.3m}{(0.0795 - 0.015)} = €4{,}826.7m$$

## 4. Pulling the elements together

### TABLE 27.7 CALCULATION OF EQUITY VALUE AND SHARE PRICE

| Example Corp in USDm (unless stated) | Year 0 | Year 1 | Year 2 | Year 3 | Year 4 | Year 5 | Year 6 | Year 7 | Year 8 | Year 9 | Year 10 |
|---|---|---|---|---|---|---|---|---|---|---|---|
| | Historical | Forecast | Forecast | Forecast | Forecast | Forecast | Forecast | Forecast | Forecast | Forecast | Forecast |
| Free cash flow to equity | | 250.3 | 258.4 | 266.1 | 273.5 | 280.3 | 286.7 | 292.6 | 297.9 | 302.6 | 306.7 |
| Terminal value using a TGR of 1.5% | | | | | | | | | | | 4,826.7 |
| Discount factors using a Ke* of 7.95% | | 0.93 | 0.86 | 0.79 | 0.74 | 0.68 | 0.63 | 0.59 | 0.54 | 0.50 | 0.47 |
| Present value of visible period | 1,866.6 | 45% | | | | | | | | | |
| Present value of terminal period | 2,246.1 | 55% | | | | | | | | | |
| Equity value | 4,112.7 | | | | | | | | | | |
| Number of outstanding shares (m) | 82.0 | | | | | | | | | | |
| Implied share price (EUR) | 50.15 | | | | | | | | | | |

\* Note that here we use 'Ke' for cost of equity whereas in most of the book we use '$r_e$'. Both are acceptable, widely used and mean the same thing. It is useful for readers to be aware of both versions as you may come across this in other readings on valuation.

We already have the cash element in the form of the FCFE forecasts for Years 1 to 10.

In practice, we often convert the risk element (the cost of equity) into discount factors. So, in order to discount the future cash flows back to their present values instead of dividing by $(1 + r)^t$ we will multiply by $\frac{1}{(1+r)^t}$. This allows us to see the impact of the time value of money: €1 received at the end of Year 1 is only worth €0.93 at Year 0 and €1 received at the end of Year 10 is only worth €0.47 at Year 0.

For the sake of simplicity, and as is often done in practice, we have assumed that the cash flows arise at the end of each year and our valuation date is the beginning of Year 1 (or the end of year Year 0).

If we multiply each of the future FCFEs by its corresponding discount factor and sum all ten products, we arrive at the present value of the visible period (Stage 1) cash flows:

$$PV_{Visible\ period} = \sum_{t=1}^{10} FCFE_t \times \frac{1}{(1+r)^t} = €1{,}866.6m$$

We already have the growth element in the form of the TV as at Year 10. It is as though we are planning to buy the entire equity in Year 0, own it for the next ten years (pocketing the FCFE it generates) and then sell it at the end of Year 10. The TV is our best guess as to what value we will be able to sell the equity for at the end of Year 10. It therefore still needs to be multiplied by its corresponding discount factor to discount it back to its present value at Year 0. Thus, we arrive at the present value of the terminal period (Stage 2) cash flows:

$$PV_{Terminal\ period} = TV_{Year\ 10} \times \frac{1}{(1+r)^{10}} = €4{,}826.7m \times 0.47 = €2{,}246.1m$$

We then simply add the present values of Stage 1 and Stage 2 to arrive at:

$$Equity\ value = PV_{Visible\ period} + PV_{Terminal\ period} = €1{,}866.6m + €2{,}246.1m = €4{,}112.7m$$

At this point it is a good idea to calculate the proportions of the equity value coming from each stage. In this case we have a 45/55 split. This weighting towards the terminal period is not uncommon as eternity is a long time. The problem would have been exacerbated if we had chosen a shorter visible period (e.g. five years) and could be improved if we chose a longer forecast period (e.g. 15 or 20 years or more). We are also more likely to obtain this kind of split if the business is already fairly mature and there is not a significant growth differential between the visible and terminal periods.

**Number of outstanding shares** – the company has 100m shares in issue but has bought back and holds 18.0m as treasury stock, giving an outstanding share count of 82m (100m – 18m).

Thus, we finally arrive at an implied share price of €50.15 (€4,112.7m / 82m).

## 5. Sense checks

As a sense check on our FCFE forecasts, we can perform a similar returns analysis to that which we did for free cash flow to the firm (FCFF) in Chapter 25 but here it makes more sense to use return on equity (ROE).

TABLE 27.8 CALCULATION OF NET OPERATING ASSET BASE

| Example AG in EURm (unless stated) | Year 0 | Year 1 | Year 2 | Year 3 | Year 4 | Year 5 | Year 6 | Year 7 | Year 8 | Year 9 | Year 10 |
|---|---|---|---|---|---|---|---|---|---|---|---|
| | *Historical* | Forecast | Forecast | Forecast | Forecast | Forecast | Forecast | Forecast | Forecast | Forecast | Forecast |
| Opening non-current assets | | 700.0 | 728.3 | 754.7 | 779.0 | 800.9 | 820.3 | 836.9 | 850.6 | 861.1 | 868.4 |
| Add: capex | | 59.4 | 58.6 | 57.5 | 56.2 | 54.6 | 52.7 | 50.5 | 48.2 | 45.6 | 42.8 |
| Less: D&A expenses | | (31.1) | (32.2) | (33.3) | (34.3) | (35.2) | (36.1) | (36.9) | (37.6) | (38.3) | (38.9) |
| Closing non-current assets | *700.0* | 728.3 | 754.7 | 779.0 | 800.9 | 820.3 | 836.9 | 850.6 | 861.1 | 868.4 | 872.3 |
| Inventories | *309.9* | 323.4 | 336.7 | 349.8 | 362.4 | 374.6 | 386.2 | 397.3 | 407.6 | 417.2 | 425.9 |
| Receivables | *232.9* | 243.0 | 253.0 | 262.7 | 272.2 | 281.3 | 290.0 | 298.2 | 305.9 | 313.0 | 319.4 |
| Payables | *(235.1)* | (243.4) | (251.4) | (259.0) | (266.3) | (273.0) | (279.2) | (284.9) | (290.0) | (294.4) | (298.1) |
| NOWC | *307.7* | 323.1 | 338.3 | 353.5 | 368.3 | 382.9 | 397.0 | 410.5 | 423.5 | 435.7 | 447.2 |
| Net operating assets | *1,007.7* | 1,051.4 | 1,093.1 | 1,132.5 | 1,169.3 | 1,203.2 | 1,233.9 | 1,261.1 | 1,284.6 | 1,304.1 | 1,319.5 |

If non-current assets were €700m at the end of the historical year, we can keep track of the running total by adding capex and deducting D&A expenses each year. If we add this to our NOWC, we have the net operating asset (NOA) base.

## TABLE 27.9 CALCULATION OF EQUITY AND ROE

| Example AG in EURm (unless stated) | Year 0 | Year 1 | Year 2 | Year 3 | Year 4 | Year 5 | Year 6 | Year 7 | Year 8 | Year 9 | Year 10 |
|---|---|---|---|---|---|---|---|---|---|---|---|
| | Historical | Forecast | Forecast | Forecast | Forecast | Forecast | Forecast | Forecast | Forecast | Forecast | Forecast |
| Net income | 273.2 | 280.9 | 288.1 | 294.7 | 300.7 | 306.1 | 310.7 | 314.6 | 317.8 | 320.1 | 321.6 |
| Net operating assets | 1,007.7 | 1,051.4 | 1,093.1 | 1,132.5 | 1,169.3 | 1,203.2 | 1,233.9 | 1,261.1 | 1,284.6 | 1,304.1 | 1,319.5 |
| Debt | (550.0) | (563.2) | (575.2) | (586.0) | (595.6) | (603.7) | (610.4) | (615.6) | (619.3) | (621.3) | (621.8) |
| Equity | 457.7 | 488.2 | 517.9 | 546.5 | 573.7 | 599.5 | 623.5 | 645.5 | 665.3 | 682.8 | 697.6 |
| Return on Equity (RoE) | 59.7% | 57.5% | 55.6% | 53.9% | 52.4% | 51.1% | 49.8% | 48.7% | 47.8% | 46.9% | 46.1% |

The company's NOA base is funded with debt and equity. If we know the NOAs and the debt, we can then calculate the equity. This is a rather rough-and-ready calculation but in the absence of a complete three-statement model, it is probably the best we can do.

If we compare the net income to the equity, we arrive at ROE, i.e. how many euros of net income does the company make for each euro of equity capital invested. In our example the numbers are quite high, starting near 60%. This is because accounting balance sheets do not capture a lot of modern assets (e.g. internally generated intangible assets, like human capital and brands). Therefore, NOAs (and equity) are understated and ROE is overstated. As a sense check, we are less interested in the quantum of ROE and more interested in its profile.

In our visible period, this is declining, suggesting diminishing returns over time. Again, we want to avoid the 'hockey-stick' profile, where returns grow significantly over time. This provides a broad feedback loop – if necessary, we can go back and dial down any/all of our net income assumptions and/or dial up our investment assumptions and/or dial down our debt assumptions until we are satisfied that the resulting returns profile is reasonable.

Before doing this, we might want to interrogate the numbers further by disaggregating (or decomposing) the returns into their component parts (i.e. the classic 'DuPont' analysis):

## TABLE 27.10 DUPONT ANALYSIS OF ROE

| Example AG in EURm (unless stated) | Year 0 | Year 1 | Year 2 | Year 3 | Year 4 | Year 5 | Year 6 | Year 7 | Year 8 | Year 9 | Year 10 |
|---|---|---|---|---|---|---|---|---|---|---|---|
|  | Historical | Forecast | Forecast | Forecast | Forecast | Forecast | Forecast | Forecast | Forecast | Forecast | Forecast |
| Net income | 273.2 | 280.9 | 288.1 | 294.7 | 300.7 | 306.1 | 310.7 | 314.6 | 317.8 | 320.1 | 321.6 |
| Sales | 1,000.0 | 1,037.5 | 1,073.8 | 1,108.7 | 1,142.0 | 1,173.4 | 1,202.7 | 1,229.8 | 1,254.4 | 1,276.3 | 1,295.5 |
| Net margins | 27.3% | 27.1% | 26.8% | 26.6% | 26.3% | 26.1% | 25.8% | 25.6% | 25.3% | 25.1% | 24.8% |
| Sales | 1,000.0 | 1,037.5 | 1,073.8 | 1,108.7 | 1,142.0 | 1,173.4 | 1,202.7 | 1,229.8 | 1,254.4 | 1,276.3 | 1,295.5 |
| Net operating assets | 1,007.7 | 1,051.4 | 1,093.1 | 1,132.5 | 1,169.3 | 1,203.2 | 1,233.9 | 1,261.1 | 1,284.6 | 1,304.1 | 1,319.5 |
| Asset turnover | 0.99x | 0.99x | 0.98x | 0.98x | 0.98x | 0.98x | 0.97x | 0.98x | 0.98x | 0.98x | 0.98x |
| Net operating assets | 1,007.7 | 1,051.4 | 1,093.1 | 1,132.5 | 1,169.3 | 1,203.2 | 1,233.9 | 1,261.1 | 1,284.6 | 1,304.1 | 1,319.5 |
| Equity | 457.7 | 488.2 | 517.9 | 546.5 | 573.7 | 599.5 | 623.5 | 645.5 | 665.3 | 682.8 | 697.6 |
| Equity (leverage) multiplier | 2.20x | 2.15x | 2.11x | 2.07x | 2.04x | 2.01x | 1.98x | 1.95x | 1.93x | 1.91x | 1.89x |
| Return on Equity (RoE) | 59.7% | 57.5% | 55.6% | 53.9% | 52.4% | 51.1% | 49.8% | 48.7% | 47.8% | 46.9% | 46.1% |

In our forecasts, the net margins are decreasing over time, as we have assumed that the cash opex margins will increase – partly due to relatively increased spending on advertising and marketing. In isolation, this would drive returns down. This effect could be tempered somewhat by Example AG's EIRs declining slightly but will be exacerbated by their ETRs increasing back towards a more normal level.

In this example, the asset turnover is very stable over time, so it is not impacting our forecast returns up or down.

The key difference between the RoIC (return on invested capital) and return on equity (ROE) disaggregation is the equity (or leverage) multiplier (RoIC is debt/equity agnostic, ROE is not). This is just another way of measuring the level of debt in the capital structure. If the company has a high NOA base and relatively low equity, then it must have relatively high debt. In line with the debt-to-EBITDA assumptions in our FCFE forecasts, these multiples are decreasing over time. This relatively lower level of debt (i.e. relatively higher equity), along with the declining net margins, is helping to pull down the forecast ROEs.

If our forecast returns were getting out of control, this breakdown would help us to identify why and enable us to correct any errors and inconsistencies in our forecast drivers.

Finally, for the sake of completeness, we can multiply through the elements as follows:

$$\frac{Net\ income}{Sales} \times \frac{Sales}{NOAs} \times \frac{NOAs}{Equity} = \frac{Net\ income}{Equity} = ROE$$

Sales in the denominator cancel with sales in the numerator, NOAs in the denominator cancel with NOAs in the numerator and we arrive back at $\frac{Net\ income}{Equity}$, i.e. ROE. For the sake of good modelling habits, we can then check that these ROE numbers agree back to the original calculations (in Table 27.9), i.e. that they net to zero. This gives us confidence that our breakdown of returns is correct.

# Stretch yourself

As with our FCFF valuation, we need to manage the uncertainty in our FCFE valuation, and we need to build in flexibility in order to achieve this. So, if we wanted, as we did in Chapter 25, we could build different scenarios (upside/base/downside cases) for our FCFE drivers and perform sensitivity analysis on our cost of equity and terminal growth rate assumptions, in order to flex our model.

# Appendix

## TABLE 27.11 THE ENTIRE FCFE DCF VALUATION

| Example AG in EURm (unless stated) | Year 0 Historical | Year 0 Historical | Year 1 Forecast | Year 2 Forecast | Year 3 Forecast | Year 4 Forecast | Year 5 Forecast | Year 6 Forecast | Year 7 Forecast | Year 8 Forecast | Year 9 Forecast | Year 10 Forecast |
|---|---|---|---|---|---|---|---|---|---|---|---|---|
| Free cash flow to equity forecasts | | | | | | | | | | | | |
| Sales | | 1,000.0 | 1,037.5 | 1,073.8 | 1,108.7 | 1,142.0 | 1,173.4 | 1,202.7 | 1,229.8 | 1,254.4 | 1,276.3 | 1,295.5 |
| Sales growth rates | | 4.00% | 3.75% | 3.50% | 3.25% | 3.00% | 2.75% | 2.50% | 2.25% | 2.00% | 1.75% | 1.50% |
| Cash operating expenses (CoGS and SG&A) | | (780.0) | (811.3) | (841.9) | (871.4) | (899.9) | (927.0) | (952.5) | (976.4) | (998.5) | (1,018.5) | (1,036.4) |
| Cash operating expense margins | | 78.0% | 78.2% | 78.4% | 78.6% | 78.8% | 79.0% | 79.2% | 79.4% | 79.6% | 79.8% | 80.0% |
| **EBITDA** | | **220.0** | **226.2** | **231.9** | **237.3** | **242.1** | **246.4** | **250.2** | **253.3** | **255.9** | **257.8** | **259.1** |
| Depreciation and amortisation expenses | | (30.0) | (31.1) | (32.2) | (33.3) | (34.3) | (35.2) | (36.1) | (36.9) | (37.6) | (38.3) | (38.9) |
| D&A as a % of Sales | | 3.0% | 3.0% | 3.0% | 3.0% | 3.0% | 3.0% | 3.0% | 3.0% | 3.0% | 3.0% | 3.0% |
| **EBIT** | | **190.0** | **195.1** | **199.7** | **204.0** | **207.8** | **211.2** | **214.1** | **216.4** | **218.3** | **219.5** | **220.2** |
| Interest expenses | | (30.3) | (30.7) | (31.1) | (31.4) | (31.6) | (31.7) | (31.7) | (31.7) | (31.6) | (31.4) | (31.1) |
| Effective interest rates (EIRs) on Debt | | 5.50% | 5.45% | 5.40% | 5.35% | 5.30% | 5.25% | 5.20% | 5.15% | 5.10% | 5.05% | 5.00% |
| **EBT** | | **159.8** | **164.4** | **168.7** | **172.6** | **176.3** | **179.5** | **182.3** | **184.7** | **186.7** | **188.1** | **189.1** |
| Tax expenses | | (46.4) | (47.9) | (49.3) | (50.6) | (51.9) | (53.0) | (54.0) | (54.9) | (55.6) | (56.3) | (56.7) |
| Effective tax rates (ETRs) on EBT | | 29.0% | 29.1% | 29.2% | 29.3% | 29.4% | 29.5% | 29.6% | 29.7% | 29.8% | 29.9% | 30.0% |
| **Net income** | | **273.2** | **280.9** | **288.1** | **294.7** | **300.7** | **306.1** | **310.7** | **314.6** | **317.8** | **320.1** | **321.6** |
| (Incr) / decr in inventories | | | (13.6) | (13.3) | (13.0) | (12.6) | (12.2) | (11.6) | (11.0) | (10.3) | (9.6) | (8.7) |
| Inventories | 296.0 | 309.9 | 323.4 | 336.7 | 349.8 | 362.4 | 374.6 | 386.2 | 397.3 | 407.6 | 417.2 | 425.9 |
| Inventory days | | 145.0 days | 145.5 days | 146.0 days | 146.5 days | 147.0 days | 147.5 days | 148.0 days | 148.5 days | 149.0 days | 149.5 days | 150.0 days |
| (Incr) / decr in receivables | | | (10.2) | (10.0) | (9.7) | (9.4) | (9.1) | (8.7) | (8.2) | (7.7) | (7.1) | (6.5) |
| Receivables | 222.5 | 232.9 | 243.0 | 253.0 | 262.7 | 272.2 | 281.3 | 290.0 | 298.2 | 305.9 | 313.0 | 319.4 |
| Receivables days | | 85.0 days | 85.5 days | 86.0 days | 86.5 days | 87.0 days | 87.5 days | 88.0 days | 88.5 days | 89.0 days | 89.5 days | 90.0 days |
| Incr / (decr) in payables | | | 8.3 | 8.0 | 7.6 | 7.2 | 6.7 | 6.2 | 5.7 | 5.1 | 4.4 | 3.7 |
| Payables | 226.5 | 235.1 | 243.4 | 251.4 | 259.0 | 266.3 | 273.0 | 279.2 | 284.9 | 290.0 | 294.4 | 298.1 |
| Payables days | | 110.0 days | 109.5 days | 109.0 days | 108.5 days | 108.0 days | 107.5 days | 107.0 days | 106.5 days | 106.0 days | 105.5 days | 105.0 days |
| **Net investment in NOWC** | | | **(15.4)** | **(15.3)** | **(15.1)** | **(14.9)** | **(14.5)** | **(14.1)** | **(13.6)** | **(13.0)** | **(12.3)** | **(11.5)** |

## Chapter 27 – Free cash flow to equity (FCFE) – walk-through and food for thought

| | | Y1 | Y2 | Y3 | Y4 | Y5 | Y6 | Y7 | Y8 | Y9 | Y10 | Y11 |
|---|---|---|---|---|---|---|---|---|---|---|---|---|
| Capex | | (60.0) | (59.4) | (58.6) | (57.5) | (56.2) | (54.6) | (52.7) | (50.5) | (48.2) | (45.6) | (42.8) |
| Capex-to-D&A multiples | | 2.00x | 1.91x | 1.82x | 1.73x | 1.64x | 1.55x | 1.46x | 1.37x | 1.28x | 1.19x | 1.10x |
| Depreciation and amortisation expenses | | 30.0 | 31.1 | 32.2 | 33.3 | 34.3 | 35.2 | 36.1 | 36.9 | 37.6 | 38.3 | 38.9 |
| Net investment in non-current assets | | (30.0) | (28.3) | (26.4) | (24.3) | (21.9) | (19.4) | (16.6) | (13.7) | (10.5) | (7.3) | (3.9) |
| Net reinvestment of net income | | (45.7) | (43.7) | (41.7) | (39.4) | (36.8) | (33.9) | (30.7) | (27.2) | (23.5) | (19.5) | (15.3) |
| Debt raised / (repaid) | | 11.0 | 13.2 | 12.0 | 10.8 | 9.5 | 8.1 | 6.7 | 5.2 | 3.7 | 2.1 | 0.5 |
| Debt | 539.0 | 550.0 | 563.2 | 575.2 | 586.0 | 595.6 | 603.7 | 610.4 | 615.6 | 619.3 | 621.3 | 621.8 |
| Debt-to-EBITDA multiples | | 2.50x | 2.49x | 2.48x | 2.47x | 2.46x | 2.45x | 2.44x | 2.43x | 2.42x | 2.41x | 2.40x |
| **Free cash flow to equity** | | 238.5 | 250.3 | 258.4 | 266.1 | 273.5 | 280.3 | 286.7 | 292.6 | 297.9 | 302.6 | 306.7 |
| Terminal value using a TGR of 1.5% | | | | | | | | | | | | 4,826.7 |
| Discount factors using a Ke* of 7.95% | | 0.93 | 0.86 | 0.79 | 0.74 | 0.68 | 0.63 | 0.59 | 0.54 | 0.50 | 0.47 | |
| Present value of visible period | 1,856.6 | 45% | | | | | | | | | | |
| Present value of terminal period | 2,246.1 | 55% | | | | | | | | | | |
| **Equity value** | **4,112.7** | | | | | | | | | | | |
| Number of outstanding shares (m) | 82.0 | | | | | | | | | | | |
| **Implied share price (EUR)** | **50.15** | | | | | | | | | | | |

### Cost of equity calculation

| | |
|---|---|
| Risk-free rate | 3.0% |
| Equity risk premium | 5.5% |
| Adjusted beta | 0.90 |
| **Cost of equity** | **7.95%** |

### Terminal value calculation

| | |
|---|---|
| Free cash flow to equity – Year 10 | 306.7 |
| Terminal growth rate | 1.5% |
| Free cash flow to equity – Year 11 | 311.3 |
| Cost of equity | 7.95% |
| Terminal growth rate | 1.5% |
| **Terminal value as at Time 10** | **4,826.7** |

\* Note that here we use 'Ke' for cost of equity whereas in most of the book we use 'r$_e$'. Both are acceptable, widely used and mean the same thing. It is useful for readers to be aware of both versions as you may come across this in other readings on valuation.

# SECTION G
# Accounting-Based Models

# CHAPTER 28

# The logic of residual income

## Bite size

Residual income (RI) measures the amount of 'abnormal' economic value (or economic value added) that a company generates for its shareholders in a given period. It is the difference between the actual net income (earnings) reported by a company under accounting standards, and a 'notional' amount of earnings that are needed to cover the opportunity cost of equity capital, used by the company to generate this net income. In simpler terms, it is accounting profit less a charge for equity capital. RI is often referred to by different names, such as abnormal earnings, residual earnings, economic profit, or economic value added.

## Practitioner focus

The concept of RI has a long history, and its early applications can be traced to the early 20th century, when General Motors and General Electric used it to measure their performance. In the late 1990s, accounting academics developed and popularised an equity valuation model that is explicitly based on the notion of RI.[24] Since then, there has been an explosion of academic research on value-relevance of RI or accuracy of RI-based valuation. And despite ample research evidence that RI and the Residual Income Valuation (RIV) model have better value-relevance and valuation-accuracy characteristics than, for example, cash flow or dividend-based valuation models, the extent of current usage and reliance on RI and RIV by valuers and analysts remains

---

[24] See: Ohlson, J. A. (1995). Earnings, book values, and dividends in equity valuation. *Contemporary Accounting Research*, 11(2), 661–687; and Feltham, G. A. & Ohlson, J. A. (1995). Valuation and clean surplus accounting for operating and financial activities. *Contemporary Accounting Research*, 11(2), 689–731.

relatively low, with only a handful of investment banks using these in their valuation practice. Despite this relatively rare use in practice, we have found that understanding RI and RIV greatly improves our understanding of multiples, the weaknesses of accounting measures and the importance and relevance of balance sheets.

# Core content

## 1. Why should we consider residual earnings?

In the context of valuation, where the focus is on measuring how much value a company is creating for its shareholders, it is the RI (rather than the reported net income) that tells us directly how much value has been created and added to shareholders. While the reported net income accounts for the cost of debt capital in the form of interest expense charge, it does not account for the implicit cost of equity capital. When a company reports a positive net income, it does not necessarily mean that the company has created an added value for shareholders, whereas a positive RI does mean that the company has created an added value for shareholders. The RI is positive when the company's net income is higher than the opportunity cost of equity capital that the company has deployed to generate this net income. And, conversely, the RI is negative when the company's net income is less than the amount needed to cover the cost of equity capital.

The following is the general formula of RI:

$$RI_t = NI_t - r_E \times BVE_{t-1} \qquad (1)$$

Where $RI_t$ is the RI for *year t*, $NI_t$ is the net income for *year t*, $BVE_{t-1}$ is the book value of equity at the end of *year t–1* (which is the same as book value of equity at the beginning of *year t*), and $r_E$ is the cost of equity capital.

Consider the following simple examples:

## Example 1

At the beginning of period a company's book value of equity capital is £20m, and the cost of equity capital (or, in other words, the required rate of return on equity capital, or the opportunity cost of shareholder capital) is 10%. The reported net income for the period is £2.3m. Has this company created or destroyed value for its shareholder in this period?

## Answer:

The opportunity cost of equity capital is 10% × £20m = £2m. This is the 'required' amount of net income that the company must earn for its shareholders to receive a 'fair' or 'normal' return on their equity capital invested in the company. However, the company's actual net income (£2.3m) exceeds the 'required' amount of net income (£2m) by £0.3m. The difference between the actual and the required net income (i.e. £0.3m) represents the additional (or 'anormal', 'residual') economic value that the company has created for the period.

## Example 2

At the beginning of period the company's book value of equity capital is £10m, and the cost of equity capital is 7%. The reported net income for the period is £0.5m. Has this company created or destroyed value for its shareholder?

## Answer:

The company has reported a profit of £0.5m, and this would seem to be good news for shareholders. But is it? Given that the opportunity cost of equity holders' capital is 7%, the company must generate net income of at least £0.7m (i.e. 7% × £10m) for the shareholders to receive a 'fair' return on their invested equity capital. However, the company's actual net income is £0.5m, and it is lower than the 'fair' return of £0.7m. This means that even though the company reports a positive net income, this amount does not fully compensate shareholders for the opportunity cost of equity capital. As a result, in the given period, we have a negative RI of –£0.2m (i.e. £0.5m – £0.7m), and a situation of negative shareholder value creation.

The above examples provide simple illustrations of why company-reported net income is not an adequate measure of shareholder value creation. The problem lies in what the reported net income actually captures, and how it is measured. Companies prepare income statements to show how various elements of income (such as revenues) and expenses (such as cost of sales, interest expense and taxation) culminate in the net income amount, i.e. earnings available to shareholders. Importantly, the net income amount is shown after deducting the interest expense charge for the cost of debt, but it does not deduct the charge for the cost of equity capital. As such, the reported net income amount only shows the 'gross' amount of economic benefit attributable to providers of equity capital, without recognising the economic (or opportunity) cost of that equity capital. It is only after the deduction of the cost of equity capital from this 'gross' amount, that we will be able to see whether the company has created or destroyed value for the providers of equity capital, and we refer to this difference as RI.

## 2. Relevance of RI to equity valuation

Consider two companies, ABC plc and XYZ plc, that are similar in all respects (e.g. same sector, revenues, types and amount of assets, capital structure, cost of capital), and the only point of difference is in the amount of the net income that these companies are expected to announce for the current reporting period. ABC plc is expected to report a higher net income than its cost of equity capital, while XYZ plc is to report a lower net income than the cost of equity capital. This means that, in the current reporting period, ABC plc is expected to generate a positive RI, creating some additional value for its shareholders, while XYZ plc is expected to generate a negative RI, destroying value for its shareholders. If you are considering investing in these companies, and you are a rational investor, will you agree to pay the same price for the stocks of these companies? The answer should be no. You would agree to pay some 'premium' for a stock that is expected to create value (i.e. ABC plc), and you would demand some 'discount' for a stock that is expected to destroy value (i.e. XYZ plc). Thus, rational markets with rational investors will command a higher valuation for ABC's stock compared with XYZ's stock.

In the context of this example, we can also refer to the notion of the premium of equity market value over its book value – usually represented by a ratio of the equity market value to book value of equity, called price-to-book (P/B) multiple (see Chapter 16). In rational markets, we should expect the P/B multiple of ABC's stock to be higher than that of XYZ's. Indeed, Table 28.1 is an illustration of the observed in-practice positive relationship between RI and P/B.

TABLE 28.1 P/B AND FUTURE RI

| Percentile groups | P/B (group mean) Year 0 | Residual income (RI) each year after P/B groups are formed | | | | | |
|---|---|---|---|---|---|---|---|
| | | RI Year 0 | RI Year 1 | RI Year 2 | RI Year 3 | RI Year 4 | RI Year 5 |
| Top 5% with highest P/B | 6.68 | 0.181 | 0.230 | 0.223 | 0.221 | 0.226 | 0.236 |
| 5% with P/B closest to 1 | 0.97 | 0.006 | 0.005 | 0.011 | 0.018 | 0.031 | 0.017 |
| Bottom 5% with lowest P/B | 0.42 | -0.090 | -0.075 | -0.066 | -0.037 | -0.020 | -0.039 |

Excerpted from: Penman, S. (2013). *Financial Statement Analysis and Security Valuation.* McGraw Hill, 5th edition, p.146.

Table 28.1 is based on 30 years of data on US public companies. Here, all companies are allocated into 20 five-percentile groups (portfolios) based on the value of their P/B multiple. Companies in the top (bottom) P/B group are valued at a premium (discount) to book value and they tend to have positive (negative) RI in future years, while companies in the group where P/B is close to 1 (zero premium) have future RIs that are close to zero.

# Stretch yourself

Presented above are the basic notion and computation principles of RI. In practice, several variants and approaches to computation of the RI exist. This is mainly because the net income and book value of equity are accounting numbers that are prepared and reported by companies based on complex accounting standards. Accounting standards, in general, promote conservatism (prudence), permit different accounting treatments, and allow managers a degree of flexibility (discretion) to exercise judgement when making their accounting assumptions and choices. Because of these 'accounting issues', the reported net income and book value numbers can present a somewhat distorted depiction of companies' 'true' economic circumstances. For example, we know that in certain sectors companies engage in extensive research and development (R&D) activities to create and maintain future growth opportunities and value. For these companies, R&D expenditures can be considered as an investment in intangible assets that can generate additional future cash flows. However, IFRS only allow recognition of a part of R&D expenditures as an asset, subject to a set of criteria (for example, see IAS 38 *Intangible Assets*). Thus, particularly in the case of R&D-intensive companies, their reported net assets (book value of equity) typically under-recognise the true value of economic assets in place. Similarly, the accounting standards do not allow companies to treat advertising expenditures as an investment in intangible assets, even though advertising can potentially create stronger brand recognition and increase future cash flows.

Other examples of value-creating assets that are not captured in the company's balance sheet are elements of intellectual capital, such as human capital and internally developed intellectual property. In financial reporting such internally generated intangible assets are not recognised on the balance sheet because they cannot be reliably measured due to the uncertain nature of the associated future benefit. They are omitted from the reported net assets, potentially resulting in a downward biased book value of equity. Because of this, two interesting effects arise.

First, unlike accountants, informed rational investors and analysts will ascribe a 'fair' value to these omitted intangible assets and incorporate their value into the market value of the firm's equity. Thus, *ceteris paribus*, there can be a consistent positive difference between the market value of equity and the book value of equity. Indeed, it is almost always the case that the market value of equity of intangible-intensive companies is significantly greater than their reported book value of equity, which translates into a large value of the price-to-book multiple (P/B) for such companies. For example, at the time of this writing, the P/B multiples of such intangible-intensive companies as Alphabet Inc. and Microsoft Corporation were 5.6x and 10x, respectively. In comparison, in the same period, companies such as ExxonMobil Inc. and Wells Fargo & Co., which mostly rely on tangible or financial assets, had P/B multiples of 2x and 1x, respectively.

The second effect is that the higher the proportion is of a company's unrecognised intangible assets, the higher the company's RI will be. This is because while the beginning of period book value of equity only captures the book value of net assets recognised on the balance sheet, the net income for the given period captures the economic result created by all – i.e. recognised and unrecognised – assets. And, as we can see from formula (1), *ceteris paribus*, a downward biased $BVE_{t-1}$ will result in an upward biased $RI_t$. Interestingly though, this bias does not invalidate the RIV model (introduced in Chapter 29), as long as the net income amount captures the company's comprehensive income. We review the notion of comprehensive income and why it matters in the context of RIV model in the next chapter.

# CHAPTER 29

# Turning residual income into a valuation

## Bite size

The previous chapter explains why residual income can be a better measure of economic value that a company creates for its shareholders in a given year than the reported net income. This implies that the company's intrinsic value should be linked to the amount of residual income that it generates. The Residual Income Valuation (RIV) model is an analytical model that translates residual income forecasts into an intrinsic valuation of the company's equity. This valuation model has many names, with different sources referring to it as residual earnings, abnormal earnings, abnormal income or abnormal profit valuation. Note that, in contrast to much of the textbook, this chapter contains numerous mathematical formulae. However, it is the broad concepts that are important rather than the derivations of these equations.

## Practitioner focus

When it comes to practical application, while the Dividend Discount Model (DDM) can only be used to value companies that (are expected to) pay meaningful dividends, RIV works for any type of company, irrespective of whether they (are expected to) pay dividends or not. This feature is one of RIV's practical advantages. Another practical advantage of RIV is that its inputs are routinely produced by analysts (e.g. earnings forecasts) and are available from companies' reported financial statements (e.g. book value of equity). Finally, the main conceptual advantage of RIV is that it estimates the value of equity by explicitly linking it to future expected residual income – an explicit measure of value creation. Despite these conceptual advantages, RIV is rarely used in practice,[25] and we allude to some of the reasons later in the chapter.

## Core content

The RIV model is an accounting-based 'reformulation' of the classical DDM and, thus, these models are analytically identical. However, for this reformulation to work, a critical assumption of 'clean-surplus accounting' must hold. Under clean-surplus accounting all changes in equity on the balance sheet, except for transactions with shareholders,[26] are entirely attributable to net income. Stated differently, under clean-surplus accounting, the net income is 'comprehensive', in the sense that there are no accounting items that bypass the income statement to appear directly in equity on the balance sheet. This clean-surplus relation can be expressed analytically as follows:

$$BVE_{t+1} = BVE_t + NI_{t+1} - \text{Net dividend}_{t+1} \qquad (1)$$

Where $BVE_t$ is the book value of equity at the end of *year t* (which is same as book value of equity at the beginning of year *t+1*), $BVE_{t+1}$ is the book value of equity at the end of year *t+1*, $NI_{t+1}$ is the net income for year *t+1*, and *Net dividend*$_{t+1}$ is the amount of all distributions to shareholders (e.g. dividends paid, share repurchases) net of all contributions by shareholders (e.g. issuance of additional equity by a company) in year *t+1*. Expression (1) essentially explains how dividends, earnings and book value of equity are linked and, thus, how dividends can be expressed through earnings and changes in book value. By rearranging this expression, we get:

$$\text{Net dividend}_{t+1} = NI_{t+1} + BVE_t - BVE_{t+1}$$

Essentially, we have expressed dividends through key accounting statement items – earnings and book values. We can now substitute this expression of dividends into the classic DDM (see Chapter 22), and rewrite the DDM as follows:

$$V_0^E = \sum_{t=1}^{\infty} \frac{NI_t + BVE_{t-1} - BVE_t}{(1+r_E)^t} \qquad (2)$$

---

25  See: Brown, L. D., Call, A. C., Clement, M. B. & Sharp, N. Y. (2015). Inside the "black box" of sell-side financial analysts. *Journal of Accounting Research*, 53(1), 1–47.
26  For example, changes arising due to contributions by, and distributions to, equity holders, such as issuance of new equity capital and payment of dividends.

Where $V_0^E$ is the intrinsic value of equity at year 0. Essentially, we ended up with an entirely new valuation model that is analytically equivalent to DDM but has no 'dividends' in it! It can be shown that by some further rearrangement of the terms in (2) we can rewrite it as:

$$V_0^E = BVE_0 + \frac{NI_1 - r_E \times BVE_0}{(1+r_E)} + \frac{NI_2 - r_E \times BVE_1}{(1+r_E)^2} + \frac{NI_3 - r_E \times BVE_2}{(1+r_E)^3} + \ldots \quad (3)$$

We call this RIV model. Why? An observant reader will recall that in Chapter 28 we referred to the term '$NI_{t+1} - r_E \times BVE_t$' as residual income ($RI_{t+1}$). And, thus, the numerators in expression (3) are nothing else than all future years' residual earnings. What this model says is that today's intrinsic value of a firm's equity ($V_0^E$) should equal its today's book value of equity ($BVE_0$) plus a 'premium' that accounts for the present value of residual income that the firm is expected to generate for its shareholders in all future years. Hence the name of the model. We can rewrite it in short form:

$$V_0^E = BVE_0 + \sum_{t=1}^{\infty} \frac{RI_t}{(1+r_E)^t} \quad (4)$$

To use this model, the valuer must forecast $RI_t$ and compute the sum of their present values. We can do this by applying a single-stage or two-stage approach to forecasting and discounting future $RI_t$.

Under a two-stage approach, the valuer would use short-term revenue and earnings forecasts to forecast $RI_t$ for a 'visible' short-term period (i.e. up to some year T) and then assume a constant sustainable (long-term) growth rate ($g$) to compute the terminal value of $RI_t$ at the forecast horizon year T:

$$V_0^E = BVE_0 + \sum_{t=1}^{T} \frac{RI_t}{(1+r_E)^t} + \frac{(RI_{T+1})/(r_E - g)}{(1+r_E)^t} \quad (5)$$

Alternatively, if the valuer has reasons to assume that $RI_t$ will grow at a constant long-term growth rate right from the first forecast year, a single-stage discounting (i.e. Gordon Growth model) can be used:

$$V_0^E = BVE_0 + \frac{RI_1}{r_E - g} \quad (6)$$

Let us put this model to a test by considering the following two examples.

# Example 1: RIV under 'unsustainable' growth rate assumptions

Here the valuer makes the following assumptions: the cost of equity capital is 10%; the company will be paying 30% of net income as dividends for all future years (i.e. earnings retention rate is 70%); and the return on equity (ROE) is constant at 20%. The opening book value of equity at the beginning of our forecast year (Year 1) is £100m. Under these assumptions the implied long-term growth rate ($g$) of the company (and, thus, the growth in earnings and book values) can be calculated using the long-term 'sustainable growth rate' formula (see Chapter 21):

$$Long\text{-}term\ g = ROE \times NI\ retention\ rate = 20\% \times 70\% = 14\% \qquad (7)$$

We use this growth rate to forecast net income [$NI_t$] for the next period, then compute the next period's dividends using the assumed above dividend payout rate (30%). We then use the clean-surplus relation (1) to forecast the beginning book value of equity [$BVE_t$] for the next period, and the residual income formula [$NI_{t+1} - r_E \times BVE_t$] to forecast the residual income. By repeating this process over and over, we generate the following model datasheet.

## TABLE 29.1 RESIDUAL INCOME-BASED VALUATION UNDER 'UNSUSTAINABLE' GROWTH RATE ASSUMPTIONS

**Panel 1**: Assumptions

|  | Year 0 | Year 1 | Year 2 | Year 3 | Year 4 | Year 5 | Year 6 | Year 7 | Year 8 | Year 9 | Year 10 |
| --- | --- | --- | --- | --- | --- | --- | --- | --- | --- | --- | --- |
|  | Present | \multicolumn{10}{c}{Forecasts} | | | | | | | | | |
| Earnings retention rate % | 70 | 70 | 70 | 70 | 70 | 70 | 70 | 70 | 70 | 70 | 70 |
| Cost of equity (r) % | 10 | 10 | 10 | 10 | 10 | 10 | 10 | 10 | 10 | 10 | 10 |
| ROE % | 20 | 20 | 20 | 20 | 20 | 20 | 20 | 20 | 20 | 20 | 20 |
| Growth rate (g) % |  | 14 | 14 | 14 | 14 | 14 | 14 | 14 | 14 | 14 | 14 |

**Panel 2**: Valuation @ 14% constant growth rate. All values in £m.

|  | Year 0 | Year 1 | Year 2 | Year 3 | Year 4 | Year 5 | Year 6 | Year 7 | Year 8 | Year 9 | Year 10 |
| --- | --- | --- | --- | --- | --- | --- | --- | --- | --- | --- | --- |
| $BVE_t$ | 100 | 114.0 | 130.0 | 148.2 | 168.9 | 192.5 | 219.5 | 250.2 | 285.3 | 325.2 | 370.7 |
| $NI_t$ |  | 20.0 | 22.8 | 26.0 | 29.6 | 33.8 | 38.5 | 43.9 | 50.0 | 57.1 | 65.0 |
| $RetainedNI_t$ |  | 14.0 | 16.0 | 18.2 | 20.7 | 23.6 | 27.0 | 30.7 | 35.0 | 39.9 | 45.5 |
| $RI_t$ |  | 10.0 | 11.4 | 13.0 | 14.8 | 16.9 | 19.3 | 21.9 | 25.0 | 28.5 | 32.5 |
| PV of $RI_t$ |  | 9.1 | 9.4 | 9.8 | 10.1 | 10.5 | 10.9 | 11.3 | 11.7 | 12.1 | 12.5 |

Valuation:
$BVE_0$ = 100
PV of all RI = infinity!
Equity value = $BVE_0$ + PV of all RI = **100 + infinity** (!)

**Panel 3**: Implied growth rates of line items

|  | Year 0 | Year 1 | Year 2 | Year 3 | Year 4 | Year 5 | Year 6 | Year 7 | Year 8 | Year 9 | Year 10 |
| --- | --- | --- | --- | --- | --- | --- | --- | --- | --- | --- | --- |
| BVE (g) % |  | 14 | 14 | 14 | 14 | 14 | 14 | 14 | 14 | 14 | 14 |
| NI (g) % |  |  | 14 | 14 | 14 | 14 | 14 | 14 | 14 | 14 | 14 |
| Dividend (g) % |  |  | 14 | 14 | 14 | 14 | 14 | 14 | 14 | 14 | 14 |
| RI (g) % |  |  | 14 | 14 | 14 | 14 | 14 | 14 | 14 | 14 | 14 |

We can see that although all our forecasted line items grow at 14% (see Panel 3), this long-term growth rate estimate is not economically viable. No entity can grow forever at a rate that exceeds the long-term growth rate of the (national or global) economy – otherwise the entity will 'overgrow' the economy. And the residual income cannot grow forever at a rate above the cost of equity capital, as we would end up with an infinite present value of this series of residual income. The above example demonstrates what happens if RIV valuation is not anchored on consistent and realistic assumptions. Most importantly, the present value of all forecast residual earnings must converge to a finite number! In reality, residual income does tend to follow a mean-reverting process and declines to long-term economically sustainable levels.[27] In addition, the rate of mean reversion is usually systematically associated with the firm's economic characteristics, and is correlated across firms in the same industry.[28] Let us consider the following, more grounded in economic reality, example.

## Example 2: RIV and 'sensible' growth rate assumptions

Here the valuer forecasts an ROE of 20% for Year 1. He also assumes that, starting from a high earnings growth rate of 14% in Year 1, the growth rate will gradually decline at a rate of 2% per year over the next six years to settle at a long-term economically sustainable constant growth rate of 2% from Year 7 onwards. The cost of equity capital is assumed at 10%, and for the first six years the company will be paying 30% of net income as dividends (i.e. the earnings retention rate is assumed at 70%). From Year 7 onwards, the valuer calibrates the earnings retention rate assumptions to 13.8% and ROE to 14.5% to ensure that they are consistent with the predicted long-term constant growth rate of 2%, in line with the expression (7) above. Following the same steps as in Example 1 above, the valuer generates the model datasheet in Table 29.2.

---

27  See: Dechow, P. M., Hutton, A. P. & Sloan, R. G. (1999). An empirical assessment of the residual income valuation model. *Journal of Accounting and Economics*, 26(1–3), 1–34.
28  Ibid.

## Chapter 29 – Turning residual income into a valuation

### TABLE 29.2 RESIDUAL INCOME-BASED VALUATION UNDER 'SENSIBLE' GROWTH RATE ASSUMPTIONS

| Panel 1: Assumptions | | | | | | | | | | | |
|---|---|---|---|---|---|---|---|---|---|---|---|
| | Year 0 | Year 1 | Year 2 | Year 3 | Year 4 | Year 5 | Year 6 | Year 7 | Year 8 | Year 9 | Year 10 |
| | Present | Forecasts | | | | | | | | | |
| Earnings retention rate % | 70 | 70 | 70 | 70 | 70 | 70 | 70 | 13.8 | 13.8 | 13.8 | 13.8 |
| Cost of equity (r) % | 10 | 10 | 10 | 10 | 10 | 10 | 10 | 10 | 10 | 10 | 10 |
| ROE % | 20 | 20 | 19 | 18 | 17 | 16 | 15 | 14.5 | 14.5 | 14.5 | 14.5 |
| Growth rate (g) % | | 14 | 12 | 10 | 8 | 6 | 4 | 2 | 2 | 2 | 2 |

Panel 2: Valuation (growth rate is gradually reduced from 14% to a GDP-consistent constant long-term rate of 2% by Year 7). All values in £m.

| | Year 0 | Year 1 | Year 2 | Year 3 | Year 4 | Year 5 | Year 6 | Year 7 | Year 8 | Year 9 | Year 10 |
|---|---|---|---|---|---|---|---|---|---|---|---|
| $BVE_t$ | 100 | 114.0 | 129.7 | 146.9 | 165.6 | 185.3 | 205.8 | 210.0 | 214.2 | 218.4 | 222.8 |
| $NI_t$ | | 20.0 | 22.4 | 24.6 | 26.6 | 28.2 | 29.3 | 29.9 | 30.5 | 31.1 | 31.8 |
| $RetainedNI_t$ | | 14.0 | 15.7 | 17.2 | 18.6 | 19.7 | 20.5 | 4.1 | 4.2 | 4.3 | 4.4 |
| $RI_t$ | | 10.0 | 11.0 | 11.7 | 11.9 | 11.7 | 10.8 | 9.3 | 9.5 | 9.7 | 9.9 |
| PV of $RI_t$ | | 9.1 | 9.1 | 8.8 | 8.1 | 7.2 | 6.1 | 4.8 | 4.4 | 4.1 | 3.8 |

Valuation:
$BVE_0$ = 100
PV of RI from Year 1 to Year 6 = 48.4
PV of RI after Year = 33.8
Equity value = $BVE_0$ + PV of all RI = 100 + 48.4 + 33.8 = £182.2m

| Panel 3: Implied growth rates of line items | | | | | | | | | | | |
|---|---|---|---|---|---|---|---|---|---|---|---|
| | Year 0 | Year 1 | Year 2 | Year 3 | Year 4 | Year 5 | Year 6 | Year 7 | Year 8 | Year 9 | Year 10 |
| BVE (g) % | | 14 | 14 | 13 | 13 | 12 | 11 | 2 | 2 | 2 | 2 |
| NI (g) % | | | 12 | 10 | 8 | 6 | 4 | 2 | 2 | 2 | 2 |
| Dividend (g) % | | | 12 | 10 | 8 | 6 | 4 | (8) | 2 | 2 | 2 |
| RI (g) % | | | 10 | 6 | 2 | (2) | (7) | (14) | 2 | 2 | 2 |

We can now see that in this scenario we have a pattern of residual income that grows at a sustainable long-term growth rate of 2% from Year 8 onwards. Because the constant growth rate of residual earnings does not start from Year 1, we should use expression (5) – i.e. a two-stage approach – to discount the residual income. We first compute the sum of the present values of residual income for Years 1 through 6, and then the present value of the growing perpetuity of residual income from Year 7. As can be seen in Panel 2 of Table 29.2, this gives us an equity value estimate of £182.2m, i.e.:

$$V_0^E = BVE_0 + \sum_{t=1}^{6} \frac{RI_t}{(1+r_E)^6} + \frac{(RI_7)/(r_E - g)}{(1+r_E)^6} = 100 + 48.4 + 33.8 = £182.2m$$

And to get to a per-share equity value estimate, we just need to divide this by the number of outstanding shares (see Chapter 23).

## Stretch yourself

Given the analytical equivalence of RIV and DDM, one might wonder whether RIV offers any conceptual and practical advantages over DDM (or Discounted Cash Flow models for that matter). DDM valuation is anchored on dividends, a measure that reflects distribution of value (i.e. the amount of cash distributed to shareholders), whereas RIV draws on residual income, a measure of economic value created for shareholders. Because the amount of dividends that the company pays to its shareholders in a given period is decided by company management, dividends may or may not be related to the company's underlying economic performance and, thus, the amount of economic value that the company has created in a given period. For example, a company might generate a positive economic value (e.g. report profits) yet management might decide not to pay out dividends or pay dividends out of line with the underlying economic performance. And vice versa, the company may underperform and create a negative economic value (e.g. report losses) yet management might decide to pay out dividends (e.g. by increasing borrowing). Thus, DDM is not based on an explicit recognition and capitalisation of future economic values that are expected to be created for shareholders, but rather on values that are expected to be 'distributed' to shareholders in the form of dividends. In contrast, RIV is explicitly anchored on the recognition of (additional) economic value the company is expected to create in all future years.

Indeed, several studies find that RIV predicts and explains stock prices better than DDM and cash flow-based models.[29] RIV is also the only model that enables the value of intangible assets, which are omitted from the balance sheet, to be ascertained from the income statement (i.e. the reported earnings) and reflected in valuation through

---

29  See: Penman, S. H. & Sougiannis, T. (1998). A comparison of dividend, cash flow, and earnings approaches to equity valuation. *Contemporary Accounting Research*, 15(3), 343–383; and: Francis, J., Olsson, P. & Oswald, D. R. (2000). Comparing the accuracy and explainability of dividend, free cash flow, and abnormal earnings equity value estimates. *Journal of Accounting Research*, 38(1), 45–70.

their capture in the residual income term of the model.[30] As compared with FCFF or FCFE models (where the terminal value component would typically account for much of the computed value), in RIV the forecasting problem is somehow reduced as a substantial part of the future expected performance is already 'captured' in the current book value. However, this reduction of terminal value forecast dependence is thwarted by an increased dependence on accounting quality of book value and earnings measurement. This is one of the reasons why RIV does not feature among the models commonly used by analysts. It is the DCF and multiples-based valuation techniques that are in common use, as valuers usually opt for valuation methods they (and their clients) are most familiar with or deem more dependable.

---

30  By applying a simplified version of RIV to two intangible asset-intensive firms, Microsoft and Dell, Penman (2009) shows that RIV can produce a fairly accurate valuation even when much of the firms' intangible assets are missing in the balance sheet. However, residual income will correctly account for the value created by off-balance-sheet intangibles only if the firm is in steady state (i.e. there is no growth in intangible assets). See: Penman, S. H. (2009). Accounting for intangible assets: There is also an income statement. *Abacus*, 45(3), 358–371.

# SECTION H
Specialist Topics

# CHAPTER 30

# Valuation in an international context – currency issues

## Bite size

Valuation of expected foreign currency cash flows can be performed in two ways: 1) either by discounting the foreign currency cash flows at foreign currency discount rates to obtain a foreign currency value, and then translating this foreign currency value into a home currency value using the spot exchange rate; or 2) by translating the expected foreign currency cash flows into expected home currency cash flows using expected future exchange rate and discounting these translated cash flows at the home currency discount rate. In equilibrium both approaches yield the same result.

## Practitioner focus

For liquid currency markets, it mostly does not matter which approach to follow. For the near-term forecasting horizon there is often enough information available to go either way. For the mid-term forecasting horizon, practitioners often have to work with assumptions about basic economic theories (interest rate parity, International Fisher Effect, etc.) as there are no quoted valuation parameters anymore. For the long-term (terminal value) horizon it is often best to assume a stable environment with fixed exchange rates.

# Core content

## 1. Deriving a home currency value for a company with foreign currency cash flows

If different currencies are involved in a valuation, it is always necessary to do translations. The typical case is a home currency valuation of a company with financial reporting and forecasted cash flows in a foreign currency. Imagine a US-based investor that wants to determine the USD[31] (US dollar) value of a UK-based company with GBP- (Great Britain pounds) denominated cash flows.

There are basically two ways of determining the value of such a foreign company in a discounted cash flow (DCF) setting:

- The first one is to discount the foreign currency cash flows (in this case GBP) with a foreign currency (GBP) discount rate[32] in order to get the foreign currency (GBP) present value. This foreign currency value is then translated into a home currency (USD) present value by using the spot exchange rate between the two currencies.

- The second one is to translate the expected foreign currency (GBP) cash flows into expected home currency (USD) cash flows using expected future exchange rates, and to discount these translated cash flows directly with a home currency (USD) discount rate. The result is here again the home currency (USD) present value.

---

31  In this chapter, unlike other chapters, we have used USD and GBP instead of their respective symbols ('$' and '£') to aid the flow of the text.
32  It should be remembered that a discount rate is linked to a particular region. For example, using the Capital Asset Pricing Model (CAPM) framework, a GBP discount rate would reflect the risk-free rate for sterling.

FIGURE 30.1 TWO DIFFERENT APPROACHES TO VALUE FOREIGN CURRENCY CASH FLOWS

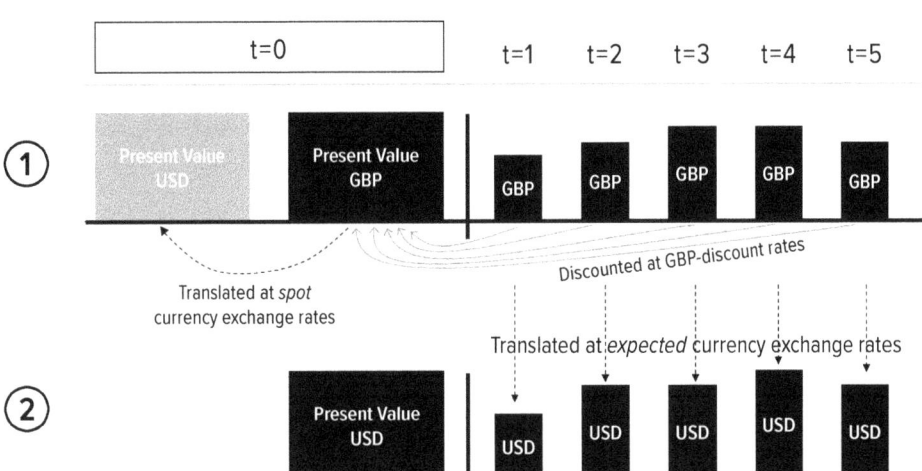

In an environment of economic equilibrium and under perfect information availability, both approaches yield the same result. In reality, this is, however, not always the case.

For the application of such translations, it is necessary to understand how cash flows and discount rates can be translated from one currency to the other. This is explained below.

## 2. Translation of expected cash flows from one currency to the other

The expected cash flow of a UK-based company for next year is assumed 100 GBP. A US investor wants to translate this GBP amount into a USD amount in order to discount this cash flow with the USD discount rate. For this exercise, there are principally three different possibilities:

### Forward rates

The current (spot) exchange rate is assumed to be USD 1.50/GBP, i.e. one gets 150 USD for 100 GBP. The currency futures (a standardised contract to exchange one currency against another one) for delivery in one year is at USD 1.42/GBP.

Using this information, next year's expected cash flow of 100 GBP here translates into 142 USD.

## International Fisher Effect[33]

According to the International Fisher Effect, the expected spot exchange rate in one year equals the current spot exchange rate multiplied by the fraction of (1 + nominal interest rate) in the respective currencies.

Let us once again assume that the current (spot) exchange rate is USD 1.50/GBP. Further assume that the one-year interest rate is 4% for USD and 8% for GBP. Here next year's spot exchange rate should be:

$$USD\ 1.50/GBP \times \left(\frac{1+0.04}{1+0.08}\right) \approx USD\ 1.44/GBP$$

In this case, next year's expected cash flow of 100 GBP here translates into approximately 144 USD.

## Relative Purchasing Power Parity (Relative PPP)

Again, let us assume that the current (spot) exchange rate is USD 1.50/GBP. The expected next year inflation rate for USA is 3% and for UK is 5%. This translates into an expected exchange rate of:

$$USD\ 1.50\ /\ GBP \times \left(\frac{1+0.03}{1+0.05}\right) \approx USD\ 1.47\ /\ GBP$$

Hence, next year's expected cash flow of 100 GBP here translates into approximately 147 USD.

Important comment: in these examples, the different ways of translating expected cash flows from one currency to the other led to different results. This might or might not be the case. In reality – in particular for such liquid currencies as GBP and USD – there are market forces tying the results of these calculations one to each other. For example, under the so-called covered interest rate parity the results from the International Fisher Effect and the forward rates approach should equal each other.

---

[33] The International Fisher Effect is an important economic theory. In essence it holds that exchange rates are driven by nominal interest rate differentials.

Chapter 30 – Valuation in an international context – currency issues

The covered interest rate parity usually holds most of the time between developed currency areas although there are deviations from time to time (e.g. in the aftermath of the global financial crisis of 2008–2009). The relative purchasing power theory is usually a good indicator of long-term exchange rates but not a very good indicator in the short run (the speed of adjustment is often slow).

## 3. Translation of discount rates from one currency to the other

Similar to the translation of expected cash flows there are also certain techniques to translate discount rates from one country to the other. Assuming that there is no country-specific risk to the foreign currency cash flows and that there are no differences in the credit-worthiness of the different countries, one can simply take the foreign currency interest rates to discount the foreign currency cash flows.

If there are differences in risk between the two countries – i.e. if differences in interest rates of the two countries mirror at least partially differences in the credit-worthiness of the two countries (i.e. if real interest rates in both countries are the same), a more generic translation of interest rates is advisable. This translation follows the so-called Fisher equation, which governs the relationship between real and nominal interest rates:

$$(1 + r_{nominal}) = (1 + r_{real}) \times (1 + Inflation)$$

Imagine that the expected inflation rates for the US is 3% and for UK is 5%. The nominal interest rate for USD is 4%. Further assuming that real interest rates are the same for both currencies then – using the ideas of the Fisher equation – we obtain for the nominal GBP interest rate:

$$r_{nominal,GBP} = (1 + r_{nominal,USD}) \times \frac{1 + Inflation_{UK}}{1 + Inflation_{USA}} - 1 = (1 + 0.04) \times \frac{1 + 0.05}{1 + 0.03} - 1 \approx 6\%$$

This generalised version of the Fisher equation states that countries with high rates of inflation should also display higher nominal interest rates than countries with low rates of inflation.

Importantly, this pure focus on inflation differentials does not mean that any potential risk impact on the foreign currency cash flows should be suppressed. It just means that for the translation of interest rates from one currency to the other, one should abstract from any risk differentials. If there is a specific risk to the foreign currency cash flows (e.g. normal risks of doing business or capital structure risk) then it must be considered as a risk factor in both (!) interest rates – i.e. that of the home currency and the foreign currency.

# 4. Valuation of a company with foreign currency cash flows in capital market equilibrium

If everything is in equilibrium in international capital markets, the valuation of foreign currency cash flows is straightforward. For the sake of simplicity below we focus on only one period of expected cash flow. Here a US investor wants to determine the USD-denominated present value of a GBP-denominated expected cash flow.

The following assumptions apply:

The forecasted cash flow of the UK-based company is 100 GBP. The spot exchange rate is USD 1.50/GBP and the quoted one-year futures rate is USD 1.46/GBP. The one-year nominal USD interest rate is 4.04% and the nominal GBP interest rate is 7.1%. The US inflation rate is 2% and the UK inflation rate is 5%.

Let us start with the foreign currency discounting (i.e. discounting the GBP cash flow with a GBP discount rate), followed by the spot exchange rate translation into USD:

$$Value_{GBP,t=0} = \frac{100 \; GBP}{1 + 0.071} = 93.37 \; GBP$$

$$Value_{USD,t=0} = 93.37 \; GBP \times \frac{1.50 \; USD}{GBP} = \mathbf{140.056 \; USD}$$

Assuming that the generalised Fisher equation holds, if we do not know the UK discount rate, we can calculate it based on the US interest rate via the inflation rate differential:

$$r_{nominal,GBP} = (1 + 0.0404) \times \frac{1 + 0.05}{1 + 0.02} - 1 = 7.10\%$$

Now, let us apply the valuation approach of translating expected GBP cash flows first into expected USD cash flows, and then discounting them at the USD discount rate. We use the quoted futures rate here as a proxy for the expected exchange rate (here we assume that the covered interest rate parity holds).

$$E(CF_{USD,t=1}) = E(CF_{GBP,t=1}) \times Forward\_Rate_{USD/GBP} = 100 \times \frac{1.457\ USD}{GBP} = 145.71\ USD$$

$$Value_{USD,t=0} = \frac{145.71\ GBP}{1 + 0.0404} = \mathbf{140.056\ USD}$$

As can be seen, in equilibrium both approaches render the same values.

## 5. Best practice valuation of a company with foreign currency cash flows

In reality, there is not always an equilibrium at capital markets and the theoretical concepts for the interaction of financial parameters (interest rate parity, International Fisher Effect, etc.) do not always hold. Therefore, the following best practice recommendations apply as long as currency markets are liquid:

- For the short-term forecasting horizon use the quoted rates, i.e. futures exchange rates, foreign interest rates, etc. Make sure that the forecast of foreign currency cash flows is based on the local (i.e. foreign) inflation assumptions.

- For the mid-term forecasting horizon it is often necessary to do your own calculations for discount rate translations and exchange rates. This is the case as quoted rates, e.g. future exchange rates, are only available for a certain time period into the future. It is advisable to apply the ideas of the International Fisher Effect and/or the different parities for performing these valuations.

- For the terminal value horizon, it is recommended to neutralise any currency effects. This means that the relevant inflation rates should be set equal for the two currency regimes (e.g. normalised at the home currency level). This assumption is useful in order to bring the company into a steady state in the terminal value horizon. If the valuer thinks that inflation differentials would exist for a longer period of time, then it is advised to extend the visible forecast phase and to enter the terminal value phase at a later point in time (when no more inflation differentials are assumed). As a matter of course, the inflation rates should also equal the inflation assumptions of nominal interest rates. This allows the exchange rates to be kept constant in the terminal value period. It is worth noting that this simplification does not lead to misvaluations as potentially 'wrong' long-term inflation assumptions for the foreign currency cash flows are perfectly evened out by the inflation adjustment in the discount rate.

# Stretch yourself

Valuing a UK-based company from the viewpoint of a US-based investor is easily manageable because of the existence of a more or less liquid currency market and there being enough information to perform the calculations. This is different for currency regimes that do not have quoted exchange rates against the home currency.

In these cases, so-called 'vehicle' currencies – often the USD – are used to calculate cross-exchange rates, e.g. indirect exchange rates between the home currency and the foreign currency using the information on the USD/home currency exchange rate and on the USD/foreign currency exchange rate.

# CHAPTER 31

# Valuation of distressed companies

## Bite size

The valuation of distressed companies differs from normal valuation settings as distressed companies show a different risk profile, have specific challenges of cash flow forecasting and valuation using multiples is difficult. The past is often no longer representative of the future. The valuer needs deep fundamental analysis skills and a good understanding of risk. Working in scenarios becomes mandatory.

## Practitioner focus

Discount rates for distressed companies are higher than for healthy companies for various reasons. Using the Capital Asset Pricing Model (CAPM) framework is only a starting point for deriving required returns. Forecasting cash flows requires a good understanding of the particular distressed situation. A dedicated financial plan that shows how companies can get through the crisis is the basis of cash flow derivation. Additionally, properly forecasting cash flows from financing (including understanding the terms of financing) is also necessary. Due to the low visibility in many distressed situations, a scenario approach is a good way of making uncertainty more transparent.

## Core content

### 1. Risk profiles of companies in crisis

Discount rates for Discounted Cash Flow and Dividend Discount models are determined on a risk-adjusted basis. In order to calculate these discount rates, the risk inherent in the cash flow forecasts has to be analysed properly.

In the context of distressed companies there are a couple of specific aspects to consider when comparing their risk profile with the risk profile of non-distressed companies. Usually, the risk is higher in distressed companies because of company-specific, valuer-specific, technical and asymmetry-related reasons:

- Distressed companies are in a special situation. Management of such companies has to make bold decisions, as longstanding processes in the company – which have proven not to be successful – have to be changed in order to (hopefully) turn the fate of the distressed company to the positive. Moreover, the reactions of stakeholders often change when companies are in crisis: employees might leave the company because they do not see a bright future in their job, suppliers might shy away from continuing doing business with the distressed company as they are scared of not being paid. Customers might be reluctant to continue buying the distressed company's products as they doubt they will receive the required ongoing maintenance services and spare parts if the company runs into insolvency, and so on. And finally, a distressed company is often standing at the crossroads with quite different paths (recovery, ongoing crisis, restructuring, etc.) to choose in the near future.

  A lot is in flux in such a corporate situation. And this means that cash flows are fluctuating heavily, too. The uncertainty of where cash flows will go in the future is usually very high in distressed companies, if only because of the high volatility of the company's future development.

- By nature of such an extraordinary situation, the visibility of cash flow forecasts for distressed companies is low. While a valuer can build on historical cash flow patterns in a stable valuation environment as a starting point for his or her forecasts and can compare the cash flow projections of non-distressed companies with the projections for peers, this is regularly not possible for distressed companies. For these companies, the past is often a bad predictor of the future and companies, which would be seen as peers under normal circumstances, are not at all comparable now because they are in a different, much healthier state. Hence, more uncertainty is added because the valuer has further problems making forecasts for distressed companies.

- From a technical point of view, distressed companies often show a higher degree of risk just because they are running at a low level of performance. For low-performing companies the *relative* changes in cash flows are higher than for normally performing companies – even if the *absolute* changes in cash flows are the same. This is the case as the absolute change is set in relation to a lower basis in the case of distressed companies. Additionally, absolute fluctuations of cash flows are already higher for distressed companies as often the amount of fixed costs (such as rents, salaries, insurance payments, etc.) stay more or less constant (or at least do not change too much). This serves as a booster to the operating leverage – i.e. as an increase in the degree of cash flow reaction to changes in revenues.

Remember: in valuation it is the risk per unit of value, i.e. the relative risk, that matters. Hence, additional uncertainty comes to distressed companies because of pure technical aspects of valuation. Figure 31.1 highlights this last point.

FIGURE 31.1 HIGHER RELATIVE FLUCTUATIONS OF CASH FLOWS IN DISTRESSED COMPANIES

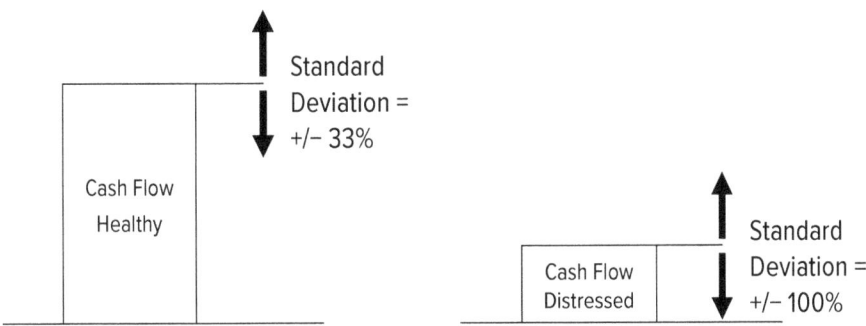

- Distressed companies sometimes run into asymmetric risk situations where going down becomes more likely than going up. There is a tipping point in a crisis situation at which insolvency risks speed up massively. This is the point where stakeholders start to react adversely – customers shying away from buying, employees leaving the firm, suppliers stop delivering – and where each negative reaction reinforces further negative reactions, leading to a vicious cycle.

## 2. Forecasting cash flows of companies in crisis

Along with the higher uncertainty inherent in forecasting cash flows of distressed companies, there are other specificities to the cash-generating process of companies in crisis that should be taken into account.

In contrast to a healthy company, distressed companies are often willing to sacrifice some margin and focus on more liquidity-driven aspects in the short run. This comes along with a different pricing policy (discounts, payment terms), extraordinary asset sales or working capital optimisation measures. Hence, the next one or two periods might be different from what the company plans to do in the mid and long term.

Special attention has to be paid to the cost composition of the company and how this translates lower revenues into an earnings or net cash flow figure. The more the company relies on fixed costs the more negative is a revenue shortfall for earnings (negative-operating leverage). Additionally, the forecasting of cash flows from financing becomes more relevant. Distressed companies often face liquidity and/or financing restrictions so that a simple revolving refinancing of loans or bonds at current terms (i.e. at current interest rates) cannot be assumed.

However, also in the mid-to-long run the structure of cash flows often changes: the composition of revenues is altered, cost-cutting programmes are in place, certain structures of the company are changed, etc. All this is the consequence of necessary adjustments in order to bring the company back to successful levels. For forecasting cash flows this means that not only the amount of cash flow components in the past is non-representative for the future but also the structure and composition of cash flows changes. Often the valuer is facing a totally new forecasting environment.

Moreover, the possibilities of learning from peer group companies and of drawing conclusions from their behaviour regarding the behaviour of the distressed company is limited. In particular, in the short run the performance and path of cash flow generation will differ quite a lot between peers and the distressed company. Even worse, it is not rare for the distressed company to experience losses in the market share, which sometimes leads to the problematic situation where peers gain in the market share, which may result in their development even going in opposite directions. However, there are also some aspects that serve well as a basis for comparison; for example, the general market developments and the demand behaviour of customers that peers are facing are, of course, also still highly relevant for the distressed company.

The lesson here is that valuers cannot use extrapolation techniques to forecast future cash flows of distressed companies. Instead, they often have to set up a new projection with quite different drivers and different compositions of cash flows.

## 3. Limits of valuation techniques

Not only do risk profiles and cash flow forecasting challenges change when valuing distressed companies, but the applicability of valuation techniques also faces new realities.

This particularly relates to valuation approaches using multiples. While DCF techniques are principally valid for the valuation of every company – although their calibration is not easy in every valuation setting – multiples valuation requires the comparability with the target company of either listed companies or companies involved in recent mergers and acquisitions (M&A) transactions. Comparability with other companies is, however, problematic, as has been discussed above. Because distressed companies regularly find themselves in a unique situation, most peers are not good comparables, neither from a risk perspective nor in terms of expected cash flow growth. Only a peer in a similarly precarious situation would qualify as a suitable comparable for multiples valuation of the distressed target company; however, finding such a peer – one that is also not mispriced – is rarely possible.

However, as double-checking the results from a DCF valuation is a good idea also (or particular) in the context of a distressed company valuation, a hybrid valuation approach is advisable. In this approach, the valuer acknowledges that, in the short term, future comparability with other companies is not easily possible but once the company has (hopefully) recovered from the crisis it will turn into a state where it becomes comparable with peers again. Hence, multiples valuation is still possible in the outer years but must be discounted back to the valuation date using a DCF approach and considering short-term future cash flows. In formal terms this means:

$$Value_0 = \sum_{t=1}^{T} \frac{FCF_t}{(1 + r_{Distress})^t} + \frac{Value_T^{Multiples}}{(1 + r_{Distress})^T}$$

Where $FCF_t$ is free cash flow in Year $t$; $r_{Distress}$ is the cost of capital of the distressed company; and $Value_T^{Multiples}$ is the (terminal) value at the end of Year T, derived by using multiples. Here, it is assumed that the company overcomes the crisis situation and returns to normal business performance at the end of Year T.

## 4. Best practice valuation of distressed companies

The valuation of distressed companies requires a fresh perspective on cash flow forecasting and discount rate determination. A valuer can no longer trust the patterns of the past, and must set up a new model, often from scratch, that considers the new realities. A lot of economic thinking is necessary, and simple extrapolation must be given up.

The low visibility that valuers face can be addressed by working with scenarios. What is the probability of ending up in a full recovery? What is the probability of suffering from a prolonged crisis? And what is the probability of going into insolvency (at least such an insolvency scenario should be part of every distressed company valuation)? The valuer must think about the riskiness of the different scenarios and develop a valuation (model) for each scenario. Often the 'doom' scenarios are riskier and require higher discount rates. And in the doom scenarios a valuation using multiples is often not appropriate as it might not be possible to project when, if ever, the company would overcome the crisis and return to normal business performance.

Distressed company valuation also requires a constant recalibration of the model as time passes, because the information environment around distressed companies is usually quite dynamic.

## 5. Simplified practical example

Let us consider a company that is facing challenging times. Two major contracts are up for renewal over the coming two years but at the date of valuation (t = 0) it is unclear whether this renewal will be successful. If not successful, the company might become insolvent. If successful, business will continue as before.

The probabilities of contract renewal are estimated at 60% in Year 1 (first contract) and 80% in Year 2 (second contract). Future cash flows dependent on the different development paths of the company are as shown in Figure 31.2 (numbers in italics indicate the probabilities of the path).

FIGURE 31.2 TEMPORARILY DISTRESSED COMPANY (EXAMPLE)

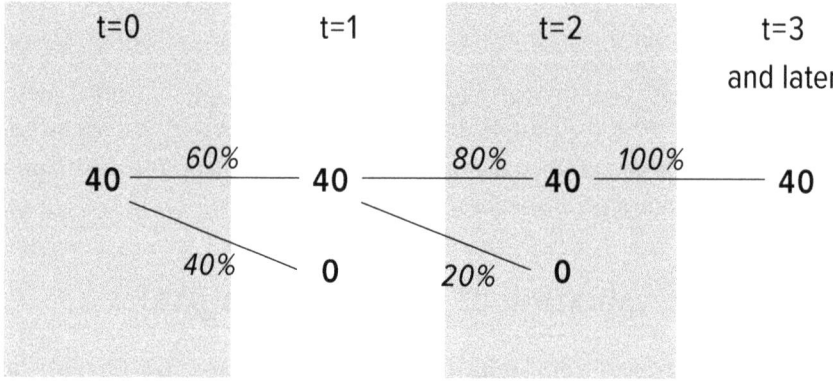

If for reasons of simplicity we do not consider different risks of different paths (i.e. we apply the same discount rate of 10% for every outcome) the value of this temporarily distressed company is determined as follows:

$$Value_0 = \frac{60\% \times 40 + 40\% \times 0}{1.1} + \frac{60\% \times 80\% \times 40 + 60\% \times 20\% \times 0}{1.1^2} + \frac{60\% \times 80\% \times 100\% \times 40}{0.1 \times 1.1^2}$$

$$Value_0 = \frac{24.0}{1.1} + \frac{19.2}{1.1^2} + \frac{19.2}{0.1 \times 1.1^2} = 196.4$$

Here, the expected cash flows are calculated as probability weighted outcomes, i.e. cash flow in Year 1 is 60% probability × 40 plus 40% probability × zero = 24. For the second-year cash flow it is important to take into account that it will only be realised if the company survives the first period and hence the path probabilities of

80% and 20% additionally have to be weighted with the survival probability of period 1 (60%), and so on.

# Stretch yourself

Because of the high path-dependency of the future development of the company – being successful in securing fresh financing increases the confidence of customers, which in turn increases the probability of better financing terms in the future, and so on – the cash flow profile often shows option-like patterns. In such situations sometimes valuation models similar to the ones for financial options (e.g. binomial trees etc.) are used. These models are, however, quite difficult to calibrate.

Sometimes a company has already left the state of distress and has become insolvent. Valuation in a concrete insolvency situation requires that many legal aspects are considered. Additionally, taxation issues become relevant, e.g. the question of whether amassed tax-loss carry-forwards can still be used in the future or not.

# CHAPTER 32
# Integrating ESG factors into valuation

## Bite size

ESG is short for environmental, social, governance. These aspects are often qualitative in nature and require a thorough analysis in order to be translated into quantitative cash flow or risk effects. For valuation purposes, it is important to assess (and quantify in financial terms) the costs, benefits and risk impacts of ESG factors.

## Practitioner focus

There are a huge number of ESG factors. For single valuation cases, however, only a few of them are relevant or material. It is recommended to first isolate the company-specific ESG topics, then to pick relevant ESG factors within these topics, and finally to integrate them into the valuation models.

## Core content

### 1. What does 'ESG integration' mean?

ESG is the abbreviation for environmental, social, governance. In the context of valuation, ESG is covering aspects that relate to the relationship of the company to the environment, its social responsibilities and corporate governance. The term ESG has an informational ('How well are companies doing in terms of ESG?'), but also an ethical ('Being ESG-positive is good!') dimension.

From a valuation point of view, the focus is clearly on the informational dimension. At the very core, a valuer wants to know how a certain corporate behaviour impacts in monetary terms. This requires a rational analysis of the expected future financial benefits, financial costs and risks of the ESG positioning of a company as a first step.

This could, for example, relate to the following:

- A company that plans to install a new, environmentally-friendly waste treatment plant faces immediate costs for the installation but will also benefit from lower ongoing treatment expenses in the future. Furthermore, there is a risk reduction with regard to future fines from environmental authorities or adverse reactions of employees, suppliers or customers to environmental misbehaviour.

- A company that shifts production from countries with low social standards to countries with higher standards may benefit from a stronger supply chain which is easier to control and audit. However, such a move will probably result in higher input costs in the future. However, this move might also lead to a reputation increase and a higher customer acceptance of its products. Here too, risks of adverse stakeholder reactions decrease.

As it might not be clear ex-ante whether a company's ESG activities are value-increasing or value-decreasing, establishing the value impact of the costs, benefits and risk associated with ESG factors, and their appropriate integration into valuation, is the job of the valuer.

## 2. Aspects valuers should look at

The number of potential ESG factors is quite big. For each of the ESG aspects there are several subtopics, and each of the subtopics has several potential ESG factors. Listed below are just a few examples of potential ESG factors:

- Environmental factors: general corporate climate policies, pollution and greenhouse gas emissions, use and preservation of resources, (toxic) waste treatment, animal welfare, product safety.

- Social factors: human rights, diversity, equality, inclusion, employee engagement, health, workplace safety, learning and development, employee satisfaction, degree of supply chain responsibility.

- Governance-related factors: strengths of the supervisory board (diversity, competences, independence), management remuneration, corporate culture, corporate values, financial reporting, general transparency, risk management in general, cyber risk management.

A special focus is necessary for companies that operate in ESG risk areas, such as power utility companies, chemical companies, companies with long and complex supply chains, companies with subsidiaries in low-social-standard countries.

# 3. Typical valuation effects of ESG aspects

Proper integration of ESG factors into valuation is not easy. In most cases, ESG integration differs from the standard cash flow forecasting and risk assessment. This is due to three important factors:

- First, ESG factors often fall within the 'non-financial information' category, i.e. they are qualitative in nature.[34] An increase in gender diversity on company boards (qualitative) is structurally different from a price increase of certain products (quantitative). The qualitative nature of most ESG aspects does not mean that they do not carry any financial (quantitative) consequences. However, their 'conversion' into value drivers and measurable financial effects – from an analytical point of view – is not a straightforward and easy task. Figure 32.1 emphasises this.

FIGURE 32.1 INDIRECT VALUE IMPACT OF ESG ASPECTS

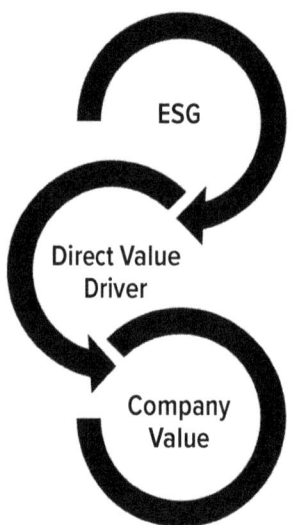

Switch to Sustainable Packaging of Products

Strengthening Diversity within the Company

Higher Customer Acceptance of Products, **Premium Pricing Possible**

Higher Motivation of Employees, **Higher Revenue per Employees**

---

34  Of course, there is also purely quantitative ESG information, such as $CO_2$ emissions. The quantitative nature of $CO_2$ emissions explains its popularity in, e.g. corporate reporting, even by companies that are not heavy $CO_2$ emitters. It is obviously more convenient for companies to report hard numbers.

The top of Figure 32.1 shows typical ESG decisions. These then may be translated into positive effects on the direct value drivers of a company (e.g. premium pricing or higher revenues, in the middle of the figure), but it is not a simple, obvious extrapolation. Once the impact on value drivers is developed, researched and clarified, we can then see the impact at a more detailed level on forecasts and valuation. For example, in this case it translates into a higher company value (indicated by the '+' sign at the bottom of the figure).

- Second, it also often takes longer for the financial and valuation effects of ESG factors to materialise. Building up corporate reputation by establishing a more positive environmental and social profile takes time, and turning an enhanced reputation into higher revenues takes even more time. Increasing the quality of the supervisory board will only gradually feed into a better performance of the company. And there are many more such examples. As a matter of course, for the valuer it is more difficult to forecast financial effects over the mid- to longer-term horizon than over the short-term horizon. In a valuation model, many of the typical ESG aspects are expected only to materialise in the terminal value phase. This requires a very high diligence when setting up ESG-integrated terminal value models.

- Third, several ESG topics do not even impact expected future cash flows, or at least it is extremely difficult to make a sound forecast of such impacts. However, these ESG aspects influence the risk profile of companies by often reducing the expected volatility of future cash flows or even by asymmetrically limiting downside risks. For example, employees might be less likely to leave the company, customers might be less likely to punish the company for bad environmental behaviour, public authorities might be less likely to fine or restrict the company, etc. In particular, a good corporate governance positioning can be seen as a protection against bad performance (similar to a long position in a financial put option). This is shown in Figure 32.2, which highlights that companies with good corporate governance may perform better because a powerful supervisory board reacts early to any bad decisions made by management or because a strong corporate culture leads to employees acting against any first signs of performance weakness. In contrast, for companies with bad corporate governance there is no such limiting barrier in place.

FIGURE 32.2 GOOD CORPORATE GOVERNANCE AS A PUT OPTION

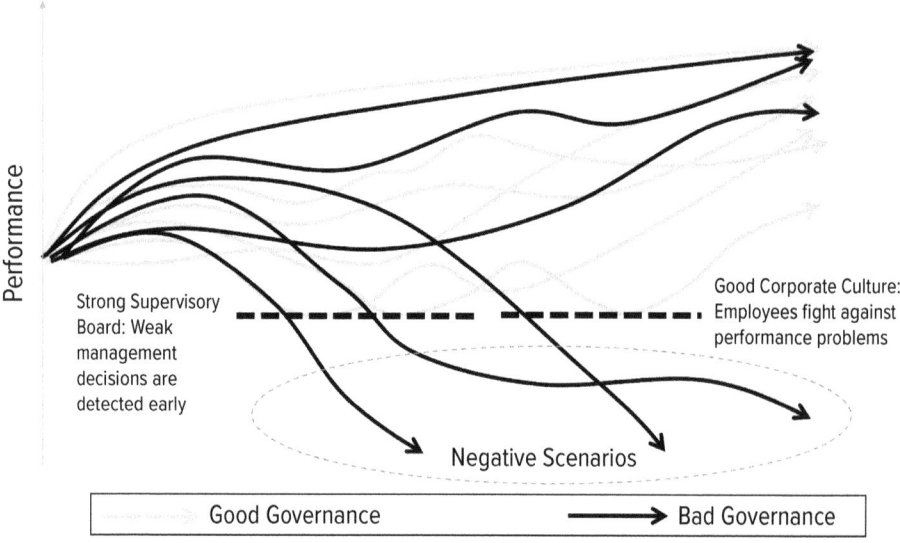

## 4. What is the ethical contribution of ESG to valuation?

From a valuation point of view ESG integration is nothing else than a rational cost/benefit analysis and quantification of ESG factors. However, three important points are worth adding here:

- First, operational exposure to environmental and social topics – e.g. developing products that help to save energy, or services that help to reduce world hunger problems – is a positive aspect as these products and services are expected to meet an increasing demand in the future. This is a positive compared with companies operating in a stable or even shrinking demand environment.

- Second, companies that are ESG-positive, i.e. that take care of the environment and society and that have a well-structured corporate governance, are usually good in risk management and have an attractive risk profile (see discussions above).

- Third, valuation is just one aspect of decision-making. Investors seeking to apply an additional ethical overlay or to contribute to the development of a better world with their investments, may indeed incorporate further ESG criteria into their decision-making process. In recent years, numerous institutional and individual investors have done so, and this can be seen as a very positive development. While it is not our intention to single out specific initiatives, there is a broad consensus that the Sustainable Development Goals (SDG) of the United Nations – a set of

17 objectives deemed a 'shared blueprint for peace and prosperity for people and the planet, now and into the future' – constitute important supplementary criteria for investment decision-making.[35]

## 5. Pitfalls in ESG integration

Integrating ESG factors into valuation has become quite popular. However, this also increases the risk of making mistakes. Valuers should avoid the following typical pitfalls:

- Risk of greenwashing by companies. The term 'greenwashing' describes companies presenting themselves in a more ESG-positive light than they actually are. For valuers the problem is that many of the rather qualitative ESG characteristics of companies are not easy to verify or quantify. Valuers should particularly answer the following questions when determining the greenwashing risk:

    - Is the ESG-picture holistic? E.g. do hotels only save water in the guests' rooms (where it is easy to spot) or also in their other operations?

    - Does research and development (R&D) spending support the ESG outlook of the management? Often the move to become more ESG-positive requires a technological shift.

    - Are there sufficient quantitative disclosures or is the emphasis on narrative disclosures? Companies can try to bring qualitative aspects into a (semi-) quantitative framework to enhance comparability and usefulness. A purely qualitative narrative may sometimes dilute the impact of ESG initiatives.

    - Are companies' explanations clear or rather vague? Expressions like 'recycled', 'supply chain audits' or 'more social than …' are often not very meaningful without further explanations.

    - Is it plausible that companies behave the way they say? Are the ESG plans of the company consistent with the cost structure of the company or the competitive situation in the industry?

- Risk of over-analysing. There is no shortage of ESG aspects and topics. Specialised rating agencies use up to a hundred (sometimes even more) criteria to assess the ESG-scores of companies. However, in terms of materiality only a few of these criteria matter for single companies, and different ones matter for different business models. Most of the criteria have no discernible cash flow or risk impact for specific companies. For valuers it is important to understand what the material criteria for the target company are, analyse these topics, draw conclusions about

---

35   United Nations (2015) The UN Sustainable Development Goals. United Nations, New York.

cash flow and risk impact, and not to waste time by analysing non-relevant aspects. It is, however, well understood that this is not always an easy task.

- Risk of ethical bias. Integrating ESG aspects into valuation requires rational and independent analytical thinking. Due to the ethical nature of many ESG aspects valuers run the risk of losing this independence and of being influenced by their perceptions of 'good' or 'bad'. Not getting distracted by ethical aspects in valuation requires training and discipline by valuers. As already mentioned, there is still room for an ethical overlay after the valuation is finished.

# Stretch yourself

Some companies are in a structural ESG conflict because of their business model. A power utility company that runs coal-fired power plants cannot change its business model within a short time. A company that manufactures and supplies plastic components for the automobile industry cannot switch to other input materials immediately. By nature of their business model such companies are limited in developing a positive ESG positioning. This, however, does not mean that they cannot show at least a partially positive development.

For analytical reasons it is worth differentiating between non-controllable ESG aspects (those relating to the core business model, at least in the short run) and controllable ESG aspects (other topics such as gender equality, waste treatment, corporate governance, etc.). In this context, it should be noted that the controllable ESG aspects are an indicator of the attitude of the management towards ESG in general and towards risk management in particular. Nevertheless, companies with a high degree of non-controllable ESG risk (e.g. companies operating in the oil or coal sector) are a big challenge for valuers as often conflicting performance and risk effects have to be adequately balanced in the valuation model.

# CHAPTER 33

# Valuation of young companies

## Bite size

The valuation of young, innovative (start-up) companies is structurally not much different from the valuation of distressed companies although the valuations take place at totally different states of the corporate life cycle. For young companies there is no past (they simply do not have one) that could be used as a basis for forecasting. Risk profiles are elevated. But opportunities are also high in some cases. Typical modern start-up business models are based on economies of scale, network effects or technological advances.

## Practitioner focus

The biggest challenge of every start-up valuation is the analysis of the business model. Founders nearly always see a huge potential of their business idea but the reality is often different. A powerful tool for valuing start-ups is the Venture Capital Method. This method uses pricing assumptions of a venture capital investor at time of a potential exit as a critical input factor and then discounts this exit value back to the valuation date, considering interim cash flows. The First Chicago Method additionally allows for taking different scenarios into account. Default probabilities help to better calibrate these models.

# Core content

## 1. Risk profiles of young companies

Discount rates for Dividend Discount models or Discounted Cash Flow (DCF) models are determined on a risk-adjusted basis. In order to calculate these discount rates, the risk inherent in the cash flow forecasts has to be analysed properly.

Young companies usually have higher risk-adjusted discount rates as compared to mature companies due to various reasons:

- Visibility is typically very low for innovative companies. And the more innovative these companies are, the less able a valuer is to make sound forecasts. This is due to the nature of innovation: new products, new services and sometimes even new markets. In many cases, there is simply no comparable situation (i.e. examples from the past) from which a valuer could derive good information for making forecasts.

- Organisational structures in young companies are regularly not well developed. Proper controlling and finance functions are often missing. Sometimes the founding team still runs the company, and they often lack management experience or background. Such structural weaknesses add to the risk profile of young companies.

- The probability of default is quite high for start-up companies. On average, after five years only 60% of companies are still operating. The main reason for this is the typically high financing need of these companies in the early years with success only becoming apparent (or not) in the later years. The risk of default is a major driver of discount rates.

## 2. Cash flow generating logics of modern start-up companies

While the business models of young, innovative companies differ quite a lot, the idea of generating cash flows in the mid to long term can be brought down to such factors as network effects, scale and technological advances. There are opportunities and threats at all of these use-case levels.

Network effects refer to the increasing attractiveness and profitability of what the company is selling through increasing uptake use of this offer. Network effects are often related to business models where interaction, particularly communication, is important. The quality of networks is often determined in business using Metcalfe's law. This assumes a proportional increase in benefit per additional network user. The classic example of network effects is the telephone. If only two people have a telephone shortly after its invention, this does not help the invention – the network is simply too limited. But as more and more people have a telephone, then values develop. The value of the network increases with each additional user. A simple network effect aims at the social benefit to participants (Facebook, Tinder, etc.). Here, the benefit of the participants increases with the increasing number of other participants. The more friends or potential partners are in a social network the more attractive it gets to everybody. Another example is a traffic app where customers (e.g. car drivers) send and receive information about the current traffic situation. Such an app also improves its performance by an increasing number of senders. But network businesses also have limits. The number of participants can at some point show a value-flattening or even value-destroying effect: too much publicity discourages participants on Facebook to reveal personal data or opinions; lowering the average offer quality on Tinder leads to higher search costs for participants. The term 'network effects' is very fashionable today, but often overused. A huge number of founders claim to develop network effects but only rarely is this actually the case. In the vast majority of cases their business at best shows economies of scale.

Many young and innovative companies with business models that emphasise scaling do so with the rationale that the growing appeal of their offerings will surpass the cost increases associated with expanding their product or service volumes. These scale effects are often data-related. For example, a credit information software application becomes more attractive and accurate as its database expands. Scale benefits extend to other software products as well: while the variable costs for each additional unit sold are quite low once the software is developed, companies can still charge the full price. Although scale can create substantial competitive advantages, they are typically not as robust as those derived from network effects.

Finally, in today's technology-driven world, many start-up businesses aim at improving lives or industrial processes.

## 3. Valuation approaches for young companies

DCF approaches are of course always applicable for young companies from a technical point of view. However, due to the low visibility and the problems of making proper long-term forecasts these approaches are often very subjective. However, a couple of other approaches are better able to capture the value in young companies from a practitioner's point of view.

The so-called venture capital method tries to mirror a typical investment situation of a venture capitalist and to translate it into a value number. The assumptions of the venture capital method are that: a) an investor in the young company has a certain assumed holding period (e.g. five years); and b) at time of exit the company will be valued based on multiples. These multiples are taken at the time of valuation and from mature listed companies or private mergers and acquisitions (M&A) transactions.

The basic idea of the venture capital method is that – although it might be difficult to value a young company during its development phase – it is much more possible to value it once it has reached a more mature state. This mature state is assumed to be reached at time of exit. Therefore multiples from mature companies at time of valuation can be applied to the exit date valuation of the target. This exit value has to be discounted back to the date of valuation. Here it is important to either take (often negative) interim cash flows into account or to assume a certain dilution (reduction of percentage ownership) over time due to future external equity capital injections (which are necessary to cover negative cash flows).

Figure 33.1 depicts the functioning of the venture capital method for an expected earnings before interest, taxes, depreciation and amortisation (EBITDA) of 200 in Year 4, an exit-EBITDA-multiple of 8x, a discount rate of 20%, and a dilution of 40%.

FIGURE 33.1 APPLICATION OF THE VENTURE CAPITAL METHOD

|  | Year 0 | Year 1 | Year 2 | Year 3 | Year 4 |
|---|---|---|---|---|---|
| EBITDA |  |  |  |  | 200 |
| EBITDA multiple |  |  |  |  | 8x |
| Exit value at the end of Year 4 |  |  |  |  | 1,600 |
| Present Value at the end of Year 0 | 772 |  |  |  |  |
| Dilution assumption | 40% |  |  |  |  |
| Value after dilution | 463 |  |  |  |  |

An often-heard critique about the venture capital method is that it only considers the blue-sky scenario of a successful exit, but in reality, there are many more – often not so positive – scenarios possible. This aspect can be addressed by either taking a success probability for the exit value into account or by actively considering more than one scenario in the valuation. If several scenarios are taken into account, the valuation approach is called First Chicago Method (named after the former private equity department of First Chicago Insurance where presumably it was first applied). The First Chicago Method determines present values for different scenarios and then sums up the probability-weighted scenario values to get the fair value of the young company at time of valuation.

For both – the Venture Capital Method and the First Chicago Method – risk-adjusted discount rates are necessary. Often these discount rates represent required returns from venture capital investors. These rates range from 40% to 60% for early-stage investments and from 15% to 20% for later-stage investments.

Finally, venture capital funds often apply the so-called Price of Recent Investment (PORI) method, which uses the price agreed in a recent financing round as a starting point for the current value of the young company. The idea here is that – if the circumstances of the last financing round indicate that the price agreed during this round equalled fair value at that time – this price can be adjusted for a) the time value of money and b) any differences in the real development of the company compared with plan. The result is an updated fair value. This approach is attractive as it does not require a full valuation and uses market-based information – the price of the recent investment – as an important parameter in the valuation model. As a matter of course, the PORI method is not applicable if there are doubts about the price of the recent financing round being a good proxy for fair value (e.g. if the financing was a rescue package or financing was provided by a strategic investor with potential synergies in mind), or if the date of the recent financing round is too far in the past.

# Stretch yourself

Investment contracts of venture capital firms are not simple plain vanilla 'price-for-share' agreements. They often entail certain additional rights to the investor, such as liquidation preferences or conversion options. In every financing round new shares with new rights are issued, which leads to a start-up company often showing several share classes that are not comparable with each other.

These rights are often of material additional value to investors (having the first right of claim in the event of a liquidation – i.e. the right to receive at least the invested amount back once the company is sold – is a clear advantage). Given a certain total value of equity of the young start-up company, those investors with more and better rights are entitled to a higher share of this equity and those without rights are entitled to a lower share. It is necessary to consider these rights if one wants to find out the value of a specific group/class of shares.

Valuation methods for single share classes are based on option pricing models (the so-called option pricing method, OPM) or scenario analysis (the so-called probability-weighted expected return method, PWERM) or a combination of both. The idea of these methods is to explicitly take the economic consequences of the additional rights into account, for example by forecasting different later transaction prices and considering the order in which the transaction price is paid to different parties.

Finally, young companies usually build up tax-loss carry-forwards in their early loss-making years. Tax-loss carry-forwards are some sort of tax credits that companies earn because of negative pre-tax earnings. Companies can use these tax credits in later years when they earn positive pre-tax earnings. The valuation of these assets is always a challenge for young companies as their later usability depends on the path the company follows. Hence, it might be necessary to deal differently with these assets in different scenarios.

# CHAPTER 34

# Valuing private versus public companies

## Bite size

Most of the models and concepts that have been discussed so far apply to publicly listed companies. For the valuation of private companies some differences apply. These relate to lower availability or quality of information, the mixing of private and business use of assets, the relevance of value components that are tied to the person of the owner-manager (i.e. personal relations of the owner-manager to customers that would get lost in the event of a sale of the company) and often inadequate corporate governance and organisational structures. Also, discount rates for Discounted Cash Flow (DCF) models of private companies are usually higher than the ones for public companies as shares in private companies cannot be freely traded at all times.

## Practitioner focus

It is usually much harder to analyse private companies than public companies because of insufficient quantity or quality of information. Often valuers have to rely more on assumptions than on hard analytical results. This requires a good understanding of uncertainty and how this uncertainty translates into quantitative value effects. In particular, discount rates must account for additional risks such as lack of transparency (usually there is much less information available about private companies than public companies) and illiquidity of shares in private companies (i.e. as they cannot be easily sold or bought, which makes them relatively less attractive for investors). The discount rates applied in valuations of private companies are usually 20%–30% higher than those of publicly listed companies.

# Core content

## 1. Structural differences of private companies versus public companies

A public (or publicly listed) company is a company that has shares of equity outstanding that are traded at an organised market such as a stock exchange. In contrast to this, the shares of a private company are not traded publicly but are in the hands of private investors. Most of the models and concepts that have been discussed so far apply to publicly listed companies. For the valuation of private companies, a range of additional issues arise that the valuer must consider.

Public companies usually have a large number of shareholders who, in most cases, are unknown to the management of the company. Due to a clear separation between the management and shareholders (owners) in public companies, a set of rules and corporate governance mechanisms are in place to ensure that management runs the company in the best interest of the shareholders. From a valuation point of view, the following different characteristics of private companies must be considered:

- The corporate governance framework for private companies is much less developed than the one for public companies. From a control and monitoring point of view, this is usually not a big problem. In private companies, the shareholder structure is usually less fragmented, and management often holds a meaningful share of the company. For valuation purposes it is worth checking whether the company has a proper risk management in place and whether management is adequately incentivised to run the company in the best interest of shareholders.

- In private companies the private and business use of assets is often mixed. This is particularly problematic from an analytical point of view if it is unclear how much of the time certain assets are used for private and how much for business purposes. The car of the owner-manager or the privately owned office building are typical examples of this. But also, the pure company-related working hours of the owner-manager are often difficult to isolate. Even private assets that are only used for corporate reasons – be it by renting them or by transferring them by a sale from the owners to the company – are an analytical challenge. A valuer should always check whether these transactions take place at arms' length, e.g. can stand a third-party comparison test.

- Another important aspect to consider is how much of the business success of a private company depends on the personal ties of its owners. For example, are there customers which only do business with the company because of the good old private relationship with the owners? Does business success at least partly depend on the personal reputation of the owners? Or, more generally, how much of the business would get lost if the company is sold to a new owner? For valuation reasons such personal aspects have to be stripped out of the analysis.

- In smaller private companies the salary of the owner-manager is often not at market conditions. This is because owner-managers can manage their income via payouts (distribution of earnings) at their discretion. For valuation reasons, it is often necessary to adjust the salary for any deviations from market norms in order to make sure that the company is valued independently of aspects associated with the owners' discretionary use of company assets.

- An important element of companies' accountability to external stakeholders is financial reporting. The purpose of reporting rules for stock-listed companies – in particular the International Financial Reporting Standards (IFRS) – is to enhance the transparency and decision usefulness of reported financial information for outside investors. Private companies, however, often rely on simplified or less complex reporting standards, such as local, generally accepted accounting principles (GAAP). This is a problem for valuers as a company's historical financial statements is a core source of information for cash flow forecasts and valuation modelling.

- The organisational structure of private companies is often underdeveloped. They might often lack important functions, such as controlling, taxation, treasury, etc. This can bring along inefficiencies, more need for external help and hence different cost structures than public companies.

- Due to the lower interest of the public in the fate of private companies, third-party information is less easily available. In particular, there are no equity analyst reports from brokers that could be taken as an analytical help.

- With all these negatives, it is worth highlighting that there are also some positives to private companies. In particular, if these companies have a big shareholder (a majority owner), the strategy is often more long-term oriented because there is no such short-termism (immediate performance pressure due to opaqueness of investors) as there is for many stock-listed companies. Moreover, in times of crisis it is easier to negotiate with the different stakeholders simply because there are fewer of them.

## 2. Discount rates for private companies

The higher analytical uncertainty and general lower visibility add to the riskiness of private companies. Moreover, as shares in private companies are not traded on a stock exchange, they cannot be traded as quickly or as cheaply as the shares of public companies. This is a negative for investors in private companies as the risk of being stuck in an unattractive holding for longer is higher. Because of the low liquidity of private company stocks and low information transparency, discounts (i.e. reductions in the valuation, also sometimes called 'haircuts') are often applied to the model-derived valuations of these companies. These discounts are called discount for lack of marketability (DLOM).

Some valuers prefer to translate the discounts directly into the model as a premium to the discount rate. This is, however, only a technical question. Academic studies show that DLOM can vary widely across companies, countries and valuers. For example, Officer (2007) finds that multiples for non-listed companies are between 15% and 30% lower than those of listed companies.[36] Koeplin et al. (2000) document DLOM of 20%–30% for US firms and 40%–50% for non-US firms, while Paglia and Harjoto (2010) suggest that DLOM on multiples for non-listed companies can be as high as 66%–72%.[37]

# Stretch yourself

There are certain company business models where it is impossible to take any valuation parameters from the capital market, because these business models are for non-scalable small businesses, such as family bakery stores, private car garages, one-man legal/tax advisory firms, private medical doctors, etc. For these cases, valuers have to frequently use analogies but also have to understand their limits ('can we compare a small tax advising firm with a large, listed auditing company from a risk perspective?').

Additionally, many of these very small private companies are extremely dependent on an individual, the single owner-manager. For example, a lawyer's office would have a value of zero (or almost zero because there would still be some assets on the balance sheet) because without the lawyer and her connections and relationships no cash flows could be generated. This high level of reliance on one person or a small group of people makes valuations emerging from a long forecast period more difficult.

---

36   See: Officer, M. S. (2007). The price of corporate liquidity: Acquisition discounts for unlisted targets. *Journal of Financial Economics*, 83(3), 571–598.
37   See: Koeplin, J., Sarin, A. & Shapiro, A. C. (2000). The private company discount. *Journal of Applied Corporate Finance*, 12(4), 94–101.
Paglia, J. K. & Harjoto, M. (2010). The discount for lack of marketability in privately owned companies: A multiples approach. *Journal of Business Valuation and Economic Loss Analysis*, 5(1).

# Index

## A

accounting policy 148, 150
accounting quality 32
accounts payable 30, 62–3, 72
accounts receivable 60–2, 72
accruals 24
   as accounting quality measure 32
   versus cash calculation 25
   concept 28
accrued expenses 30
adjusted betas 102
amortisation 29–30, 63–5, 71, 192, 221, *see also*
   depreciation and amortisation (D&A); EBITDA
asset turnover 202–3
assets
   adjusting for difference across 143–4
   on the balance sheet 35–8
   capital structure and 35–44
   changes in 30
   classification 17–18
   content 37
   current 17–18, 38–9
   finding comparable 142–3
   fixed 51, 127, 178
   intangible 42–4, 63–4, 241–2
   net operating 67, 107–8, 204, 228
   non-current 17–18, 39–41, 63–5, 67–8
   non-operating 122, 188, 198, 211
   tangible 40, 50, 67

## B

balance sheet 17–19, 25
   assets on 35–8
   components of 17
   enterprise value and 109–10
   forecasting 57–68
balance sheet values 109–10
beta 92, 99
book equity capital 114–16

book value 18, 109–10, 139, 155, *see also* equity value;
   price to book (P/B) ratio (multiple)
business model 87, 92–3, 165

## C

called-up share capital 115
Capital Asset Pricing Model (CAPM) 89, 95, 194,
   216, 263
   as the core model 90–2
capital expenditure 36, 64–5, 74, 193, 224
   capex-to-D&A multiples 193, 224
capital intensity 127
capital structure 41–2, 101–2
   assets and 35–44
   avoiding influence of 153
   impact on multiples 126–7
   neutrality 110
   price to book value multiple and 149
   price to earnings multiple and 147
   using enterprise value when different 126–7
capitalise 36, 43
cash 18, 39, 51
   surplus 42, 123
cash conversion 31
cash flow 9, 171
   of companies in crisis 265–6
   Discounted Cash Flow (DCF) model 131–3, 212, 217,
     266–7, 278
   earnings versus 27–34
   forecasting 69–77, 164–5, 265–6
   foreign currency 256–7, 260–1
   future 81–2, 85–6
   generating logics 278–9
   importance of 27–8
   operating 21, 31, 66
   statement *see* cash flow statement
cash flow statement 17, 21–2, 28–30
cash flows relating to financing (CFF) 74–6
cash flows relating to investing (CFI) 74

287

cash flows relating to operations (CFO) 70–2
cash operating expense margins 192, 221
clean-surplus 244
common stock 115
components of financial statements 17
compound annual growth rate 55
Conceptual Framework 23
consensus estimates 47
conservatism 23–4
consistency 24–5
consolidated net income 149
content assets 37
corporate governance 273–4, 283
cost of debt 101, 193–4
cost of equity 94, 128–9, 194, 224, 238–9
cost of goods sold (CoGS) 50–1, 59–60
cost of sales 33
credit risk premium 194
crisis
   best practice valuation of companies in 267
   forecasting cash flows of companies in 265–6
   limits of valuation techniques 266–7
   risk profiles of companies in 263–5
currency effects 261
current assets 17–18, 38–9
current liabilities 38–9

## D

debt 65–6, 68, 76, 188, 198
   cost of 101, 193–4
   debt-to-EBITDA multiples 65–6, 216, 224
   effective interest rates (EIRs) on 221
   finance and firm maturity 42
   finance and industry 41
   net debt 42, 108–12, 123
debt-to-capital ratio 41, 65
debt-to-equity ratio 41, 65
deferred revenue 29, 37
depreciation 29–30, 63–5, 71, 171, 192, 221, *see also* EBITDA
depreciation and amortisation (D&A) 29–30, 63–5, 71, 154, 171, 184, *see also* EBITDA
   as a % of sales 192, 221
   capex-to-D&A multiples 193, 224
   expenses 65, 71, 184, 192, 215, 221
dilutive securities 117
discount for lack of marketability (DLOM) 285
discount rates
   basic framework of model 90
   Capital Asset Pricing Model (CAPM) 89–92, 95, 194, 216, 263
   for distressed companies 263, 267–8
   impact of risk 81–8
   practical perspectives on risk-adjusted 96–102

   for private companies 284–5
   standard approaches to determine risk-adjusted 88–95
   translation of between currencies 259–60
Discounted Cash Flow (DCF) model 131–3, 212, 217, 266–7, 278
discounting 245, 260
distressed companies
   best practice valuation of 267
   forecasting cash flows of 265–6
   limits of valuation techniques 266–7
   risk profiles of 263–5
   valuation of 263–9
diversification 90–1
Dividend Discount Model (DDM) 131, 150, 243–5, 250, 263, 278
   how it works 177–81
   logic of 168–76
dividend payout ratio 74–5, 151
dividends 74–5, 150–1
   deriving from corporate accounts 177–8
   money not paid out as 172–4
   turning into value 169
   understanding future path of 178–9
   where they come from 170–1
DuPont analysis 204–5, 229–30

## E

earnings
   cash flows versus 27–34
   forecasting 47–56
   importance of 27–8
   price to earnings (P/E) ratio (multiple) 20, 125, 127–8, 139, 141, 147–9, 150–1, 159
   residual *see* residual income
   retained 116
earnings before interest and taxes *see* EBIT
earnings before interest, tax, depreciation and amortisation *see* EBITDA
earnings normalisation 148
earnings per share (EPS) 20, 147, 153
EBIT 31, 125, 127–8, 155
   EV/EBIT 154, 158
EBITDA 125, 127–8, 155
   debt-to-EBITDA multiples 65–6, 216, 224
   EV/EBITDA 154, 157, 158, 185
economies of scale 142, 192, 205
effective interest rate 52–3, 194, 221
effective tax rate 53–4, 192, 221
enterprise value 12, 138–9
   advantages of using 110–11
   balance sheet values and 109–41
   bridge to equity value *see* enterprise value bridge
   definition of 105–12

different pathways to 108–9
enterprise value bridge to 120–3
operating enterprise value 112
total enterprise value 112
when to use 124–9
enterprise value bridge 105–8, 111–12, 120–3, 198–9
enterprise value multiples 152–6
  EV/Barrel of reserves 159
  EV/EBIT 154, 158
  EV/EBITDA 154, 157, 158, 185
  EV/IC 154–5
  EV/Revenue 158
environmental, social, governance *see* ESG factors
equity 18, 75–6
  book equity capital 114–16
  book value of 18, 109–10, 139, 155, *see also* equity value
  cost of 94, 128–9, 194, 224, 238–9
  debt-to-equity ratio 41, 65
  free cash flow to 123, 214–16
  multiples 140, 146–52
  return on 174, 230
  statement of changes in shareholders' 23
equity financing 41, 74, 110, 112
equity multiples 146–52, 160
  price to book (P/B) ratio 18, 149–50, 240–1
  price to earnings (P/E) ratio 20, 125, 127–8, 139, 141, 147–9, 150–1, 159
equity risk premium 164
equity valuation 11, 160, 237
  relevance of residual income to 240–1
equity value 12, 113–19, 125, 138–9, 226
  enterprise value bridge to *see* enterprise value bridge
  when to use 124–9
*Ertragswertverfahren* 213
ESG factors 270–6
ESG integration
  definition of 270–1
  ethical contribution to valuation 274–5
  pitfalls in 275–6
  valuation effects of 272–4
ethical aspects 276
exchange rates 255–62
expenses
  depreciation and amortisation 65, 71, 184, 192, 215, 221
  operating 50–1, 56, 221

## F

financial crisis 259
financial leverage 87–8
financial reporting 16, 241, 284
financial statements
  components of 17–23
  fundamental accounting concepts 23–5
  notes to 23
  structure of 17
firm maturity 42
First Chicago Method 277, 280
Fisher Effect 258, 261
fixed assets 51, 127, 178
fixed costs 88, 264–5
flow multiples 140–1
forecasting
  balance sheets 57–68
  cash flows of companies in crisis 265–6
  completing cash flows 69–77
  earnings 47–56
  key elements of accounting needed for 32–4
  need for accuracy 133
  net income 220
foreign currency cash flow 256–7, 260–1
forward multiples 132, 133
free cash flow 9, 94, 131–2, 178, 267
  to equity *see* free cash flow to equity
  to the firm *see* free cash flow to the firm
free cash flow to equity 123, 214–16
  food for thought 219–31
  talk-through 212–18
  walk-through 219–31
free cash flow to the firm 123, 182–5
  food for thought 202–12
  forecasting 190–3
  talk-through 182–9
  walk-through 189–99

## G

generally accepted accounting principles 16, 284
going concern 24
Gordon Growth model 98, 173, 180, 186, 196, 208, 217, 225, 245
greenwashing 275
gross long-term debt 123
gross profit 20, 33
gross profit margin 33
growth rates 185–7, 216–18, 225, 248–9
  compound annual 55
  sales 48–50, 192, 206, 220, 225
  terminal 208–10, 225
  'unsustainable' assumptions 246–7

## H

historical cost 24

## I

IASB 23
IFRS 16, 241, 284
illiquid stock 95
illiquidity 282
impairment 43
implied share price 206–8
income statement 20, 36, 53–4, 72–3, 140–1, 214
inflation 259–61
intangible assets 42–4, 63–4, 241–2
interest expenses 51–3, 72–3
interest rates
   effective 52–3, 194, 221
   nominal 259–61
   parity 255, 258–61
   real 259
International Accounting Standards Board 23
International Financial Reporting Standards 16, 241, 284
International Fisher Effect 258, 261
intrinsic valuation 9, 13, 243
inventory (asset) 18, 30, 39, 71–2
inventory days 60, 70, 192, 222
inventory turnover 59–61
invested capital 139, 203
   EV/IC 154–5
   incremental 208–9
   return on 155, 204, 230

## L

levered and unlevered taxes 184, 215
liabilities 18
   changes in 30
   current 38–9
   financial/non-operating 188, 198
   operating 107–8
liquidation preferences 281
liquidity 266, 285

## M

M&A 48–9, 266, 279
margins analysis 32–4
market capitalisation 116
market portfolio 91–3
market value of equity 18, 108–10, 116–17
market-risk premium 93, 98–9
mergers and acquisitions 48–9, 266, 279
mortgage 106–8
multiples valuation 266–7

## N

narrative (valuation) 12, 13
net asset value 159
net assets 114, 241
net debt 42, 108–12, 123
net income 71, 139, 149, 153, 178, 238–41
   calculation of 214
   consolidated 149
   forecasts 220
   key drivers of 215
   paid out 172–5
net operating assets (NOA) 67, 107–8, 204, 228–9
net operating profit after tax (NOPAT) 154, 183–4, 193, 208–9
net operating working capital (NOWC) 38, 58–9
   increases/decreases in NOWC items 71–2
   net investment in 222
   NOWC cycle 70
net profit margin 34
network effects 278–9
non-controlling interests 122–3, 148–9, 188, 198–9
non-current assets 17–18, 39–41, 63–5, 67–8
non-operating assets 122, 188, 198, 211
normalisation 54–5
   earnings 148
notes to the financial statements 23
number of outstanding shares 188–9, 199, 227

## O

operating cash flow 21, 31, 66
operating enterprise value 112
operating enterprise value (OEV) 112
operating expense margins 50–1
   cash 192, 221
operating expenses 50–1, 56, 221
operating profit margin 33, 205
operating working capital *see* net operating working capital
option pricing method (OPM) 281
options 117–18
ordinary shares outstanding 117

## P

payables days 63, 70, 193, 223
payables turnover 62–3
P/E ratio (multiple) 20, 125, 127–8, 139, 141, 147–9, 150–1, 159
PEG ratio (multiple) 159
perpetuity 9, 85–6, 106, 216
personal aspects 283–4
Porter's five forces 57–8
preferred stock 115

prepaid expenses 19
prepayments 39, 59
present value 27, 82, 169–70
　calculation of 85–6
　models 130, 131–2, 163–7, *see also individual models*
　of perpetuity 106
　stages in models 163–7
　USD/GBP 256–7
Price of Recent Investment (PORI) method 280–1
price to book (P/B) ratio (multiple) 18, 149–50, 240–1
price to earnings (P/E) ratio (multiple) 20, 125, 127–8, 139, 141, 147–9, 150–1, 159
price to tangible book (multiple) 159
probability of default 278
probability weighted expected return method (PWERM) 281
property, plant and equipment (PP&E) 22
purchasing power parity 258–9

# R

rate of return 85, 176
receivables days 61–2, 70, 192–3, 222
receivables turnover 61
regression analysis 92
relative purchasing power parity 258–9
relative valuation 8–9, 125, 138
research and development 43–4, 241, 275
reserves 114, 116
residual income 237–42
residual income valuation 243–51
retained earnings 116
return on equity 174, 230
return on invested capital 155, 204, 230
return on net operating assets 204
revenue expenditure 36
revenues 30, 88, 158, 169–71, 265–6
risk 81–8, 224–5, 259–60, 273
　in context of valuation 84
　definition of 82
　example of 86–7
　importance of 82–4
　TVM concept 85–6
risk aversion 82–3
risk premium 90, 93, 194
　market-risk premium 93, 98–9
risk profile
　of companies in crisis 263–5
　of young companies 278
risk-adjusted discount rates
　basic framework of 90
　CAPM as core model 90–4
　need for 90
　practical perspectives on 95–102
　standard approaches to determine 89–95

risk-free rate 90, 93, 97, 194–5
RoIC 155, 204, 230
RoNOAs 204

# S

sales 48–50, 55, 139
　D&A as % of 192, 221
sales growth rate 48–50, 192, 206, 220, 225
scale 142, 143, 279
　economies of 142, 192, 205
scenario analysis 10, 199, 206, 281
scenarios 206, 263, 267
　negative 267, 274
selling, general and administrative costs (SG&A) 20, 192, 221
sensitivity analysis 207–8
separate entity 25
share premium 114, 115
share price 117, 147, 187, 207, 226
shareholder equity 17, 139
spot exchange rates 255–60
start-up companies 82, 277–82
　cash flow generating logics of 278–9
　risk profiles of 278
　valuation approaches for 279–81
statement of cash flows 17, 21–2, 28–30
statement of changes in shareholder equity 17, 23
statement of financial performance 20, *see also* income statement
statement of financial position *see* balance sheet
stock multiples 141, 150
stock options 117–18
straight line depreciation 40
surplus cash 42, 123
sustainability 174, 246–7
Sustainable Development Goals 274–5

# T

tangible assets 40, 50, 67
tax rate, effective 53–4, 192, 221
tax shield 94, 194
terminal growth rate 208–10, 225
terminal period 185–6, 212, 216–18, 227
terminal value 166, 185, 195–6, 209, 225, 261
time-value-of-money (TVM) concept 85–6, 186, 218
total enterprise value 112, 156
trailing multiples 132–3, 141
transitional period 166–7, 212
Treasury Stock Method 118

## U

uncertainty 81–4, 206–8, *see also* risk
unlevered taxes 184, 215

## V

valuation multiples 137–45
   basic structure of a multiple 138–9
   intrinsic versus relative value 138
   need for 140
   steps in using 142–4
   types of 140–1
valuation narrative 12, 13
value of equity 108
   book 18, 109–10, 139, 155
   market 18, 108–10, 116–17
value of net debt 108–10, 125
value of net operating assets 108–10
variable costs 56, 88, 279
venture capital 280–1
Venture Capital Method 277, 279–80
visible period 185–6, 212, 216–17
volatility 117, 128

## W

weighted average cost of capital (WACC) 94, 185, 195, 207
working capital 38–9, 58–63
   net operating 38, 58–9, 70–2, 222

## Y

yield-to-maturity 52, 101
young companies 82, 277–82
   cash flow generating logics of 278–9
   risk profiles of 278
   valuation approaches for 279–81

www.ingramcontent.com/pod-product-compliance
Ingram Content Group UK Ltd.
Pitfield, Milton Keynes, MK11 3LW, UK
UKHW051813270725
461243UK00014B/167